TREASURES
of
DARKNESS

TREASURES
of
DARKNESS

Power Perfected in Weakness

Marja Kostamo

XULON PRESS

Xulon Press
555 Winderley Pl, Suite 225
Maitland, FL 32751
407.339.4217
www.xulonpress.com

Xulon
PRESS

Treasures of Darkness by Marja Kostamo

Dedicated to:

My husband Tuomo,
who prayed almost daily for this book to be written,
saying these stories need to be told.

Endorsements

In "Treasures of Darkness" our good friend Marja Kostamo takes us on her own personal journey of prayer. What began as a wilderness season, teaching her to lean on God, soon became a treasure hunt full of adventure!

Chapter by chapter, story upon story, Marja's journey is transparent and real, personal and practical. From the early beginnings, to praying for nations, her own life story is a testimony to the fact that God loves to take ordinary people and use them to do extraordinary things! A must read for all generations.

~ Dr. Dick and Joan Deweert,
Founders and Pastors of Third Day Victory Church, Lethbridge, AB
Founders and Leaders of Dominion Media
Exec. Producers and Hosts of LifeLine Today, as seen on Daystar Canada TV

Anyone who says, "Lord, I want to have a life of adventure!" is in for the ride of their lives. Marja, in her new book, has invited us into the journey of a lifetime of prayer and the dynamic way in which God has met her along the way. She doesn't stop there. Her heart is to encourage us all to simply pray and open the door to the miraculous nature and hand of God in our own lives.

She reminds us all that one learns to pray when one begins praying. She adds that great men and women of God say that the best way to learn about prayer is to actually do it.

Marja is a long-time friend whose life truly bears witness to the stories she has penned. Read it, and be encouraged. What God has done for her He can do for you.

~ Steve Schroeder,
President, Christian Ministers Association of Canada

I found this book absolutely fascinating and once I started, I really was enthralled by it. I should admit that the title didn't really capture me at first but once I was reading, the lights were coming on for me. What Marja has created is a treasure map of how to persist in our walk with the Lord through the valleys of life to reap the delicious fruit we all long for. I was struck by the fact that all the seasons of her life, many of which were dark, have contributed to the unfolding of a rich lifetime of the miraculous interventions and intimacy with God she now has.

Marja Kostamo has been a person of prayer both in her private life and on national stages and because of that we would expect that she would teach us to pray. What she has actually accomplished in this book, however, is to provide us with a roadmap of developing a deep and vibrant relationship with Jesus. For each of us our journey to intimacy with Jesus is going to be different, but the cost is going to be the same. Here is a story of how God refined, prepared, and used a humble wife and mom to become a person whose prayers have changed the trajectory of lives and helped birth movements of God's Spirit in our generation.

Marja is one of the most valiant people of faith I know. It has been obvious to me over many years of friendship that she has a vibrant walk with the Lord and a large faith not just for herself, her family and church, but for the cities she has lived in and nations she has prayed for. She has an ability to be quiet and unassuming and yet God continually thrusts her into significant times and places where she speaks, leads or stands for Him. I thought I knew her well, until I read this book and discovered just how she was quietly learning in secret from the Lord and being transformed into one of God's generals for our generation.

Many times we see the multitude of challenges that lay before us and complain. But God doesn't work through our complaints. He births vision, miracles, and breakthrough out of our intimacy with Him. Could it be that this challenging season in your life is one where Jesus is drawing you into deeper intimacy and a greater dependence on Him? As you read her book, Marja's journey will undoubtedly become an encouragement and possibly a guidepost for you as you seek to be transformed by Jesus.

~ *Greg Paulson,*
Lead Pastor, Gateway Christian Ministries,
Prince George, BC

Well done Marja! This book is aptly named "Treasures of Darkness" – it is full of gems and nuggets! Full of scripture, saturated with stories and testimonies.

If you want your faith to be strengthened and your knowledge to increase, read this book. You have an opportunity here for your life to be changed. Rev.4:1 comes to mind, "come up here". If you read and apply the things thatMarja shares here, you will be lifted up higher in your journey with God.

I recommend that you read it *slowly*, with a highlighter or a notepad.

Thank you, Marja.

~ Peter Ziemer,
Pastor, The Well, Prince George, BC
Serving on the Watchmen for the Nations Leadership Team

A must-read page–turner! Follow the trail of the writer's lifetime of ups and downs, successes and challenges. As with the author's earlier writings, Marja takes the reader on and incredible journey. A journey of inspiration, intrigue and introspection. Relax as the Holy Spirit prompts and nudges the spirit in you. Be prepared to laugh, cry and be stretched to new dimensions of your faith and walk with God. Enjoy!

~ John Abraham,
Founder of Global Outreach Foundation
International Missionary, Evangelist, Teacher and Author

Table of Contents

Prologue

When we think back on the wonders of God in our lives—all His answers to our prayers—our faith and vision are renewed and we **know** He will do it again!

This book is a necklace of many links of amazing answers to prayer. Not instant answers, necessarily. Some took persistent contending with fasting added to the mix.

Our lives are meant to be an adventure with God.

Early in my life I prayed, "Oh Lord, I want to have a life of adventure!" And it has been such, with many twists and turns, mountains of blessing and valleys of despair. And always He has shown up.

The people in the Bible were often told to "tell the generation to come" the stories of God's miracles and wonders, His interventions, His answers to their prayers and cries, so that they would put their trust in God.

When I have read these verses, I have heard a strong whisper from heaven repeatedly saying, "Write the stories. Tell of My wonders in your life."

That is why this book.

Part One

Tell the Stories

Speak of His wonders
Remember…His marvels and
the judgments uttered by His mouth
Psalm 105:2, 5 nasb

Chapter One

God said, "Tell the Stories"

Things happen when you pray, that don't happen when you don't pray.

I am going to tell stories of what only God could have done. But He did it in partnership with me, with us.

He does that if we pray.

He said He will heal our land, *if* we humble ourselves and pray. Our part.

Some of these stories are answers from praying alone, others of people praying together, sometimes persistently and for a long time.

He has shown up in many miraculous ways.

There are many ordinary days in between. Well, not. Because to be breathing is a miracle, snowflakes are miracles, to see is a miracle, to be born is a miracle.

We start to see miracles all around.

But, these stories are exceptional.

God said to me, "Tell it to the next generation."

This will be written for the generation to come,
that a people yet to be created may praise the Lord.
Psalm 102:18 nasb

Tell to the generation to come…His wondrous works that
He has done.
That they should put their confidence in God.
Psalm 78:4, 7 nasb

To pray, be like a child

E. M. Bounds speaks of prayer being "a trade to be learned," going on to say, "We must be apprentices and serve our time at it. Painstaking care, much thought, practice and labor are required to be a skillful tradesman in praying."[1]

But this mastery is baffling.

Because it is so simple.

It is always childlike faith that moves God's heart.

Often when I am stumped about how to pray, I think, "Be a child." Simple. Just ask.

When something seems complicated, difficult, I think, "Be like David." When things were too difficult for him, he leaned against God, like a weaned child leans against his mother (Ps. 131). Don't try to figure it out, just rest. He is bigger. He has the answer.

I am far from perfection, and often struggle with my shortcomings. But I have come to know that it is not perfection that gets you answers. It's **believing** that God hears and answers prayer.

As I have read the Bible from cover to cover—many times since I was a child—I began to realize that all the Bible people, except Jesus, fell short of perfection. When that realization dawned on me, I celebrated. Why? Because I fit in. *I am one of them!* They are just like me! Though they fell short, God talked to them, heard them, answered them, worked with them, and disciplined them. Yes, He *loved* them and *walked* with them. So I knew I had the same access to the Father they'd had. I can come to Him boldly as His beloved child even though I mess up and fall short. Not that we justify our shortcomings. We ask forgiveness, get up, let Him dust us off, and carry on. We are a work in progress. He is forming us.

Just like parents. We love our kids. They mess up. We discipline them and teach them. But we love them.

How much more does God love us and want us to come to Him and talk with Him!

O Lord, my heart is not proud, nor my eyes haughty;
Nor do I involve myself in great matters, or in things too
difficult for me.
Surely I have composed and quieted my soul;
Like a weaned child rests against his mother.
My soul is like a weaned child within me.
Psalm 131:1-2 nasb

Afflictions eclipsed by glory

How often we miss the eclipse.

We fight the pain, the anxiety, trying to find our own solution to escape it, run away, self-medicate.

Even Jesus struggled. He was human like us, and wrestled with the weight of His assignment to carry our sins to the cross. He prayed, "Father, if You are willing, take this cup from Me; yet not My will but Yours be done (Luke 22:42 niv).

He didn't run away. He didn't escape. He went to the cross.

And GLORY came!

My story: a third child was born into the middle of two shaky businesses, with two brothers just stair steps older. We were barely scraping by financially on a continual basis, and the phone and doorbell rang a lot because we ran the businesses from our home. The uncertainty and chaos made me feel like I was losing my mind.

I cried out to God for help. He said, "You only give me five minutes a day. I want an hour."

How do I find an hour in my already endless, crazy day??

I was desperate, so I began.

What at first were hours of dry praying and reading the Bible, **suddenly** opened up into a treasure hunt because God started to **answer my prayers**. I began to hear the voice of God.

That was 48 years ago. God helped me stay with it, though not perfectly, forming a prophetic intercessory calling in my life.

If you are overwhelmed with anxiety, this book is especially for you.

Do not be anxious about anything, but in every situation,
by prayer and petition with thanksgiving, present your
requests to God. And the peace of God, which transcends
all understanding, will guard your hearts and your minds
in Christ Jesus.
Philippians 4:6-7 niv

This was the pathway to peace. Order began to come into my chaos. God will do His part but He expects us to do our part.

To give Him our time.

Don't quit!

Prayer is simple really. You ask and you receive. If you don't receive, keep asking. Don't stop. I learned this. It is not rocket science.

My life seemed impossible—I could barely keep my head above the water—I felt like I was drowning all the time.

I cried out to God to help me. As I wrote in the previous page, He answered, "I want to help you, but you only spend 5 minutes a day blessing your family and reading a chapter or two from the Bible. I want an hour a day."

I knew that I knew He was speaking.

I obeyed. I began to pray an hour a day and saw answers to prayer that stunned me. Some prayers were not answered and still remain unanswered, but because of the answers I *have* received, I have faith that He is hearing every single one of my prayers and will answer in due time. Some perhaps won't be answered in my lifetime, but they will be answered.

I have realized that my prayers and God's answers were the beginning steps of a cleverly designed journey by Him. To get to know Him. He wants to be *known.* Answered prayer is not the end all—it is part of the journey of discovering God. What an amazing, wise, thoughtful, kind, merciful, creative, ingenious, redemptive, forgiving, full of longing, detailed, multi-tasking, story-creating, planning, responsible, talented, surprising, lavish, just, rewarding, generous, serving, clever, original, intelligent, listening, hearing, answering, partnering, inclusive, exclusive, stepping-in-to-do-it-for-us-because-we-can't-get-it-done God He is!

He is a Person who wants to be loved. By us.

Just like us. We want to be loved. Because we are created in His image.

I started to realize along this prayer journey, that God wants to share the things on His heart with me. Not just me talking to Him and asking for His help and intervention, not just me needing Him. He also has things on His heart that He wants to speak about. He wants friends He can be comfortable to share the deep things of His heart and mind with. It stunned me, really. I am a weak and broken human being, and *You, the God of the universe*, want friendship with *me?! You* want to tell *me* things?!

He began to tell me things when I was still struggling in so many ways. I felt like I was in grade one, and yet He trusted *me* to tell *me* things?! It awed me. Think about it. He chose Mary, a teenaged girl, to be the mother of *His* Son. The mother of *God?!* A young teenaged girl! He **trusted** a teenaged girl to be the mother of His Son. Selah. He trusts a heart that seeks Him and is committed to Him and His ways. A heart that is wanting to run after Him up that dark, misty mountain—a heart that wants to follow Jesus, though not doing it perfectly. He is drawn to such ones and takes risks, giving us responsibilities that are staggering, really.

It made me want to pray more and read the Bible more. With this new-found revelation, I began to understand the Bible more, to understand His plan and to get glimpses of *Him*. I learned to pray the words of the Bible, to pray His plan: to align with what is on His mind and pray those things. The Bible tells how He feels about things: what makes Him happy, what makes Him sad, what makes Him angry. I thought, *I want to pray what He wants to see happen. I want to care about what He cares about. If something is important to Him, I want it to be important to me.*

I realized that a lot of things in life are designed—quite cleverly by Him—to get to know Him. To know how He feels about things, and what it is like *for Him*. For example, becoming a parent. Oh, so *that's* how *You* feel about raising us, *Your* kids. Some great and wonderful times, and some very frustrating and painful times. Celebrating the maturing process and milestones of our kids growing up, but also suffering through heartaches, too. That's what *You*, God, go through with us. You love us and take out our garbage again and again. Just like parents do things for their kids. For kids who are oblivious and often uncaring about what all it takes to raise them. A sacrifice of love.

That's what God is like.

Marriage is another ingenious design by God to show how much He loves us. Tenderly, like a bridegroom loves a bride. Marriage is about partnering together in life to raise a family, and as a family being part of a larger community to advance God's purposes. We are called to be a bride, to be loved by Him and to partner with Him in His purposes. He wants to do life with us, to do His kingdom plans with us, to include us, to share the deep things of His heart with us, like a husband and wife.

Many other things have begun to make sense when I realized He let me go through this or that to feel what He feels. So instead of trying to resolve them, I embraced them. Some suffering was meant to be so that I could walk in the fellowship of *His* sufferings. I can't really know Him if I don't know that part too. Because He is a God who has suffered.

Sometimes He tenderly woos us, awakens us, patiently waiting until we "get it". Other times He is running and looking over His shoulder, shouting, "Are you coming?! Hurry up! Get going! Now! Or you are going to miss the moment!" He is predictable and unpredictable. Sometimes a gentle wind. Sometimes a tumultuous storm. Sometimes seemingly distant in times of darkness, and other times suddenly so very near, surprising us with unexpected blessings. Blessings with His signature written all over them.

I often "see" Him running up a mountain path in a fog, and me running behind, trying to keep up. He is a little higher up on the path, so I keep my eyes on the hem of His garment and on His feet because that is all I see through the dense fog. And I keep running. As long as I see Him, I am OK.

He calls us to be His friends, and yet we are aware of His majesty. He is God, we are not. We walk respectfully, with the fear of God, recognizing

His greatness, His vastness, His eternity. The mystery. The beautiful, awe-inspiring mystery that we, broken human beings, are invited to be a part of. He comes so close that He comes to live *in us* if we say "yes" to Him—to fulfill His kingdom plans through us. Chosen and called by God to be a part of His family, His kingdom, to work with Him to fulfill His plans.

From time to time I get glimpses of this and am struck by wonder.

It all begins with prayer.

Prayer is conversation with God.

This book is about that, the things that have happened since I started having conversations with God.

How do you pray for nations?! It was beyond my reach

When at 21 years of age I was drowning in my chaotic life, out of sheer desperation and in obedience to what God said to me, I started to pray that one hour a day. Little did I realize—in those days of prayer that felt like chewing cardboard—that one day I would be praying for nations, become an ordained prayer pastor, establish a house of prayer, and travel and minister in a number of nations.

In my early 20's I attended a *Change the World School of Prayer* seminar in the basement of the Connaught Hill Lutheran Church on Patricia Boulevard in Prince George, British Columbia. The sessions were on film reels. Dick Eastman was the speaker on film and we all (maybe 50 of us from various churches) had little blue binders that we made notes in as he taught. I still have that blue binder. I remember him saying he had a prayer place—a playhouse in his backyard that he had converted into his "house of prayer". With a map of the world tacked on one wall, he spent four hours a day praying.

I thought, *4 hours a day? How does one pray for Afghanistan? How do you pray for a nation?* It was too far above me…but…a seed was sown that slowly began to sprout and grow.

How do you build a wall around a city? One brick at a time.

God showed me that each prayer we pray is like a brick—whether it is for a loved one to be saved, a prodigal to come home, a church to get on fire for the Lord, or a city or nation to come into great awakening and revival. We may not see results after one prayer. It is just one brick in the wall. When every brick is laid in place, the job is complete. You just don't give up! One day, at the appointed time, His answer comes and your joy will know no bounds.

Forty some years later, I reflect on how God has sent me to many towns, cities, and nations, to either pray there, or to preach, teach…and always pray. I have been in 54 airports in 20 countries of the world in my travels. There are many who have done much, much more than that, but this was the surprising journey God took me on.

This began with a young 20-something-year-old looking at a map of the world, puzzled, and thinking, "How do I pray for nations?" I stepped into a life of prayer, knowing God would lead me and He has, one step at a time. I discovered that the places you pray for regularly, He also sends you to, to pray on site. I write about that in further chapters.

Those who sow in tears will reap with joyful shouting.
He who goes to and fro carrying his bag of seed
Shall indeed come again with a shout of joy,
Bringing his sheaves with him. Psalm 126:5-6 nasb

To be fulfilled Christians, prayer is the main thing. It is, simply put, talking with our bridegroom, Jesus (how hard is that?). He longs for our conversation with Him. He desires us, our closeness. Our lives begin to unfold with purpose, adventure, and destiny once we enter into this ongoing conversation.

This first chapter gives snippets of what this book is about.

God called me to an hour a day. However, it is not a magical number. Each person needs to listen to what His call is for them. What is He asking you to do? Also, it can change in different seasons of our lives. Over the years in my life, the hour has increased, but at the beginning, He called for a *sacrifice* of time. Time that was costly because I had so much on my plate. But I discovered the secret: as we give, He gives back—pressed down, shaken together, running over. He helped me get things done in a day that normally took three days to do, or He brought hands and feet to help me get them done. And He taught me about priorities—what was important and what was not.

Mary knew when it was time to sit at Jesus' feet. She was not distracted by all the things clamoring for her to do, and Jesus affirmed and blessed her choice by saying:

> *"...but only one thing is necessary, for Mary has chosen*
> *the good part,*
> *which will not be taken away from her."*
> *Luke 10:42 nasb*

Chapter Two

The Treasure Hunt

You will seek Me and find Me when you search
for Me with
All your heart. Jeremiah 29:13 nasb

I love how He talks!

I was at a prayer conference in Kelowna, British Columbia in 2012. Though it was a national conference, praying for Canada, God ambushed me personally in an unusual and wonderful way. He began to rearrange my life and point me in a whole new direction.

During worship time at one of the sessions, I had my hands raised with my palms upward, my eyes closed. I was experiencing the sweet presence of the Lord. As I worshiped, I felt a tangible, physical weight on my hands. At first I thought it was my imagination, but it persisted and increased. It felt heavier on one hand than the other.

Having walked with God for many years, I know when He does something like this, it "means" something. There is an interpretation. It's not just a cool experience. So I began to ask the Lord what He was telling me, asking Him for discernment, understanding, interpretation. Nothing came. I knew He would speak in His good time so I had a sense of anticipation in my spirit.

The next day I joined the pre-service prayer time in an upper room. I noticed a tall side table along a wall. On the white table cloth lay a very long, pewter-colored sword. After everyone left the room I walked over to the table, picked up the sword, and held it across my upraised palms.

Suddenly I realized this was exactly what I'd felt during worship the day before. The weight on my hands was like holding a sword, the hilt end being heavier than the blade.

Again I asked the Lord for revelation as my mind had not yet comprehended His message. My spirit was alive with God hovering on me but my mind was not getting it.

He often does it this way, speaking to our spirit, fully bypassing our mind.

He lets our mind catch up later.

He loves to give clues, taking us on a treasure hunt. My expectancy level heightened because I knew God was about to reveal something significant.

That evening was the last session of the conference and the order of the service was different. After worship the facilitator introduced several prophets and explained that they were going to minister to the conference attendees by prophetic ministry.

The first prophet asked those who were carrying a "book or books" inside them, those who were sensing a call to write, to stand up. I stood as I had known this for a dozen years or more. I knew it deep inside and it had already been confirmed by prophetic words. I noticed a few others stood also.

She began to prophesy saying, "The PEN is MIGHTIER than the SWORD." Oh, my! Oh, my! I was astounded. Here it was. The sword. He had dropped the hints and clues a bit at a time, and then, when my longing to understand had peaked, He spoke loud and clear.

Now I **knew** He wanted me to write beyond a shadow of a doubt.

When the word comes, the sweet presence of the Lord hovers along with it. I was experiencing that sweetness.

But I also knew it would require obedience and action on my part—a response. He does His part and we do our part. When He speaks, it is glorious. We feel we can conquer every mountain. However, the walking out of what He speaks is not all that easy. Since my desire is to walk in whatever He is calling me to do, I immediately began to pray for help to walk this out, asking God to show me how to order my life to write.

This was not a new word to me. I had heard it repeatedly in my spirit for many years and it had been confirmed. But my life was busy with many things: leading Prince George House of Prayer, being connected with the nations with the prayer movement, organizing semi-annual prayer retreats for the ministerial in my city, as well as organizing citywide prayer events and conferences. Besides that, I was a mother of five children and sixteen grandchildren (now nineteen, and three great grandchildren)—all who are very important to me, important enough that I have endeavored to give quality time to each of them.

How was I going to have time to write? I had tried to write, but all these other commitments kept me from it. I wrote a regular newsletter but I knew it was more than this. The Lord was asking for books.

After the prayer conference I had a day in between before I attended a second conference in Vernon, BC, a 30 minute drive from Kelowna. This second one was a Christian Ministers' Association conference, one that I attend almost yearly. My ordination papers are through this group. That year, 2012, these two conferences happened to land back to back.

During the day in between, I had time to think and pray. I knew I had to take some drastic measures to make time to write. I asked the Lord to direct me, to help me.

The CMA conference was uplifting and good. At the very end the Lord dropped something further into my spirit, something very profound and jolting. It was a further challenging word added to all He'd been speaking the last few days. He was really on my case.

The speaker was Ken Blue who had been an associate pastor alongside John Wimber. In the last session, at the very end of his talk, he had us stand up. He'd been speaking about fulfilling God's purpose in our lives, saying some of us might not be doing what God actually wants us to be doing. As we were standing, he said he would make a statement and then have us be silent for a few minutes, thinking on it.

"If you were brave, what would you do?" he asked.

Immediately I began to think on how to rearrange my life to write. I knew God would not do that part. I needed to do that. I had a deep sense that if I don't take action, this moment of opportunity may pass.

After we had been quiet for a few minutes, Ken said, "The first thought that came to your mind is most likely what you should be doing."

Boom!

God's voice was loud and clear.

Within a year I had transitioned from leading the Prince George House of Prayer, having turned the reins over to a faithful woman of God who had been attending for seven years, and who carried PGHOP in her heart. I also stepped down from the executive of the Prince George Ministerial Association, an assignment I had carried for eight years. Within two years of that encounter with God in Kelowna and Vernon, I had written, illustrated, and published my first book, *A True Tale of a Returning King.*

Why did I write this chapter, this story from my life? Perhaps you are in that place of needing to take a step of faith into a whole new focus and season in your life. What has God been whispering to you?

If you are brave, what would you do?

Part Two

The Call

For consider your calling
...that there were not many wise according to the flesh,
Not many mighty, not many noble
1 Corinthians 1:26 nasb

Call to Me and I will answer you, and I will tell you
Great and mighty things, which you do not know.
Jeremiah 33:3 nasb

Chapter Three

The Visitation

We do not know how to pray as we should.
Romans 8:26 nasb

God called me to prayer at an early age.

I didn't know that was what He was doing when I had a very unusual visitation. I wasn't even born again. I was about eight or nine years old.

My sister, Miriam, who is two years younger, and I were lying on the floor propped on our elbows coloring in a shared coloring book. We were chattering away, as little girls do, enjoying the moment.

Suddenly I was in another realm. My sister's voice faded into the background and I could hear a song being sung:

I won't forget,
I won't ever forget
Your suffering.
I saw you there on Your knees
In Gethsemane.

I heard this song in the Finnish language which is my mother tongue. This familiar, minor key hymn was sometimes sung in church. That day, though, it was not being sung by a human—it was coming from another realm entirely. I was gripped.

My sister chattered away, completely unaware that I was hearing something else. I heard her voice in the distance, but this song overrode everything else and overwhelmed me.

"Marja! Marja!" my sister's voice came through with an edge of annoyance. I realized she had asked me something and was irritated because I didn't answer. The "visitation" faded and I was back in this earthly realm. I did not tell her what had happened because I was not able to explain it. It left an indelible mark on my soul and I pondered it.

It was not until a few of years later that I gave my life to Jesus in response to His Spirit drawing me.

Learning from older praying people

When I was 11, my parents started me on piano lessons. We didn't have a piano at home so my dad, being the pastor of the church, gave me a church key to practice there. I walked a mile three times a week or so, to the little church at the end of our long street. For a short season I tried praying after those practice times, kneeling down at one of the wooden pews to pray for about 15 minutes. Alone in the church, I attempted to seek the Lord. I knew prayer was something people who truly knew God did, so I started. I did this for maybe a few weeks but didn't carry on.

I learned to play the piano because there was no pianist in the congregation. Within two years I was accompanying the hymns as well as the choir, though my playing was quite bumpy at times. On Wednesday nights there was a prayer meeting which I attended to accompany the singing. I listened to the older saints pouring out their hearts in prayer as we kneeled at the old wooden pews and it left a deep impression on my heart. I knew this was holy ground, this seeking of the Lord.

My parents went to God in prayer

My parents were praying people, not just at church but at home also. We went through many trials and my parents knew where to go for help—to God.

Mom prayed daily. In the morning, she made breakfast for dad and saw him off to work before getting us five children ready for the day. After that, she shut her bedroom door to pray and read her Bible for about an hour before starting her daily tasks. I had deep respect for that and it left a lasting mark on my life.

One time no one was at home except my dad and I—a rare moment, considering we were a family of seven. I was upstairs in my bedroom when I heard my father crying out to God in deep, earnest prayer. It was a type of prayer that was not just a quiet conversation with the Lord. It was earnest supplication with tears. I heard the tears in his voice. It was a breathtaking moment as he poured out his heart to God. I knew there was some trouble at the church, so I guessed my dad was going to the Lord about it.

My parents were far from perfect but they were the real deal. They knew where to go—to God. I learned this walk of prayer by observing their lives.

I wanted a prayer life

But it was not to be until a few years later that I started on that journey.

At 21 years of age, my husband and I had three children and two floundering businesses. We had moved from Ontario to British Columbia, two thousand kilometers from my family. I was drowning in the weight of responsibility and overwhelmed with anxiety because our finances were very tight. I was at the cusp of a nervous breakdown.

I was desperately crying out to God for help because I felt hemmed in with walls all around me. However, there was no ceiling, so I looked up and cried out to God. He spoke to me, saying, "I want to help you, but you only come to Me five minutes a day. I want your time. Come spend one hour a day with Me." I knew this was God speaking. It was true I read a chapter or two from the Bible almost daily and then would say quick, "bless us" prayers for all the family. But He wanted a greater depth of relationship with me.

How was I going to fit an hour a day with God in the midst of three little ones, and two businesses?

However, my heart was set to make it happen somehow. Though I didn't start right away, it was my goal to get there one way or another. I knew if God was asking me to do it, He would empower me. He wasn't going to ask me to do something I wouldn't be able to do because the Bible says, "I can do all things through Christ who strengthens me" Philip. 4:13 (web).

God is so good. He knows the intentions of our heart, hearing the weak prayers for help as we try to move in the direction He has spoken. His help came through a book which fell into my hands in an unusual way, and it launched me into the life of prayer I had wanted to have for a long time.

God works hard behind the scenes to help us, more than we realize. His Holy Spirit is called the "Helper". He wants us to fulfill His dream for our lives and He coaches, woos, and helps us along with many clues and hints. He keeps talking to us in many ways and from many angles and sources, confirming what He is saying. The book, the help from God, came to me in this way:

One of the businesses we were doing was Amway. My husband started Amway to tide us over during the slower months of our primary business, Home Electric and Finnish Sauna.

Our Amway business had grown to include a number of distributors whom we trained, one couple living about 180 kilometers away. We encouraged them to organize a training weekend and we would come train their growing team.

We had three little boys at that time. We left the two oldest at home with a babysitter and took the baby with us.

Our hosts lived in a mobile home with their three children. They generously gave us the master bedroom for the night. As we were nearing bed time, they told us Saturday was their "sleep-in" morning and asked us not to get up until 10 am, their home being so small that if someone got up and started bustling around, it would disturb the others. We happily complied as our next training meeting wasn't until the afternoon. Our baby was a good sleeper, so I thought I was in for a treat—I could sleep in with no toddlers to get up for!

I slept soundly, but at 7 am I woke up. I tried to sleep some more, but to no avail. I was wide awake. I wondered what I was going to do for the next few hours, as I could only lie there.

Because our host family lived in a mobile home with limited storage space, there were a lot of unpacked boxes neatly piled on one side of the room, each neatly labeled in large letters. I spent some time reading the labels from bed, but that only covered a small segment of time. Then I looked over the books on the bedside table. One book, titled *How Do You Find the Time,* caught my eye. My very dilemma! I flipped to the back cover to read about the author. It had a picture of a very pretty lady, well-dressed and well-groomed. *I bet she doesn't have kids. What does she know about time?* I began to read her bio and was shocked to find she had TEN children. I was sold. I began to devour the book, reading most of it by 10 am.

This book launched me into a life of prayer. The author, Pat King, wrote how her life had been basically like mine, in chaos and losing her mind until a priest helped her to order her life.. He counseled her to put GOD FIRST. Give Him time. Then give time to your husband, then to your children, and then to work or ministry. She began to do the same as my mom had for years—after getting her husband off to work, her kids off to school, and organizing the little ones to play, she spent 15 minutes a day with the Lord. Even before she cleaned up the breakfast bowls.

Her life began to come into order and peace.

I *knew* God was speaking to me!

I felt God asking me for one hour a day. Jesus' words to the disciples in the Garden of Gethsemane when they had fallen asleep while He prayed in agony, were: "Could you not watch with me one hour?" (Matt. 26:40 nasb). I felt He was saying these words to me.

It was still another three months before I launched into prayer, though I was committed. I wanted to be inwardly prepared so that I would keep at it, not wanting to start something and then quitting. I guess that would be called "counting the cost".

After "counting the cost" I finally began

It was September of 1977 when I finally started to pray an hour a day, doing it in the afternoon during the kids quiet time/nap time. There were four of them now, as I was babysitting a little 2 year old boy alongside my three boys who were 4, 2, and 1.

The first few months were like chewing cardboard—very dry. In ten minutes I had prayed everything I could think of, and nothing more would come. Because I was determined to keep my hour, I read my Bible and then a good teaching book to fill up the time.

After two months of this I had a *breakthrough!*

I was burdened for some new believers who were attending our church and prayed for them. It was like I entered a river of prayer. Something took over. It was the Holy Spirit praying through me, as Romans 8:26–27 (nasb) states:

> *...for we do not know how to pray as we should,*
> *but the Spirit himself intercedes for us with groanings*
> *too deep for words;*
> *and He who searches the hearts knows what the mind*
> *of the Spirit is,*
> *because He intercedes for the saints according to*
> *the will of God.*

I was in a spirit of prayer. I thought ten minutes had gone by, but when I looked at the clock, it was an hour. I was exhilarated. And not just because I had prayed an hour with a flow of the Spirit, but also because I **knew** in my spirit the Lord had heard and He would answer.

Sure enough, I began to see God answer these prayers. Though I didn't tell these people I was praying for them, I had the privilege of watching my prayers being answered. It built my faith to keep asking—to keep praying. I felt like I had discovered a priceless treasure: the gift of prayer. A whole universe of possibilities had opened up to me. "Ask and you shall receive." I was eager and ready to keep going, to keep asking. I was sold. I was in!

The further unpacking mystery of it all was that some of these ones I was praying for came asking me to pray for them, and some asking me to counsel them. I was overwhelmed as I did not know anything about counseling. One young woman, in particular, who was four years older than me, wanted counselling. I told her the only thing I could counsel her about was on how to connect with God in prayer. She was willing, so I, in my early 20's, taught her what little I knew and she began to do it. Her life was a mess—drugs, depression, and a difficult marriage. She began to pray and learned to prevail in prayer, because she was determined to know her God. About 12 years later she went to Japan as a missionary with her 13 year old son. Within a few years, she was ordained, and pastored a small congregation in Nagoya, Japan for over 20 years until her death in 2019. This formerly depressed young woman who had spent a lot of time in bed, learned the power of prayer. She became an ordained pastor, led people to the Lord, discipled, helped and prayed for many people, as well as traveled to several nations to minister. In Zambia, the First Lady (the President's wife) attended a conference where my friend spoke, and invited her for tea. "Do you see a man skillful in his work? He will stand before kings." (Prov. 22:29 esv). She became skilled in the art of prayer and God led her in unusual ways.

Unfolding adventures

God has had me on an adventure with Him ever since I learned the power and delight of prayer. Over the years I have seen many miracles.

At age 31 I wrote a teaching manual about prayer called *Power Perfected in Weakness.* My pastor arranged my manuscript to be typed and printed and I taught it at our church's Bible School for many years. God also opened doors for me to teach it in three Bible Schools in Africa: in Malawi, Zimbabwe, and Zambia as well as in a number of churches in towns and cities of Canada. When I teach this course, I tell many stories from my own life, my family, and from the team of intercessors I prayed with, to show the application of the Bible truths of prayer.

As I wrote, in chapters one and two, God spoke to me to write these stories. He also spoke to write about the principle of birthing. The stories are not written in the teaching manual because I tell them verbally when I teach. This book is both a stand-alone book, and also a companion book to the manual—a written account of these stories.

My prayer is that this book will inspire you in your life and journey of prayer and that you will grow in intimacy with the Lord. Also I pray you will have an ongoing conversation with your bridegroom, Jesus, and with the Heavenly Father, allowing the Holy Spirit to pray through you.

My whole life has been a journey of prayer and a journey of mobilizing, stirring, and encouraging the bride of Christ to be a praying bride—because things happen when we pray!

It wasn't until later in my prayer journey that I learned what actually takes place when we pray. For years I just did it and had great faith because I saw answers. But I have come to see that prayer is the very tool God left with us to advance His kingdom purposes. His kingdom comes, advances, grows as we pray. Prayer is talking with Jesus, our bridegroom, and creating things with Him through words spoken in faith. He has called us to partner with Him through prayer, and the actions that follow, to build His kingdom.

In the next chapter I write about birthing. If you are a man, and think that chapter is for women, please know that Jesus likened His death, burial and resurrection to a woman in the process of birthing (John 16:20-22). And Paul, a man, said:

> *My dear children, for whom I am again in the pains*
> *of childbirth*
> *Until Christ is formed in you. Galatians 4:19 niv*

Part Three

In the Dark Night of the Soul We are Birthing

If anyone wishes to come after Me, he must deny himself,
and take up his cross and follow Me.
Matthew 16:24 nasb

For we who live are constantly being delivered over to
death for
Jesus' sake, so that the life of Jesus also may be
manifested in our mortal flesh.
So death works in us, but life in you.
2 Corinthians 4:11-12 nasb

My grace is sufficient for you,
for power if perfected in weakness.
2 Corinthians 12: 9

Chapter Four

Birthing

As I wrote earlier, when I was a young mother in my early 20's, I felt overwhelmed—a lot—with two active little boys, expecting a third and managing two businesses from our home. The phone rang constantly and clients were often at the door. Finances were sporadic. Some months were okay, but other months were terribly lean. I had a lot of anxiety because bills remained unpaid at times and because of our topsy-turvy life. On top of this, our marriage was strained. I was struggling with resentment toward my husband for adding these businesses to my busy life of just being a mom of toddlers and keeping up the house. This was the circumstance that started me praying. Desperate praying to keep me from drowning.

In the midst of this desperate praying, God began to teach me to be specific in prayer, so I asked Him why life had so many problems. It seemed you just worked through one set and another loomed on the horizon. There didn't seem to be a lot of "aaaah" moments where you could just kick back and feel the joy of life. It was "go-go-go" from morning to night. You just got everything cleaned up and then you had to start all over again. My daughter, who has 4 children, said it well: "The majority of my life is about food. I grocery shop, put the groceries away, cook, feed the family, wash dishes, and then start all over again."

It wasn't just the work load that was demanding. There were obstacles and trials continually interspersed in the middle of it all.

For about nine months I asked the Lord this question: why so many problems and difficulties? I was pregnant with my third child at the time, and when it was time to birth, God answered me. It wasn't audible words He spoke. It was a revelation.

He said, in essence, "Everything of value in life is birthed. There are labor pains to bring forth life. This principle works in the natural realm. You give birth to children through a process of conception, gestation, labor, and birth. It is painful but the child is a treasure, and far outweighs the pain a mother suffers to give birth. In the same way, to bring forth life in the spirit, you go through conception, gestation, labor and travail."

After this revelation I began to notice that whenever we faced trials, sometimes seemingly unbearable ones, something was being "birthed". As a result, rather than being hopeless, helpless, and despairing, it gave me hope. Rather than looking at the bleakness of the trial, I began to look ahead to see *what was being birthed through it.*

I knew she was a ripe fruit ready for picking!

One early spring weekend was especially dark and bleak in many ways. The days were unpleasant, cloudy, chilly, and gloomy, and our little hobby farm acreage was a muddy mess as the snows were melting. We had several goats and one of them went into labor, a first birthing for her, but she could not deliver. Our boys had become quite attached to her so it was upsetting for them to see her in such distress. My husband had grown up on a farm and knew something of these things but he finally called a veterinarian for help because the labor was going on far too long. He was informed they would not come during the weekend. The labor pains continued into the night but the goat could not deliver. The youngest boys finally fell asleep but our oldest son was too grieved to sleep, weeping inconsolably. The baby goat died in the process and my husband had to remove it from the mother's body. She barely survived the ordeal. It was all very sorrowful. Very tragic.

On Sunday we went to church as usual, and after service I talked with a friend, Andrea*, asking her about a mutual friend whom she worked with at a seniors' home. A few weeks earlier Andrea had told me about

---

* *names changed*

Olivia*, saying she was very close to asking Jesus into her life. Olivia had been asking a lot of questions. I encouraged Andrea to lead her to the Lord, saying I would pray for her as she did this. So now at church I asked her how this was going. She said she hadn't led her to the Lord yet. Suddenly I knew I needed to call Olivia myself.

Later that day I called and asked if I could visit. She was happy to have me come and we set a time. A few days later I arrived at her home and we began to chat. Before long I told her about a family who was known to both of us, telling her how the husband had recently given his life to the Lord. As I told the story, I noticed she was sitting on the edge of her seat, so to speak, wanting to know everything. She was drinking it in. *I knew she was a ripe fruit ready for picking.* I finished the story, asking if she also wanted to ask Jesus into her life. She immediately said, "Yes!" No ifs, ands, or buts. She was absolutely ready to become a Christian. I prayed with her and she asked Jesus into her life, receiving forgiveness of sins. It was a joyful moment. A divine appointment.

As I drove home, I praised the Lord—I was ecstatic! A new child had been born into the kingdom of God. My joy was similar to the joy I had experienced immediately after giving birth to my children. An immediate flood of joy and exhilaration, of great happiness, had overwhelmed me after each birth. I pondered this. I felt that same sense of joy and exhilaration for this new birth. We had gone through several bleak days of "birth pains": the death of the baby goat during those dark, dreary days followed by a new birth. It had been dark and now the lights were on brightly. The sun was shining again. I saw the correlation: pain preceded birth. I thought of the scripture "so death works in us, but life in you" 2 Cor. 4:12 (nasb).

A broken leg on a ski hill led to the salvation of a Satanist

Some years later, when two girls had been added to our family, we made a holiday trip to Smithers, BC for a day of downhill skiing. We had worked tirelessly for 8 weeks as volunteers, campaigning for the federal election to

---

* *names changed*

have a good MP voted in. After the push, we were exhausted and due for some quality family time. We were living on a shoe-string budget so a holiday like this would normally be out-of-question. However, my cousin had visited Canada from Finland and when she left, she gave us her left over Canadian dollars. It was just enough to make this trip. Another friend lent us her van to more comfortably accommodate our family of 7. We arrived in the evening and settled into our hotel room for the night. The next morning we headed out to the mountain which was about 20 kilometers away. We wanted a whole day of fun so we left early to take in every possible minute.

I had been there once before as a chaperone for our church's youth group and recollected a breathtaking moment from the top of the mountain. It had been a gorgeous, sunny day. The sky was bright blue and the snow-covered vista stretched for perhaps 50 kilometers. It was brilliant and sparkling white against a backdrop of blue sky and dark green coniferous tree—so beautiful that it moved me. The scene and accompanying emotion were etched into my soul and I was hoping to relive that moment.

However, it was not to be. Instead of sunshine, big flakes of snow were falling—thick and heavy—from grey, low-hanging clouds. Well, we weren't going to let that stop us, so we donned on the skis. Tuomo said he would do the first shift with the girls, who were 6 and 4 years old, to teach them basics of skiing at the bottom of the hill. I headed up the lift with the boys for the first run. Near the bottom of the hill I was aghast to find Helena, who was 6, with a broken leg! The ski lodge first aid attendants carefully placed her on a sled, and skied down the hill, gently pulling the sled to our van. Tuomo, as he was leaving to drive her to the hospital, told us to keep skiing. Though I would much rather have gone to the hospital, one of us needed to stay with the rest of the kids and let them get some enjoyment from the day. It certainly was not enjoyable for me. My heart was with my little girl who was suffering, and the bleak, gloomy day added to the feeling of despondency. A cloud hung over us but the kids did many runs down the mountain in spite of this set back.

Finally around 3 pm, the van pulled into the lodge parking lot. Helena lay in the back seat with a cast that reached to her thigh, and in spite of her pain, was in quite good spirits. Surprisingly, Tuomo had picked up a hitchhiker who was sitting in the front passenger seat. This young woman had been out in the wilderness, many miles from anywhere, hitchhiking with her dog. Tuomo felt a prompting from the Lord to give her a ride. She was headed out further past the ski lodge to her uncle's cabin. Very quickly the conversation had turned to God. She claimed to be Satanist and asked how many commandments God has, going on to say Satan has 13. She had grown up in a Satanist family—that was all she knew. The Holy Spirit led Tuomo to share Christ with her. She was open to listen, and after some more questions, she wanted to receive Him into her life. They had just gotten to that part when they arrived at the parking lot. We all piled into the van and Tuomo introduced Rose*, sharing the gist of their conversation with us and then saying that we are going to pray because Rose wants to receive Jesus into her life. So we prayed together—a car full of kids, one in a cast fresh from the hospital—and were thus able to participate in a new birth. It was glorious to be present when a child was born into God's kingdom.

The dark night of the soul was turned into glory!

Though Helena missed out on the fun of skiing and later swimming at a waterslide pool, she endured her circumstance with patience. At school she was hailed a hero and came home with many names autographed on her white cast.

Death works in us, but life in you

I began to see the following scripture at work in our lives, and memorized it because God was writing it upon my heart:

> *But we have this treasure in earthen vessels,*
> *so that the surpassing greatness of the power will be of*
> *God and not from ourselves. We are **afflicted in every***
> ***way, but not crushed,***
> ***perplexed but not despairing, persecuted but not***
> ***forsaken,***

---

* *name changed*

struck down but not destroyed,
always carrying about in the body the dying of Jesus
that the life of Jesus also may be manifested in
our body.
For we who live are constantly being delivered over to
death for Jesus' sake,
that the life of Jesus also may be manifested in our
mortal flesh,
so death works in us but life in you. 2 Corinthians
4:7-12 nasb

These two stories are about new births that took place as a result of birth pains. However, birth pains are not just for salvation of souls. It is for anything God has called us to do. Some may be long-term life callings that are often preceded by a long season of birth pain. In the next chapters I talk about how God prepared the Bible characters for their callings by years of trials, and I tell some of our story which seemed to have no end of trials and testing. But God was forming something…

Chapter Five

The Fellowship of His Sufferings

Whenever we have pain and suffering, it is an
invitation to the knowledge of God. Pain is often the
escort to know Him

These difficulties I wrote about were not just to be endured and gotten out of the way so we could get on with the business of the kingdom. No, rather, God was at work using these *very difficulties* to bring life. Through much tribulation we enter the Kingdom. (Acts 14:22). These are the necessary birth pains.

To truly know Jesus as an intimate Friend, we need to walk—even partly—where He walked

That I may know Him and the power of His resurrection
and the fellowship of His sufferings, being conformed to
His death. Philippians 3:10 nasb

To have resurrection power, we need to also to be identified with Jesus' suffering. How can we understand someone until we have walked, even partly, where they have walked? Until we have felt some of their pain?

Rejection may be a privilege

I think of rejection, for example. If we go through that in some form, it is actually a high privilege. We are given the experience of being identified with Jesus because He was the most rejected Person, and still is. Even now God is not wanted in most governments of the world, though He was the one who created these earthly rulers and gave them the authority they have (Rom. 13:1, 4). He gives breath, food, shelter, and favor to the very ones who are denying and rejecting Him. They devise their own ways to govern independently of the God who makes their hearts beat.

In Hebrews it says we are to go out to Him, outside the camp, and bear His reproach. He was rejected. He was put outside the camp. So if you feel that you are rejected, feeling like you are not included, that you are an outsider, consider this: you are identified with the Lord. Jesus came to earth the first time as a suffering servant, but He will come again as Bridegroom, King and Judge and will govern this earth with righteousness and justice.

If you just wait a little while. If you keep turning to Jesus in your pain, asking for His healing grace and comfort, and praying for and blessing those who reject and hurt you, the tables will turn in your life. God tests us to see if we will walk through these difficult, unjust things His way. He has reigning in mind for you. Some of it will be here on earth in this age, but some in the age to come. You are going to rule and reign with Him.

Jesus response to unjust treatment is an example for us

When Jesus was terribly and unjustly treated this was His response:

> ...*And while being reviled, He did not revile in return;*
> *while suffering, He uttered no threats, but kept entrusting*
> *Himself to Him who judges righteously. 1 Peter 2:23. nasb*

When He was insulted and wrongly treated, He did not give it back, but kept committing Himself to God, knowing God will make the right judgment in due time. Rather than retaliating, He said, *"Father, forgive them; for they do not know not what they are doing"* (Luke 23:34 niv). They were blinded and did not know how wrong—how terribly wrong—they were in hurling accusations, beating, and crucifying Him, the very One who came to help, rescue, and save them from their sins. The one who came to heal them from brokenness, give them a future, a hope, and eternal life with Him.

Our responses in this life matter for the life to come

Jesus was our example in all things. He modeled for us how to live, how to respond in life's situations. There is more to life than these 70 or 80 years here on earth, an eternity of billions of years. Not everything gets resolved here, but nothing goes unnoticed by God and everything will be resolved one day. How we live in this age matters. How we respond to situations will determine our authority in the spirit realm here and now, but also in the future.

God wants us to live with an eternal, long-term perspective, being confident that He sees—He does not let anything go past Him unnoticed— and He will bring justice.

God *is* a God of justice, He *will* deal with it

So if unjust accusations are hurled at you, God sees, and your response matters. He wants you to know *He will deal with it*, but in His own way and His own time. Our job is to trust Him, not take vengeance, or to try to vindicate ourselves. Yes, there are times we are to speak up, but other times we need to be silent and wait for God to move. If we go to Him in prayer, He will show us which way to respond.

Those who remain faithful to Him in this age, even while suffering, will rule with Him, as Paul says that if we suffer, we will also reign with Him (2 Tim. 2:12). It seems the pathway to authority in the spirit realm is to walk in suffering also. This authority is for both the present age and the age to come when He comes to establish His physical government here on earth. This long term vision helped me greatly. I knew there would be justice one day because God is a just God.

Reading through the Bible over and over opened my eyes to see the way God dealt with His people, particularly those whom He had called to walk in leadership. God loved them and was moved by their response of trusting Him through their times of suffering and trials.

Joseph

The story of Joseph has always moved me. I remember reading it to my girls when they were under 5 years of age, sitting on my lap in our overstuffed armchair. I read it from Arthur Maxwell's Bible series books for children. The part that still moves me the most is when Joseph's brothers, who had terribly rejected him and sold him into slavery 20 years earlier, were now on their knees before him. They didn't recognize him because he was now a ruler in Egypt. Speaking to each other in Hebrew, they lamented their mistreatment of him, saying they were reaping the consequences. He understood what they were saying though he pretended to speak Egyptian only. Joseph could no longer contain his emotion and quickly left the room. He cried so loudly that his voice was heard throughout the palace by the servants. I had to stop reading at this point because emotion welled up in me so strong that I couldn't contain it either. I sobbed. Joseph loved his brothers in spite of everything they had done and he forgave them.

Joseph had gone through terrible, unjust treatment. God was behind all this, having in mind this plan to make him a ruler in Egypt for the purpose of preserving his own family who were the beginnings of the nation of Israel, and who carried the Messianic seed in their lineage. And God, through Joseph, saved Egypt from famine also.

It's very interesting that the Genesis story of Joseph—where 20 some years are covered in 13 chapters—is mostly from a human point of view, saying the brothers sold him as a slave, and Potiphar sent him to prison. He went to Egypt because of his brothers' sinful actions, and into prison because of Potiphar's wife's lie. But in Psalms 105, the story is told from God's perspective. The brothers are not even mentioned. It says *God sent* Joseph to Egypt. Wow! It was planned! He even planned the famine!

*And **He called** for a famine upon the land;*
He broke the whole staff (provision) of bread.
***He sent** a man before them, Joseph, who was sold*
as a slave.

They afflicted his feet with fetters, he himself was
laid in irons;
until the time that His word came to pass, the word of the
Lord tested him.
Psalm 105:16-19 nasb

Man is often the instrument that brings us pain, but God is behind the scenes, using those painful things to form us into His masterpiece.

For you have tried us, O God; *You have refined us as*
silver is refined.
You brought us into the net; You laid an oppressive burden
upon our loins.
You made men ride over our heads; *we went through*
fire and through water, **yet You brought us out into a**
place of abundance.
Psalm 66:10-12 nasb

God has a long-term plan and outcome. He wants to bring us to a place of abundance, and into a place of reigning, which Joseph's story illustrates.

David

David was another one who went through many years of affliction, being chased by Saul and his army of 3,000 soldiers on assignment to kill him. When David was a teenager, he had been anointed by Samuel, the prophet, to become the king God had chosen, but it took 20 years of trials and testing before he stepped into his full rulership in Israel.

David was real in his conversations with God. I held closely to some of his words because they gave me hope in my own long-term trial. Also, by reading the Psalms and Job I realized I can be real with God: I can tell him how much it hurts and how desperate I am for Him to bring me a breakthrough. David was honest, he was real, he didn't pretend.

How long, O Lord? Will You forget me forever?
How long will You hide Your face from me?
How long shall I take counsel in my soul,
having sorrow in my heart all the day?
How long will my enemy be exalted over me?
Psalm 13:1-2 nasb

Do not hide your face from me...
I would have despaired unless I had believed that
I would see the goodness of the Lord in the land of the
living. Wait for the Lord; (he is talking to himself)
be strong and let your heart take courage;
Yes, wait for the Lord.
Psalm 27:9, 13-14 nasb

I memorized Psalm 27 at one time because it was a lifeline for me in the dark tunnel that seemed to have no light at the end. I saw from scripture how things ended up for David. He was not killed by Saul. He finally became king over all Israel. So it gave me hope that there was an expected end for my situation too.

There had to be!

Daniel

Daniel also suffered many things in preparation for the great heavenly visitations and revelations which came in his senior years, visions that are for us, for our generation now in the end times.

Job

Job became a very precious book to me, giving me hope. Job was a God-fearing, righteous man, the wealthiest man in that era. Satan said to God that Job worshiped Him because He blessed him so much. God gave Satan permission to shake up his life to show that this man didn't seek and worship Him just for the blessings. As a result Job lost his wealth, his children, and his health, and yet he stayed true to God and trusted Him. He brought his suffering and complaint to God, but he did not lose his faith and trust in Him. I love these words he spoke (Job 1:21 nasb):

> *The Lord gave and the Lord has taken away. Blessed be the*
> *name of the Lord.*

In his suffering he kept talking to God.

> *Oh that my request might come to pass,*
> *and that God would grant my longing! Job 6:8 nasb*

You can hear his desperation for God to release him from his painful ordeal.

> *Though He slay me, I will hope in Him, Nevertheless I will*
> *argue my ways before Him. This also is my salvation, for a*
> *godless man may not come before His presence.*
> *Job 13:15 nasb*

God desires us to keep talking to Him, even bringing our complaint to Him. He wants us to be open and real. He delights in us staying close to Him through both good times and hard times. Many pull away from God during hard times. Those are the times we should press in all the more, like Job who said, "Though He slay me, I will hope in Him."

The restoration of Job came when he prayed for his friends, even though they had been poor comforters.

> *The Lord restored the fortunes of Job when he prayed for*
> *his friends,*
> *And the Lord increased all that Job had twofold.*
> *Job 42:10 nasb*

Paul

Paul the apostle talked about suffering, saying he was well content with difficulties and trials. Not at first though. He had been given a "thorn in the flesh, a messenger of Satan to torment" him, which some commentators say was a physical ailment. It was given to keep him from getting proud because he had been taken up to heaven and given visions and revelations which he was not allowed to talk about.

He implored the Lord to remove this "thorn". Three times. That may have been three seasons of fasting and prayer. God spoke to him, "My grace is sufficient for you, for power is perfected in weakness" (2 Corinth. 12: 9 nasb). Amazing words. God said "No" to Paul's request, but said, "I will give you sufficient grace to bear up under this because power is perfected in weakness". It really is a thing to meditate on. When God gives us a word, we can bear things. It sustains us. Paul goes on to say:

> *"Most gladly, therefore, I will rather boast about*
> *my weaknesses,*
> *so that the power of Christ may dwell in me. Therefore*
> *I am well content with weaknesses, with insults, with*
> *distresses, with persecutions, with difficulties,*
> *for Christ's sake; for when I am weak, then I am strong."*
> *2 Corinthians 12:9-10 nasb*

There is an expected end to suffering, a future and a hope

Reading about these Bible people who went through suffering, and who came through to an expected end, gave me much hope in the long season of testing we walked through. These verses became very dear to me. I hung onto them, because they showed the end of the story—the good outcome of their suffering.

These afflictions eclipsed by glory[2]

The depth of suffering equals the height of glory. The song, *Oh, How He Loves Us* by John Mark McMillan, has a line that says it well: *"these afflictions eclipsed by glory."*[3] I love those words—so powerful! Somehow in this process of affliction there comes a moment of eclipse when we have a revelation of His great affection for us. *If* we just hang in there, wait, and trust. He never lets us down.

I found a treasure of a scripture showing that God does not thresh forever. When whatever He is perfecting in us is done, the threshing ends:

Give ear and hear My voice. Listen and hear My words.
Does the farmer plow continually to plant seed?
Does he continually turn and harrow the ground? Does he
not level its surface, and sow dill and scatter cummin, and
plant wheat in rows, barley in its place, and rye within
its area?
For his God instructs and teaches him properly.
For dill is not threshed with a threshing sledge,
nor is the cartwheel driven over cummin;
but dill is beaten out with a rod, and cummin with a club.
Grain for bread is crushed, indeed,
he does not continue to thresh it forever.
Because the wheel of his cart and his horses eventually
damage it,
he does not thresh it longer.
This also comes from the Lord of hosts,
who has made His counsel wonderful and His
wisdom great.
Isaiah 28:23-29 nasb

God may harrow and turn the ground of our lives and later thresh BUT He knows exactly when to stop. He doesn't do it forever and it is for a very specific reason that He threshes—to bring fruitfulness, a harvest from our lives. There is an end to the trial.

For the Lord will not reject forever, for if He causes grief,
then He will have compassion according to His abundant

lovingkindness. For He does not afflict willingly or grieve
the sons of men. Lamentations 3:31-33 nasb

How comforting it is to know that He knows the depth of our suffering, walking alongside us, feeling our pain:

In all their suffering He also suffered. Isaiah 63:9

If you have been walking in faithfulness toward God and yet have been going through perplexing and excruciating long-term trials, I hope this chapter and these passages from the Bible are an encouragement to you. God is birthing something in and through your life and will bring you out, as Psalm 66:12 says, into a place of abundance at His appointed time.

When He has tried me, I shall come forth as gold.
Job 23:10 nasb

Chapter Six

The Dark Night of the Soul– Birthing a Vision

Through pain and struggle we give birth; wine comes only by the crushing of grapes

In Chapter 3 I wrote two stories from our lives about "birthing". They were shorter experiences of trials for several days preceding a birth. But what if you are going through years of testing that does not let up? Like Joseph. Like David. Perhaps God is birthing a calling or ministry in your life, something more long-term (this may not be pastoral ministry, but some service that will be a blessing to many people). I am going to tell you about the long-term, seemingly endless trial we went through, and what God brought about through it.

Before I do, I want to talk a bit more about birthing.

As I wrote in Chapter 3, through pain and struggle we bring forth life. This happens in both the natural and spiritual realms.

We know that everything God made has been waiting until
now in pain,
Like a woman ready to give birth. Romans 8:22 NCV

Childbirth is a painful process. At times the woman giving birth feels like she is dying. "An expectant mother often feels she is at the very brink of death during childbirth…the pain is necessary and might be labeled as the dying part of a mother's experience. Only as she willingly suffers and works can new life come forth."[4] This suffering turns into great joy.

*Whenever a woman is in labor she has pain, because her
hour has come;
but when she gives birth to the child, she no longer
remembers the anguish because of the joy that a child has
been born into the world. John 16:21 nasb*

Jesus likened His death and resurrection to a woman giving birth

When talking to His disciples, He described the emotions they would go through very shortly, likening them to what a woman goes through in birthing. At that point they didn't understand what He was talking about.

*(Jesus said) "Are you trying to figure out among
yourselves what I meant when I said, 'In a day or so you're
not going to see me, but then in another day or so you
will see me'? Then fix this firmly in your minds;* **you're
going to be in deep mourning while the godless world
throws a party. You'll be sad, very sad, but your
sadness will develop into gladness. When a woman
gives birth, she has a hard time, there's no getting
around it. But when the baby is born, there is joy in
the birth.** *This new life in the world wipes out memory of
the pain.* **The sadness you have right now is similar to
that pain, but the coming joy is also similar.** *When I
see you again, you'll be full of joy, and it will be a joy no
one can rob from you."*
John 16:19-22 Message

Valleys of pain can lead to mountains of delight and joy

The child brings great joy and delight to his mother and father, but he is birthed through pain. This same principle exists in the spiritual realm. Whenever God wants us to bring life to others, we must go through a process of "death" which is painful. It may not be physical pain, but it can be. It can be mental torment, upheaval of circumstances, a feeling of loss of vision and direction, great despairing and hopelessness, a feeling of failing in areas you have been good at before, a loss of a job or possessions, a sudden negative reversal of finances, loss of a loved one, or being rejected.

There is an IF

These difficult, painful things may be God's gateway to ministering life to others through you. I say "can be", because there is an "if" in the equation. Our response. How do we respond to these trials? Some become bitter and hardened. Others turn to God and trust Him through the trials. *If* we continue to seek Him and trust Him like David, Joseph, Job, Jesus, and Paul did, then life will be birthed through these "death" experiences.

Painful reversals may be a birthing process, bringing life to others

This "death" process may take a day, several days, several weeks, or even some years. It depends on what God is birthing. If there have been several years of darkness in your life, God may be calling and forming you for effectual ministry, not just for one person's life but to many.

There is no victory without a battle.

There is no joy without sorrow.

There is no gain without pain.

John and Paula Sanford write about how God took them through this process in their book, *The Elijah Task*. They had faithfully and successfully pastored for many years, but then things took a turn. They felt like they were crashing down a mountain. Suddenly they were failing at everything they used to do well, and went through fiery trials for a period of about seven years. When they finally came to the "bottom of the mountain", a prophetic calling had been added to their lives.

So don't be surprised if this happens to you too. You may have been serving faithfully and joyfully in the purposes of God, and sudden reversal seems to take place. You seem to be failing at everything you were good at before. God is birthing you to a higher realm of spiritual effectiveness. You are going through the "death" process which will bring "life" to others.

*We are **afflicted** in every way, **but not crushed**,*
perplexed but not despairing, persecuted but not

forsaken; struck down but not destroyed, always
carrying about in the body the dying of Jesus,
that the life of Jesus also may be manifested in our body…
So death works in us, but life in you.
2 Corinthians 4:8-12 nasb

This "death" means the afflictions, perplexing circumstances, crushing and persecutions. This "life of Jesus" means the help that comes to people through us. It can take the form of a word of encouragement, exhortation, prophecy, teaching, deed of mercy, healing, word of wisdom, etc. Whatever help it is, because it has been birthed through death in us, it brings life—it stirs life in the person who is the recipient. Comfort, strength, renewed vision and hope come to that person, and because we have "birthed" life, it also brings us great joy. Our heart is satisfied when we do the will of God. Jesus said, "My food is to do the will of Him who sent me."(John 4:34 nasb). The most satisfying moments are in finding myself doing the will of God.

God comforts us in our trials so we can bring comfort to others
There is much in this following passage to help us in our trials. Please read it slowly.

Blessed be the God and Father of our Lord Jesus Christ,
*the Father of mercies and **God of all comfort, who***
comforts us in all our affliction so that we will be
able to comfort those who are in any affliction with
the comfort with which we ourselves are comforted
***by God.** For just as the sufferings of Christ are ours*
in abundance, so also our comfort is abundant through
Christ. But, if we are afflicted, it is for your comfort and
salvation; or if we are comforted, it is for your comfort.
2 Corinthians 1:3-7 nasb

What we go through brings comfort and help to others if we walk our trials through with the Lord. John and Paula Sanford's story brought great comfort to me. It helped me see the light at the end of my tunnel—that there was purpose in my trials. God was forming something. In the same way, your and my trials will turn around to bring comfort to others as we trust Him for His comfort in the middle of them.

Paul Billheimer, in his book *The Mystery of God's Providence*, says: *"The longer the time God takes with our training and the harder the discipline the larger will be life's service when it is finished."*[5]

I am taking quite a bit of space writing about this preparation: these trials—the sufferings and afflictions that God's kids go through in smaller and larger scales. I felt God wanted this emphasized because some of you feel like Joseph in a dungeon, or like David being chased around by Saul, despairing even of life at times, or like Job with seeming endless suffering and trials. On top of that, you are being told you must have sin in your life or are lacking faith, to add to the pain. Be comforted. Just like Joseph, David and Job, God is preparing you for something and He knows exactly when to stop. He knows when you are threshed grain, ready to be baked into bread that will nourish many.

Your "death" will bring "life" to others.

Chapter Seven

Our Dark Night of the Soul

The ravens will feed you

Before I married Tuomo, he told me about a prophecy given to him in Finland before he moved to Canada. He was told he would go through a time when the "ravens would feed him." "Are you sure you want to marry me?" he asked. There was absolutely no hesitation on my part. I gave the prophecy little thought.

Our first few years were good financially. As newly-weds, we moved from Thunder Bay, Ontario to Prince George, British Columbia. Tuomo landed a job easily in his field of being an electronics technician. His income was double what it had been in Ontario and we were able to buy half a duplex. A few years later he began his own business, *Home Electric and Finnish Sauna*. The first few months were reasonably good, but after Christmas there were very few client calls. I was getting worried. February came and Tuomo added Amway as a second income to tie us over the hard months. I gave birth to our second son in the middle of this. I felt overwhelmed. Our first few peaceful years were moving into a storm of uncertainty, irregularity, unpaid bills, and lots of work with babies, bookkeeping and phone calls.

A brief interlude of prosperity

After a few years of fluctuating businesses, Tuomo took a job as an office equipment salesman. He did quite well, and Amway was proving to give us some second income, though keeping us quite busy. One year we had $10,000 in the bank after all the bills were paid. We bought a house, and because of this extra money, Tuomo bought three more houses as investments. ($10,000 was worth almost four times more than now).

The season of ravens feeding us began

In 1981 the economy took a drastic downturn. It was very difficult to sell houses, and rental payments did not cover the mortgages. In the midst of this, Tuomo lost his job. We now had five children, three boys and two girls: mouths to feed and school payments to pay. He looked for work daily, but jobs were not available. Finally we had to resort to welfare assistance for six months. When tree planting season opened up, he left home several weeks at a time to work alongside university students in a distant wilderness.

After a few weeks of this exhausting labor, he was brought to a hospital in an ambulance. Following extensive testing locally and in Vancouver, he was diagnosed with Meniere's syndrome, a debilitating condition he suffered with for 20 years. This complicated his and our lives a lot. Then God healed him, and he has lived in much better health in his senior years.

In spite of his health situation, he went brush cutting that fall, worked as a caterer for a logging company, and then became a car salesman. He did anything and everything possible to keep food on the table: sold used items in garage sales (some he picked up from the side of the road), sold copper wire he harvested from electrical equipment, shoveled roofs in the winter, and collected dew worms with the kids late at night, selling them to gas stations in containers. The dew worm money was our bread and milk money.

Feeding a big family on a shoe string budget with wild game and fish

No matter what we tried, we got behind more and more. For a long time my allotted grocery budget was about $25-$35 a week. I always shopped the sales, used coupons, and bought the least expensive brands.

We had moved out-of-town to a 5 acre property which was one of the houses Tuomo had purchased. With the boys he planted a big garden of potatoes and carrots. Tuomo was a good hunter and fisherman, so our freezer was full of moose meat and trout. He often went fishing with the boys and took some of our young nephews along as well. The fishing rules back then stipulated you could take 10 fish a day per person, so an overnight fishing trip, with all those boys, meant a harvest of a hundred fish or so in the freezer. God blessed us this way. Our meals consisted of many forms of wild game, fish, potatoes and carrots.

Praise God for saskatoons!

For dessert we had saskatoon berries in many forms: fresh, cooked or baked into pies. When our first daughter was several months old it was saskatoon season. There was a big line of trees, lush with these juicy berries, at West Lake, not too far from our place. I packed the kids into my beater car many days in a row to pick the berries. I lay a blanket on the ground near the lake, placing the baby on it, and each of us had a 15 minute shift taking care of her while everyone else picked saskatoons. When the buckets were full, the boys were allowed to swim and play. These saskatoons were packaged and put into the freezer.

No such thing as going out for coffee

We didn't have money for extras. I remember our pastor talking about a fund raiser, suggesting people give up going for coffee for a time. It was completely foreign to me to have such a luxury as to actually go out for coffee. I was not able to do that for many years.

We didn't talk about our difficult situation to many people because it seemed everyone else was doing well. They had money for things like coffee, and lawn mowers. We at times were without a functioning one and our grass grew to shameful heights, adding stress because we were elders and were to be an example even in how we took care of our properties.

At times I cut off and discarded the black parts of old rotting potatoes, salvaging what I could, because there was nothing else to cook.

Christmas miracles

Christmas times were the hardest. I hoped for even a little extra to buy the children presents, even meager ones, and to buy some special groceries. One year was especially tight. We had no money at all to buy gifts for the boys; our daughter was so little she would not miss getting a present. We had a tradition of getting together for Christmas with extended family who lived in our city, so I knew the boys would get some presents from the family. I was able to give gifts to our relatives from our left over Amway stock—there were jewelry pieces for women, men's gift soaps, and items for the nephews and nieces—so our dire situation was not fully known. A card with some money arrived from my parents. I was able to buy pajamas for each of the boys, something they needed, but which they probably didn't appreciate as much as toys. But sure enough, they received gifts at our family celebration. These gatherings of celebrating Christ's birth, eating a special meal together, and exchanging gifts were highlights.

When we came home that evening, Tuomo handed me 50 beautiful roses in many, lovely colors. I was stunned. How could he do that? He told me he had gone to a flower shop late on Christmas Eve with a few dollars, hoping to buy one rose. The proprietor asked if he would like all the roses in the shop because they were closing over the holidays, and those roses would have been thrown out. It was amazing! I saw God's hand in it, blessing us and showing His desire to give us good gifts especially when we couldn't.

Chocolates in answer to our six year old daughter's prayer

God came through many times in amazing ways during the 16 years of excruciating financial hardship.

Truly the ravens fed us. We often found boxes of food on our doorstep. A church group in a nearby town had a unique ministry of helping out families in need of groceries, keeping a big supply of food specifically for that purpose. They would pray, asking God who to give to. Someone from this group often showed up at our door, through the most difficult years, with several boxes of groceries each time. These would come *just when we needed them the most*. They truly heard from God.

One time my youngest daughter, Keziah, who was 6, asked if we could buy Easter chocolates. Sadly I told the girls we had no extra money for that, but I said, "Why don't we pray and ask God for chocolates?" The three of us joined in prayer and asked. A few days later a box of groceries arrived at our door, and there was a basket of chocolate Easter eggs included. My heart sang and I thanked the Lord. It was a lesson for my girls that God hears and answers *their* prayers. It also showed me that God does not mind us having some treats like chocolates—we can even ask for that!

Getting my eyes off my misery and praying for those worse off

Our house was heated with oil, much too expensive, so Tuomo planned to build a wood-boiler furnace. He thought it would be done over a weekend. The weekend turned into 3 weeks with no furnace during the month of February, a very cold time of the year. We had two fireplaces and one space heater. Tuomo and the boys were gone most of the day to work and school where they were warm, but I struggled to keep our baby and myself warm. I put the space heater in the baby's room and huddled on the fireplace ledge as close to the fire as possible. The wood was not good burning wood, giving off very little heat, so I sat wrapped in a blanket, getting more and more miserable.

My eyes fell on a church bulletin which was lying on the fireplace ledge near me. I picked it up and began to read. There was an inserted World Vision brochure which drew my attention. On the front was a picture of a young, severely malnourished African boy sitting on the ground, hunched over. All his ribs were visible and he had little energy to barely sit up. My heart broke for him. I began to pray heartfelt prayers for those suffering this way in the world. My heart was painfully moved; I was groaning for them, agonizing for them. After praying for some time, I realized the heaviness about my own situation had lifted—yes, our situation was harsh compared to most in our culture, but it was not to the level this little boy was going through. God arranged for me to see this brochure, *just at the right time!* He moved my heart to pray for him, and others like him, and in so doing, He broke the heaviness off me. New grace flowed into me to carry on.

The well pump broke and there was no money to fix it

The 16-year journey was a continual walk of faith, needing to trust the Lord for basic things like water, even. Our well pump broke. There was no money to fix it. That meant no showers, no flushing toilets, no drinking water, and no water for washing dishes or laundry. How does one deal with that with a family of 6, a baby in diapers, to boot? Disposable diapers were out-of-question because of the expense. Tuomo started hauling 2 five gallon pails of water on his way home from work each day, which provided for meals and sponge baths. We put snow into the toilet bowls and tanks and the boys went outdoors for their bathroom business. We had an outside wood-heated sauna, which we used to bathe in, washing ourselves from basins of water.

But laundry? Friends who lived a few kilometers past us, and who attended our church, heard about our situation and offered their laundry facilities and showers to us. Once a week I took our baby and laundry and headed to their place while their house was empty, because both parents worked and their children were at school, as were our boys. I washed all my laundry but didn't use the dryer as I had one at home. I bathed the baby and had a shower myself, feeling so good to be clean and have the laundry washed. But when I arrived home, I could have cried. Our old Suburban SUV had a back window that did not close completely, a 4-inch gap remaining open and sucking in exhaust. All my laundry, my baby, and I reeked of engine exhaust!

It seemed we were continually being hit with discouraging things. God gave us grace to keep walking through this, but one time, one of the pastors' wives asked me how I was doing. She looked close into my eyes and asked, "How are you *really* doing?" I crumbled, began to cry, and told her our situation. Not long after, a couple contacted us, offering to loan us money to get the well pump fixed with no deadline for repayment. It was such a relief! After the work crew left, I headed for the shower, planning to enjoy it to the fullest. When I turned it on, only a tiny trickle came for a short while and that was all! Another setback. The work crew had to come back to fix the problem. Finally the well pump was fixed and we had water again.

The sump pump broke, then the dryer

Then, to our dismay, the sump pump broke. Tuomo had another smaller pump, which he inserted temporarily in the pit in our garage floor where the sewage was pumped from. Because this pump didn't have strength to pump to the lagoon underground, he had it pumped above-ground into a ditch near our house. Our house and neighborhood constantly smelled of sewage. Fortunately we lived far enough from our nearest neighbors so they didn't have to smell it. I dreaded people visiting, embarrassed by the smell. Eventually we could afford a new one, solving that problem.

Then our dryer broke so I hung laundry all over the house. It was winter, so diapers hung on lines across the living and dining rooms.

Encouraged by the Psalm-writer's despair

This chapter ends like Psalm 88. Almost all the Psalms, no matter how hopeless the psalmist was at the beginning, end in hope, thanksgiving, and confidence in God's answer. Psalm 88, however, ends in seeming despair. Somehow even that was an encouragement to me. Someone else had gone through endless pain and struggle. I am not alone!

Chapter Eight

God Kept Us Busy During Our Dark Years

During our 16 years of deep trial, I discovered how to walk through it from the Bible. One of the things God taught me was to reach out and help others, even when my own circumstance was bad. Isaiah 58 speaks about the fast we should do—a fast to help those who are helpless—going on to say that our situation will change when we do the things listed in that chapter, one of the results being: "your darkness will turn into noon day sun". I hung onto promises like this. I saw this happen when being directed by God to pray for those much worse off than us. When I did, my heaviness lifted even though my circumstance did not immediately change.

I once read about a famous psychiatrist who was asked what he would do if he knew he was going to have a nervous breakdown. His reply was that he would find someone in worse condition and try to help them.

I hung onto words like this because at times I felt like I was going to have a nervous breakdown.

Abraham Lincoln said, "To ease another's heartache is to forget one's own."

The Lord spoke these words to Jeremiah to speak to the people who were in captivity:

> *Seek the welfare (peace, prosperity) of the city where I*
> *have sent you into exile (maybe your situation feels like a*

captivity or being in exile) and PRAY to the Lord on its
behalf, for in its welfare (peace, prosperity) you will have
welfare (peace, prosperity). Jeremiah 29:7 nasb

God kept me busy praying for our city: praying, and leading prayer groups for the unity of the churches, for the pastors, and for revival. That was the burden of the Lord for me. As I did, He gave grace. I saw from that verse in Jeremiah that when we pray for our city, we will be blessed in return.

I saw from scripture, that when Job prayed for his friends, his dire situation turned around into double blessing.

The Lord restored the fortunes of Job when he prayed for
his friends,
And the Lord increased all that Job had two-fold.
Job 42:10 nasb

Even though I didn't see immediate breakthrough, I believed these scriptures. I knew the rewards would come in due season. And they have. I will go into it later.

A single mom who gave her last

The story of the widow of Zarephath always intrigued and challenged me (1 Kings 17). She was a single mom who gave her very last to a prophet and it resulted in a tremendous breakthrough for her. The prophet had a word from the Lord for her to first bake him a loaf of bread and give him a drink, before baking for her son and herself. He said if you do, your flour and oil will not run out until the day the Lord sends rain. She obeyed, taking a big step of faith because it was her last flour and oil. The widow gave her very last in obedience to God and it brought a *double reward*. She not only had ongoing provision, she later was the first person recorded in the Bible to experience a resurrection. Her son came back to life. God rewards us when we obey His commands—His written commands in the Bible, and those He speaks to us personally by the Spirit directly or through a prophetic word, like Elijah's words from God to the widow. In verse eight we read that God had already spoken to her before Elijah came. *"Go to Zarephath, in Sidon and live there. I have commanded a widow there to take care of you."*

It was the principle of giving that was in operation. Give and it shall be given to you, pressed down, running over...

I hung onto stories like this, knowing I serve and love the same God they did, and therefore He will take care of us too, if we obey Him.

When you are at the point of desperation, as we were, the words of the Bible become more and more real and meaningful. I found treasures there, promises that I desperately clung to.

I loved and hung onto Psalm 41:1-3, which says:

> *How blessed is he who considers the helpless*
> *The Lord will deliver him in a day of trouble.*
> *The Lord will protect him and keep him alive,*
> *And he shall be called blessed upon the earth;*
> *And do not give him over to the desire of his enemies.*
> *The Lord will sustain him upon his sickbed;*
> *In his illness, You restore him to health.*
> *Psalm 41:1-3 nasb*

Chapter Nine

When I Ran out of Grace God Stepped In

God didn't deliver us from financial difficulty for a long time, but during that time He was proving to us that He would strongly support us in it and through it. I treasure these words:

> *For the eyes of the Lord move to and fro throughout the earth that He may strongly support those whose heart is completely His.*
> *2 Chronicles 16:9 nasb*

Where are You, God??

It seemed I had grace to endure most of the time, but there were times I ran out. One time I was at the end of it. Tuomo was at work and the boys were in school and I was at home with the girls, who were 4 and 2 years old. I was in the kitchen at the end of my rope. It seemed our situation had been going on far too long, too much! I wept, then looked up and shouted to God, "I hate my life! I hate my life! Where are you??? It says to seek first the kingdom of God and Your righteousness and all these things will be added to you. I have been doing that!" I bent over in grief and pain, sobbing uncontrollably. The girls ran to me from their bedroom where they had been playing happily. Alarmed and concerned, they clung to me. Their attempt to comfort me was so sweet.

Later Tuomo and the boys came home as I was preparing supper. Tuomo settled in and after a while casually said that something happened that day. Because I was emotionally drained from my day of grief and despair, I responded half-heartedly, acknowledging his comment. He quietly said his dad had given him $5000, going on to say he'd given that amount to all the siblings, not just us. His dad wasn't aware of the extent of our situation. He had just decided to give out some of the inheritance.

I immediately knew God had heard my cry!

I felt like Hannah. He'd heard my desperate prayer when I was at the end of my rope. Some have asked me, "Did you feel ashamed or bad because you shouted a God?" No. Not a bit. I felt *heard* and *loved* by Him.

God heard Hagar in the wilderness where she had fled when she was pregnant with her son. God appeared to her. He saw and heard her. He told her to go back to Sarai, and told her to name her son Ishmael, meaning, "God hears". Later He appeared to Hagar again, when Ishmael was 13, and was languishing of thirst in the wilderness. He said He had heard the lad weeping. Truly He is a God who hears. (Genesis 16 and 21).

There are times we can come to God to withdraw from our account in heaven. If we have been faithful in sowing, we will reap.

My friend, a widow, complained to God and was heard

My friend, who was a widow with two daughters, worked hard to provide for them. For a season she cleaned houses. At one time she was at the end of her rope—tired from all strain of taking care of everything—emotionally, mentally, and physically spent, and to top it off, her lawn was six inches high. While standing in the bathtub of one of her employers, scrubbing the walls, she shouted to God saying, "You are supposed to be my husband. My lawn needs mowing and I don't even have a lawn mower!!" When she returned home, her lawn was mowed. A neighbor had taken care of it.

These stories are not to condone us shouting at God but rather to show that He responds even when we are upset with Him. In both cases He showed us He hears and answers even if we might not do our part perfectly. He understood the depth of pain we were in. It built my faith in God. It built my love for Him. It increased my confidence in coming to His throne of grace. It showed me He is a covenant-keeping God. He will do His part.

David and Job talked to God this way, at times, asking, "Where are You?"

When I prayed for someone else, my heaviness lifted

Living out-of-town, the outdoors had become my sanctuary of prayer.

I had learned to appreciate the quietness of those country roads and because we were quite isolated, very few cars ever drove by. A perfect set up for praying out loud while walking along.

One time on my prayer walk on this country road, my own burden was heavy, but the harder I tried to pray about it, the thicker the wall. I wasn't getting anywhere. I knew it was time to forget about myself. If God was not answering, He must have a very good reason. I knew He would come through in His time; I just needed to wait patiently. I needed to focus on Jesus and take on His burden because at this moment He had something on *His* heart that He wanted me to pray about—not for my situation. *"Seek first the kingdom of God and His righteousness and all these things will be added to you."* (Matt. 6:33). Sure enough, I began to pray for a person in our church who was going through a very difficult time. As soon as I began to pray, I felt a strong anointing, completely different from the feeling I had while trying to pray for our situation. I prayed with a flow. The spirit of prayer was on me. Later the Lord directed me to share some words of encouragement with her—God's words acquired in that place of prayer.

I also realized that my heaviness had lifted after praying for someone else. Nothing changed in our circumstance at the time, but my spirit was lifted. I had new grace. God's help had come.

Chapter Ten

My Teenaged Daughters Fasted While I Spoke at a Women's Luncheon

If I take on the burden God gives me, His grace carries me

Rather than going into depression, we kept an outward focus by God's grace. He directed me to start a prayer meeting in our home. I prayed for and with my friends who had very difficult situations. We grew into a team of prophetic intercessors and prayed through many things for our church, city, nation and nations. We experienced many powerful answers to prayer.

My husband and I led a home group, and we prayer-counseled many people. Sometimes people poured out their financial woes to us. We prayed for them and helped them, though we were worse off than they, which they did not know.

When we did this, it kept our heads above water. We continually participated in the church, using our gifts and callings, leading home groups and prayer groups and mentoring people. This upward and outward focus kept us going. Always the Lord was reminding me to take on His burden. His burden is light. If I looked at the stormy waves, focusing on our problems, God's grace lifted off me and I was tempted to draw back from ministry. But if I took on His burden, His grace carried me. The only way I could move forward was by keeping my eyes on Him, obeying Him, and doing His will. He would give just enough grace for the moment, for each assignment, and for our lives.

Our daughters' response to bare cupboards was incredible

I was invited to speak at a Christian Women's luncheon in Quesnel, a city about an hour south of our city, Prince George. When the day came, our situation was dire. Our daughters were now in their early teens and I was homeschooling them. There was no food for even a proper breakfast or lunch. I was bemoaning this to the girls but they said not to worry, saying they were going to fast and pray for me while I spoke at the luncheon, and also for God to provide us with groceries. It gripped me. My daughters' response was incredible.

Not only were the cupboards bare, there was only enough gas in the car to get *to* Quesnel, but not back again. My husband said he would come with me as he had a client to see there. I told him I was going to receive a $25 honorarium, so if we cashed it right away in Quesnel, we could pick up enough gas to get home, and also buy a few groceries.

The luncheon was lovely. *I am eating while my girls are fasting,* was my thought. I spoke about the call to prayer, feeling God with me as I shared, but I did not share about our situation. When it was time to leave, the organizers got busy putting things away and tidying up the hall but they forgot to give me the honorarium. $25 is not much, except when you are depending on it to get back home! I thought, *I am not going to ask for it,* and stepped outside to wait for Tuomo to pick me up. I waited for about 5 or 10 minutes, and just as Tuomo drove into the parking area, one of the ladies ran out the door and said, "We forgot to give you the honorarium!" Just in time!

We cashed the check, picked up gas and bought a few groceries. A day or so later, there was a check in the mail which I immediately cashed and bought plenty of groceries. When I arrived home, the girls met me with excitement, saying that boxes of groceries were brought to our door while I was shopping. We had so much food that we shared with another family in need, gladly giving from this abundance.

God was teaching our kids through these trials—not just us parents. Because of the abundant answer to their prayers and fasting, their faith grew. While I was groaning inwardly that we couldn't provide better, God was using this ideal, fertile, frustrating circumstance as a lesson for our children to grow in *their* prayer lives. They saw the power of fasting and prayer for themselves, it becoming a personal experience for them.

Chapter Eleven

God Called the Broken Ones Together to Intercede

During this time, a number of hurting, broken women would call me for prayer and counseling. I was teaching them how to pray—how to do what I was doing, praying and reading my Bible for at least an hour a day. Many times people want you to pray for them, but the most important thing for them to learn is how to pray themselves. They need to learn how to connect with God and how to wait on Him until they get answers. It is the best way for people to grow in their Christian life. Two of the women I mentored, without knowing about the other, both said I should start a prayer group. It was confirming something I had been sensing. My husband and pastor were both supportive, so I began a group that met weekly at our place. Most of them were like David's men who gathered around him: in distress, in debt, or discontented (1 Sam. 22:2). As we prayed together, we saw the power of prayer. Most of them are still powerful intercessors today, after almost 40 years. Some have gone to their heavenly home to be with the Lord.

There were about 12 of us who met regularly, a few men joining us as well. We prayed through for many things. The main prayer focus was that our church would become a praying church. So often there are all kinds of meetings, but no prayer meetings. It troubled me. God's mandate was that His house was to be a house of prayer for all nations (Isaiah 56:7). If we are to be pleasing to Him, we should care about what is important to Him. Jesus cared about what was important to His Father. He chased the money changers from the temple and said "My Father's house is to be a house of prayer." He knew what his Father wanted, and zeal for His Father's house consumed Him.

Because the boys were at school, my 7 month old daughter was the only child at home when I began the prayer meetings. She was a good napper most of the time. I began by reading 15 minutes from the *Change the World School of Prayer* book to build and strengthen our faith. Then I shared the prayer focuses and we would pray. We formed into a solid group of intercessors who had many, amazing answers to prayer, which I write about in further chapters.

Nothing is happening, I thought

After we had been meeting for some time, an associate pastor's wife began attending. In preparing for the meeting, I had felt God wanted us to kneel and be silent before Him for an hour. That was the first meeting she came to. During the silence I had a hard time focusing, thinking maybe I had made a mistake. *Nothing is happening. This is the first time this pastor's wife is here, and she probably won't want to come back.* The enemy was attacking me with these negative thoughts and doubts; however, the opposite was actually happening. God was speaking to her deeply, confirming a call to intercessory prayer, which she told me about later, and she began attending on a regular basis.

Our family members were not the only ones God was forming and preparing for future assignments through these times of testing. He was forming a company of intercessors. He was strengthening all our spiritual muscles and growing in us in faith, trust, fasting and prayer and teaching us the power of praying together.

Chapter Twelve

Travailing for the Unborn

At that time, one of the things I carried deeply in my heart was a terrible sin in our nation (and in many nations), the sin of shedding innocent blood. Abortion. It became such a deep burden I could hardly bear it. I saw from scriptures that God's judgment came on Israel because of idolatry and the shedding of innocent blood—the sacrifice of babies. He took the nation of Israel into captivity for 70 years. (Ps. 106:37-42, 2 Kings 17:17-18, 23, 2 Chron. 33:6, 9-11). I knew "judgment" was written over Canada as well, because of this continuous murdering of children.

A book that rocked my life

I began to travail, weep, and pray for several years because of this. Tuomo picked up some pro-life literature from one of the people in our church who was part of a pro-life group. He brought it home but I was the one who read it all and it deepened my burden. I knew I had to fight for our nation's future, and for our own children's and grandchildren's future, because God would not keep looking the other way for long. Not that He ever looks the other way. He knows exactly what is going on and is very grieved about it. Judgment is hanging over our nation. I read a book called *Abortion: The Silent Holocaust* by John Powell, S.J. where he wrote that the extermination of Jews during WW II was part of an evil progression It first began with abortion, then euthanasia, then the killing the mentally and physically disabled, and then it moved to the killing of 6 million Jews. I thought, *we are on this slippery slope here in Canada*. If something is not done, another holocaust is on its way because we reap what we sow. I wanted my children to have a future and a hope, so I was in much travailing prayer.

Don't be offended if others don't "see" what you "see" or you will lose your effectiveness in the spirit realm

Before sharing this burden with the prayer group, I shared it with the pastors. However, they didn't have the same response of grief I had, and neither was it talked about on Sundays from the pulpit for some time.

Later on I understood God's pattern: He usually burdens the prophetic intercessors first. Then as they pray through, the rest of the church takes on the burden also. I was in a learning curve. It was also a time of testing. Do I become offended because they don't step up to the plate? No. If you become offended and pull away, point fingers and criticize, you lose your effectiveness in the spirit realm. That is not God's way. God's way is to pray, bless, and honor.

I was carrying a heavy weight in that season of my life. I did not talk about the financial difficulty we were in with the intercessory prayer group (though during the weeks we were without water, I casually mentioned there might not be water when they flush the toilet because our water pump was broken). Neither did I talk about the weight of the abortion burden I was carrying. Not yet.

A dam burst. I couldn't talk, just weep uncontrollably. Then God stepped in to speak to me

One Tuesday, when it was time to lead the prayer group, I couldn't lead. Everyone was gathered in the living room and I started to speak, but I couldn't. I just wept. It was like a dam burst and there was no end of tears. I couldn't speak but only cry in front of everyone. The pastor's wife stepped up and called everyone to gather around me and lay hands on me and pray. Before they prayed, she read Psalm 27.

As she read, *I felt God breaking in and speaking those words to me personally. It was the word of the Lord for me!* She had no idea what I was going through, and just read those words by the leading of the Holy Spirit.

I had begun to live in the dread of the weighty judgments that were coming on the land. Would Canada go into captivity? Even come under an oppressive government?

As she read, it was like balm to my soul. God spoke directly to me through her reading His words, that even if terrorism or war came, we did not have to fear. He was personally assuring me through His word which became a rhema—a living word for me that day:

> *The Lord is my light and my salvation; whom shall I fear?*
> *The Lord is the defense of my life; whom shall I dread?*
> *When evildoers came upon me to devour my flesh, my*
> *adversaries and my enemies, they stumbled and fell.*
> *If an army encamps against me, my heart will not fear; if*
> *war arises against me, in spite of this I am confident.*
>
> *One thing I have asked from the Lord, that I shall seek:*
> *that I may dwell in the house of the Lord all the days*
> *of my life,*
> *to behold the beauty of the Lord and to meditate in*
> *His temple.*
>
> *For in the day of trouble He will conceal me in His*
> *tabernacle; He will hide me in the secret place of His tent;*
> *He will lift me upon a rock. And now my head will be*
> *lifted up above my enemies around me, and I will offer*
> *sacrifices in His tent with shouts of joy…*
>
> *…I would have despaired if I had not believed that I would*
> *see the goodness of the Lord in the land of the living. Wait*
> *for the Lord; be strong and let your heart take courage. Yes,*
> *wait for the Lord. Psalm 27:1-6, 13-14 nasb*

These words were so powerful that I memorized the whole Psalm and spoke it over and over again. I used the word of God to war against the sense of despair I felt because of our financial situation and because of Canada having such a weight of national sin that God's judgment was hanging.

The last two verses gave me hope. I kept declaring that I would see the goodness of the Lord in the land of the living. Yes, to wait for the Lord.

The goodness of the Lord has been in my life, as He promised

That deep, dark trial was almost 40 years ago. Though our journey was very difficult for many years (we lost all those houses Tuomo had purchased), today we are living in a lovely home overlooking a river valley, on 5 acres, fully paid for. Truly God has brought us through to see His goodness in the land of the living, and in the midst of those many years of trial, He did many miracles. Not only have we been blessed with 19 grandchildren and 3 great grandchildren, He led me to travel: to pray, preach and teach in many cities and nations. Tuomo and I made a trip to visit a number of missionaries in three nations to encourage and pray for them. Each of our children made missionary journeys to minister in other nations. Financially, how did all that happen? God showed us that nothing is too difficult for Him. All these took steps of faith. If we had done it based on our circumstances, these things would not have happened. He wanted to show us that He is a God who supplies all our need according to His riches in glory. If we seek first His kingdom and His righteousness, all these things are added to us. (Matt. 6:33)

Why the years of darkness?

I pondered why the Lord allowed me to go through these years of darkness, even despairing at times. By reading the Bible, I found I was not alone: Abraham, Jeremiah, and Habakkuk were given revelations of impending judgments, and experienced "darkness and terror". Though I'm not saying I am at their level, the scriptures say that God's sheep do hear His voice (John 10:27) and He reveals things to His friends (John 16:15).

In Genesis 15 God made a covenant with Abraham to confirm His promise that He would make him into a great nation, and give his descendants the land he was standing on. Abraham fell into a deep sleep, and "terror and great darkness fell upon him" (Gen. 15:12). God told him that his descendants would be enslaved and oppressed in a foreign land for 400 years, but afterwards, God would judge that oppressing nation and they would come out with many possessions. I realized that God at times lets us experience things like this because it is a prophetic walk. He let Abraham actually feel the oppression that was coming on the nation.

Jeremiah, too, wept much because of the prophecies of judgment that God was giving him for the nation. Habakkuk was another prophet who felt overwhelmed at times because of the judgments coming on the land. Yet he ends by saying:

> *Though the fig tree should not blossom,*
> *and there be no fruit on the vines…*
> *though the fields produce no food…*
> *I will rejoice in the God of my salvation.*
> *The Lord God is my strength.*
> *Hab. 3:17-19 nasb*

What God worked in me through this time was to give me a great burden to fast and pray for revival for Canada (which I have done for four decades), to teach about and lead prayer in small and large gatherings, and to participate in countless large gatherings and conferences where corporate prayer for Canada has taken place.

I saw from scripture that prophecies of judgment were at times conditional. Moses interceded and God changed His mind about destroying the rebellious Israelites. Also Amos prayed and God changed His mind about the type of judgment that was coming.

I believe this word:

> *If My people who are called by My name shall humble*
> *themselves and pray and seek My face, and turn from their*
> *wicked ways, then I will hear from heaven, forgive their*
> *sin and **heal their land!***
> *2 Chron. 7:14. nkjv*

I understood from this scripture that there was the possibility of healing for our nation, so I determined to do my part, and also join with other watchmen on the wall to fast and pray. In the book of Ezekiel, God talks about looking for a man to stand in the gap for the nation. I felt that call, as have many other intercessors.

In further chapters I write what God spoke and led us to do from that place of fasting and intercessory prayer, things I never expected. God is a God of surprises. He is able to do far more abundantly beyond all that we ask, think or imagine (Eph. 3:20).

Eye has not seen, nor ear heard, nor have entered the heart
of man the things which God has prepared for those who
love Him. 1 Corinthians 2:9 nkjv

I felt the Lord wanted me to write about our long, dark trial because perhaps you may be going through something similar and this will encourage you in your journey. There is an expected end. God is good and will show you His goodness in the land of the living at His appointed time for you. He has promised. In the meantime, His grace is sufficient for you. As you keep praying, He will whisper words to you that will give you comfort, direction and light for your path. He will never leave nor forsake you and He strongly supports those whose heart is completely His.

Chapter Thirteen

Don't Quit until It's Finished!

God said, "You haven't even fasted about this yet!"

Was my husband's annoying idea from God?

Backing up a few years to a time when our family had grown to five children—we had been blessed with two cute girls in addition to the blessing of our three boys—God called me to another level of prayer. The boys had been attending a Christian school, but after a few years we could no longer afford the school fees. Tuomo began suggesting homeschooling. I had three active boys, a 2-year old toddler and an 8 month old baby. And I had no desire to homeschool. My plate was full just managing my family, thank you very much. Homeschooling was at a pioneering stage, so there were very few people doing it. There was no distance learning through computer like these days. I would be on my own teaching, marking, and organizing their academics, besides carrying all the other responsibilities of a busy mother.

I had also been leading the prayer group in our home for a year and a half, and the hand of the Lord was evident on this ministry. I couldn't see myself homeschooling plus the prayer ministry. And I didn't sense God wanting me to stop the prayer group.

I felt hemmed in, a place I had been in before. There seemed to be no options. Public school was not an option for us, something we had decided at the beginning of our marriage. I was walled in on all sides except the ceiling. Look up and cry out to God! I had learned that.

Staying up all night to hear from God

For six weeks I was irritated and uncomfortable, frustrated that Tuomo was suggesting this for me to do. Finally I decided to stay up all night if I had to, asking God to speak *His* will in this matter. After everyone was in bed, I first listened to a couple of teaching tapes. I needed an attitude adjustment because I had been quite angry about the whole situation. I asked God to forgive me, asked for a heart to really hear from Him, and I was willing to do whatever He spoke for me to do. I felt inadequate about homeschooling and felt no grace for it whatsoever. I *had to* hear from God. I knew He would equip me for the task, no matter how difficult it would be, *if* it was His will.

I had learned to be specific in asking, to arrange my request before Him. I pictured, at times, opening file folders and having them all laid out before the Lord. I asked Him these questions: 1. Is it Your will I homeschool the boys (not just Tuomo's idea)? 2. Do You want me to stop leading the prayer group, if it is?

I didn't hear anything from God that night, which I wasn't concerned about because I knew He would speak to me soon. I finally went to bed around 5 am. I didn't hear anything the next day either. But a few days later, when I woke up in the morning and sat on the edge of the bed, the Spirit of the Lord fell on me. In a minute I heard him speak, "It is my will for you to do homeschooling *and* to keep leading prayer". Accompanied with God's words was a flood of grace, a knowing that I could do it, as well as great joy. When God speaks, there is peace and joy. All the frustration, anger, and anxiety was replaced by new peace.

Juggling homeschooling, family, and prayer ministry

I launched into the year having to be super-organized as the homeschooling took a lot of time. The girls were easy going, so I was able to manage both the younger and older ones, but that first year took everything I had to juggle it all. The second year was a little easier because the Christian school allowed homeschooled kids to attend on Tuesdays for the full day. This way the homeschoolers were able to be a part of chapel time and other school activities as well.

You haven't even fasted about this yet!

In the meantime, I continued to lead intercessory prayer. We prayed continually for a revival of prayer because I knew that historic revivals had been preceded by revivals of prayer. We prayed that our church would be a praying church. One time I was fervently praying about this on my own, asking God when He was going to answer our prayers. The Lord spoke to me saying, "You haven't even fasted about this yet!" It stopped me short. I knew what He meant. It wasn't a one day, or three day fast He was asking for. I knew it would be a 3 week fast.

Help! Could I do it? Yes. If God was asking for it, He would also give me the accompanying grace.

I began to prepare myself mentally and spiritually. It took six months before I was ready. I knew I couldn't do it during school season because I needed full strength for it, so I waited until summer when the demand on me was not as intense. I was tired from the load of responsibility I carried, so summer was a reprieve. I didn't know if I had strength to homeschool another year, so I tried to regroup, waiting until the end of summer before I launched into the 3 week fast.

I did a cleansing fast: lemon, maple syrup and a pinch of cayenne pepper mixed into water—many glasses a day. After four days I felt so weak I could barely get any work done. I remember lying in bed and crying out to God for help. I heard him say, "Drink carrot juice." I drank about a 1/3 cup a day and it gave me a boost. I understood later that my body was getting rid of toxins so the first 5 days or so were the most difficult. I began to feel much better and by God's grace I kept going.

Is it finished, yet? Is it finished?!!

On around day 11, I was on my knees in my bedroom crying out to God, "Is it finished, yet? Is it finished?!!" I really wanted to end it, but somehow God gave me perseverance. A few days later, on Sunday, my pastor preached a sermon, titled, *"Don't Quit Until its Finished!"* I was astounded. *Wow, God! You sure speak loud and clear. You answer my cries. You talk to me!* I don't remember the rest of the sermon as I was in a daze. After the service, I dashed to the washroom not wanting to talk to anyone until I could say *Thank You! Thank You! Thank You!* I reveled in how intimate God was that He would speak to me this way and I didn't want to lose the moment. I felt His love and presence. I understood and loved that He was working with me on this assignment. It was all I needed to complete the 3 week fast.

God pays well and gives bonuses

My last day was the following Sunday. We invited our pastor and his wife to our home for a visit after the evening service. After I got the children settled and refreshments served, our pastor mentioned someone had anonymously come forward to pay for our boy's schooling at the Christian school for the year. We were speechless. This was a most surprising, unexpected offer. Perhaps thinking we didn't want to have the children go to the Christian school, he quickly went on to say that, of course, it was up to us if we wanted to receive this, considering I might want to homeschool. No! Yes! We were overwhelmed and wanted to receive this with great thankfulness and appreciation. It was beyond our wildest dreams. Unthinkable!

God was *showering* us with His glory.

After our guests left, I went downstairs to our oldest son's bedroom. He had been telling us he wanted to go to the school; he had a lot of friends there and wanted to be with them. I couldn't wait until morning to tell him. He was already in bed, but still awake. I sat by his bed and asked if he still wanted to go to the academy. He said, "Yes!"

"Well," I said, "Someone has paid for our family's schooling for this year." He was overjoyed.

This was not what I'd been fasting for. I knew in my heart this was a *bonus* from the Lord. He was showing His delight in me earnestly seeking Him with fasting and prayer. I have seen this over the years: He gives *bonuses*, or paydays, as one of my friends calls them, when we press in deeper.

God responded to the fast

As the fall season progressed, answers to this fast began to unfold. Every fall and spring our church ran a Bible school, offering numerous classes on Tuesday nights. That fall a course on prayer was offered for the first time, called *Communion with God*. I signed up because I was thrilled, knowing this course was part of the answer, and I wanted to see this "new baby" for myself. On the first night of the course, during break, when everyone headed to the open area for coffee and goodies, I stayed in the classroom alone. I wept tears of thankfulness that prayer was being taught in our church. *"Thank You! Thank You! Thank You!"* bubbled up in my spirit.

After Christmas our pastor began a new preaching series on Sundays. It was on *PRAYER*! He stayed on the subject for six whole months teaching it in three series back to back. God was answering!

Writing began

However, the fast unfolded something more in my life regarding prayer. I felt a call to write. I realized then why I had not received grace for that year of home schooling. God had another plan.

Thoughts began to percolate about writing a book on prayer in the form of a teaching manual. I had written some articles for our church newspaper, called *The Vine*. Other times I had written a page here and there when a flow hit me, and had filed them in a "Seed Thoughts" file.

I had homeschooled three young boys for two years while juggling the care of my two little girls. It had taken supernatural strength and organization to do, something which God had graciously provided. So now, with the boys going to school every day, it seemed I had time on my hands. Every morning after Tuomo and the boys left, I cleaned up, got the girls needs tended to and set them to play. They were good playmates, now being 4 and 2 years old, so the mornings went by quite pleasantly. After lunch I put them down for a nap/quiet time. These mornings and afternoons gave me time to write. I pulled out my filed "seed thoughts", spread them out on my coffee table and started writing. There was an anointing from the Lord that caused my pen to flow easily.

A book was born: Power Perfected in Weakness

Very quickly I had the outline of the book and then filled in the rest. In six weeks or so I had written a book as neatly as I could in long hand on three-ringed lined paper. I titled it *Through Pain Comes Anointing* which was later changed to *Power Perfected in Weakness*.

I felt the Holy Spirit urging me to take this manuscript to my pastor but I was quite nervous about it. So I prayed and prayed (I always had to pray a lot for courage). The sense to take it to him persisted, so after Christmas I made an appointment. I showed him the manuscript, recounting how God had given me this book. He perused it, flipping through the pages. I held my breath. He was quite moved by it, recognizing the hand of God on it, and immediately recommended I get it typed and then the church would print it into a book. He said it could be typed on one of the church computers.

I did not own a computer, so I wasn't familiar with using one. However, the Lord placed a person on my mind to ask. She had sincerely offered to do any typing Tuomo or I might need because we had helped her by counseling and praying for her and her family at times. One time she and I had done some serious warfare prayer for one of her family members who was suicidal. After the two of us agreed in prayer, this person was completely freed from that spirit of suicide. My friend was very grateful and offered to do anything for us we needed, specifically mentioning typing.

I asked her and she was happy to oblige. The church staff set her up at a computer desk near the office of one of the associate pastors. He walked by her office often, seeing her working. Before long, she was hired on as an office assistant for him. She later became the executive administrator for the senior pastor and worked for over 20 years at the church—all from typing up the manual for me. God blessed her as she blessed me. God opens doors to those with grateful, servant hearts.

Another result of this fast: a prayer teaching ministry locally, nationally, and internationally

The manuscript was printed into a book, *Power Perfected in Weakness*, a book about prayer, fasting, intercession, revival, and birthing. I taught this course every year, sometimes twice a year for 16 years, at our church Bible school. In 2001 I was invited to teach it in Africa at three Bible Schools in Harare, Zimbabwe, in Lilongwe, Malawi, and in Lusaka, Zambia over a three week span of time, one week in each Bible School. Another church in Prince George had me teach it as a 12 week course. I have also taught shorter versions of it at weekend seminars in cities and towns in Canada, in Merrit, Fruitvale, Mackenzie, Fort St. John, Regina, Aldergrove, and Edmonton, as well as single messages in a number of churches in Canada, USA, and Thailand.

I had been praying and fasting for our church to become a praying church. I didn't expect part of God's answer was that I would teach about prayer at our church, in our nation, and internationally.

I was amazed at how God moved this way. He told me to fast, so I did (it wasn't easy), and all this began to unfold. It built my faith in the power of prayer and fasting.

Some years later I became the prayer pastor of our church and was ordained. I had no idea, during those previous, difficult, dark years that this would happen. I served on staff for 8 years teaching and mentoring in the area of prophetic intercession as well as leading and overseeing many prayer groups at our church. I also served on our city ministerial executive, helping organize many citywide prayer and worship events, as well as organizing and helping facilitate ministerial prayer retreats twice a year.

Later the Lord directed us to establish a house of prayer in Prince George, a citywide ministry. I also made many prayer journeys to other nations, taking intercessors with me.

Unexpected, ongoing, unfolding results from the 3-week fast

When we enter a fast which God has called us to, there are ongoing, unfolding results over a long span of time. We are called to this life of adventure, but it takes dying to self—at times dying to comforts, like food.

Through this 3-week fast, not only did things begin to happen in the area of prayer in our church, but I received the bonus: our boys schooling was paid by an anonymous, generous person. As a result of their schooling, I was able to write the book. A 20 plus year ministry of service opened up for a friend who gave her time to type the manuscript. A ministry of pastoring, leading, and teaching on prayer opened up for me in my church, nation and nations. This domino effect took place. God is amazing.

I am writing this to encourage you if you have prayed and prayed about something, and no answer has come, that perhaps God is saying to you, "You haven't even fasted about this yet." I know this may sound abrupt, but that is how He spoke to me—abruptly. It launched me into these amazing things that unfolded. If you have fasted, know that it is duly noted to your account to be answered at an appointed time. God has not forgotten. He will answer you and show you great and mighty things in His time.

> *Call to me and I will answer you, and I will tell you*
> *great and mighty things, which you do not know.*
> *Jeremiah 33:3 nasb*

Chapter Fourteen

Jesus Experienced Distress

I noticed some words in the Bible that encouraged me greatly. These words are about Jesus, words that indicate His humanness: "deeply moved in spirit and troubled", "deeply grieved to the point of death", "very distressed and troubled". I marveled. The Son of God is like us. He was truly human. He felt grief, anxiety, sorrow, distress, and worry.

*When Jesus said this, He became **troubled** in Spirit.*
John 13:21 nasb

*He was deeply **moved in spirit and troubled**.*
John 11:33 nasb

*Jesus **wept.** John 11:35 nasb*

*And began to be **grieved and distressed**. Then He said to them, "My soul is **deeply grieved to the point of death**". Matt. 26:37-28 nasb*

*And He took with Him Peter and James and John, and began to be **very distressed and troubled**, Mark 14: 33 nasb*

*Now **my soul is troubled**, and what shall I say? "Father, save me from this hour'? No, it was for this very reason I came to this hour." John 12:27 niv*

*And **being in agony** He was praying very fervently.*
Luke 22:44 nasb

For we do not have a high priest who cannot sympathize
*with our weaknesses, but One who has been **tempted in***
***all things as we are**, yet without sin. Hebrews 4:15 nasb*

*...He offered up both prayers and supplications with **loud***
***crying and tears** Hebrews 5:7 nasb*

Jesus was God but became a human and experienced the same feelings we do. He was not just gliding through life on a cloud of heavenly glory. He became anxious, deeply distressed, and heavy in spirit just like we do at times. He modeled for us how to walk through the valley of the shadow of death to new life being birthed in and through us.

Seasons of pain precede seasons of new life

Our lives go through times of death, burial, and resurrection. When we are at the brink of death (not necessarily literal death, but a death of a vision, a death of a relationship, a death financially), we often feel those same feelings that Jesus as a man, felt. Feelings of great distress, heaviness, anxiety, worry, fear, oppression, and depression. Those feelings come when we are in transition labor, so to speak, often at the brink of "death", but at the same time at the brink of a "birth"—a breakthrough, a resurrection. Through that pain, something new is being birthed. Like a woman in transition labor, she is in great pain, but soon a child is born and she has joy.

These preceding verses are about two deaths and resurrections. The first one was the death of Lazarus, one of Jesus' good friends. He felt the grief of loved ones to the point that He also grieved. Death is grievous. But He resurrected Lazarus moments later and the grief was turned to incredible joy.

The next verses are about Jesus' own approaching death. Passion Week was not an easy time for him because there was an escalation of demonic activity around Him. Evil plans to kill him were being concocted behind closed doors. At one point Jesus said, "The ruler of the world is coming." He knew what was ahead.

Jesus likened His death to a woman in labor, His resurrection to a child being born

I wrote about this in Chapter 6, but I am bringing another aspect here.

Jesus likened the dark days ahead to a woman in painful labor, in anguish giving birth (John 18:20-22). It would be hard, but then it would turn around to great joy, just like a mother experiences immediately after a child is born. He was laboring to bring about salvation for the whole world, to everyone who believes. That was what was being birthed. He likened the distress the disciples would experience during those days of His arrest, death, and burial, to a woman in labor. They didn't understand that He was going to die, but He told them this because later they would understand. And then when He was resurrected, they would rejoice. Their deep sorrow would be turned into joy, just like with a natural birth.

I found strength for my painful situations by seeing this principle, that something is being birthed through these trials. The long term trials we go through are birthing something long term down the road. The shorter ones are for some more immediate victories. Jesus modeled for us, as the Son of Man, a human, how to walk through the valleys of death. He let us see Him in Gethsemane through the eyes of the disciples. There may be those moments when you are travailing in the Garden of Gethsemane, and you want to escape the cup of suffering that God the Father has planned for you to drink momentarily. Let us remember Jesus. Though He was tempted to escape, even asking the Father to take this cup from Him, if possible, He yielded to the cross saying, "Not My will, but Yours be done."(Luke 22:42 nasb). Even those words of hesitation about going to the cross, asking the Father to remove the cup, are an encouragement. Jesus was human like us.

God sends help from heaven: sometimes angels

An angel from heaven appeared to Him, strengthening Him. (Luke 22:43) Wow! God does not forsake us. When we are at the end of our rope, He sends help from heaven. I know of times in my life when I have been strengthened by an angel sent by God. When we feel we cannot go one step further, He sends help if we keep trusting Him, and are willing to walk out His will even if it means momentary suffering.

We need to keep our eyes on Jesus and on what is being birthed, not on the suffering

Jesus kept His focus on what God was birthing through His great suffering. It says, "Who for the joy that was set before Him endured the cross" (Heb. 12: 2 nasb). He knew the suffering was for a purpose—He was anticipating the baby that was to be born: salvation for the world, for whoever believes.

Likewise, if we ask the Lord to help us see the joy, the outcome of the suffering, we are able to endure.

> *Therefore we do not lose heart...for momentary light*
> *affliction is producing for us an eternal weight of glory far*
> *beyond all comparison. 2 Corinth. 4:17 nasb*

A woman in labor keeps focused on a baby being born. She endures the pain for that purpose.

There is a purpose

There is a purpose to the suffering. Some of it is for this time on earth and some for eternity. Years ago, in my 20's, I read some of Paul Billheimer's books, which greatly encouraged me because he articulated the purpose of suffering very well. If you want to read them they are titled: *Destined for the Throne, Don't Waste Your Sorrows*, and *The Mystery of God's Providence*. God faithfully brought the right teaching to me at just the right time.

He will do that for you also, if you keep seeking Him by spending time in prayer, reading the Bible, and doing the things He whispers for you to do. He will bring the right message at the right time: through a book, a Youtube teaching, a movie, nature, Facebook, a message preached at church, a person saying the exact Bible verse you need, or someone telling a story that is exactly what you need to hear though they may not realize its impact on you. He strongly supports those whose hearts are completely His. (2 Chron. 16:9)

A strange dream prepared me for an unusual assignment

I had an experience of this on a smaller scale.

In a dream, early one Sunday morning, the letters PM88 appeared along with the meaning of the letters and numbers: PM meant Pressing Matters, 8 meant 8 Issues and the second 8 meant 8 Untimely Deaths. All this was in my dream.

I told Tuomo my dream, not understanding what it meant and neither did he. I went for a prayer walk to the Nechako River trail, where I often went. I had a heavy feeling of hopelessness which I could not shake nor understand. Little did I realize I would be walking into the middle of a suicide attempt and would be praying with the wife, mom, and niece of a man who was about to jump off the bridge! He was standing on the outside edge of the railing at the center of the Cameron Street Bridge that spans Nechako River in Prince George.

Police arrived and tried to talk him out of jumping. Another Christian showed up. I recognized him as the leader of a Catholic prayer group. He began to pray in tongues quietly and spoke encouraging things to the family. I felt encouraged realizing that God had sent two of us who know how to pray, to be there. *God must have a plan to stop this.* As we continued to pray, the suicidal man finally climbed back over the railing onto the bridge.

The Catholic man then told a story of what had once happened to him. An oppressive feeling had overwhelmed him suddenly like a wet blanket. He began to pray in tongues and prayed and prayed. He drove home from work to find that his 12 year old son had rescued three people from the river.

In the same way, God had let me feel the hopelessness of this man who wanted to end his life.

An intercessor often takes the hit

That is how intercessory prayer works. The intercessor takes the hit, often not knowing why he or she is going through those feelings. If we just kick into prayer, praying in tongues or "groans too deep for words", when we don't know how to pray in our natural language, God acts and things unfold.

God showed me in the dream that a *pressing matter* was taking place, an attempted *untimely death*. He let me feel the heaviness of this man but He moved it from "death" into "life". I continued to pray for this family by name for some time, naming each of them in my prayer journal.

Thank You, Jesus, that You came to live among us as a man. You felt the same feelings we feel and You modeled for us how to walk through these trials, dark as they may be at times. Thank You for Your word, for the Holy Spirit, for angels, for dreams and visions, and for the gifts of the spirit that all help us. You never leave us alone.

Chapter Fifteen

God's Hurt Heart– He Knows What Wrenching Pain Is

One time I heard the Lord speak one word: "crushing". When I asked Him what this means, I heard these words in my spirit: "sweet wine comes from the crushing of grapes".

Some of you have walked this walk of being crushed and experienced the outcome of sweet wine. Others may be in the middle of crushing and need encouragement to persevere.

Suffering has a purpose

Being a Christian doesn't mean suffering ends. It means that suffering has a purpose.

Jesus went to Gethsemane. We, as disciples, are not above our Master. If Jesus was called to Gethsemane, then we will at times be called there, also. Paul said:

> *Now I rejoice in what I am suffering for you, and I fill*
> *up in my flesh what is still lacking in regard to Christ's*
> *afflictions, for the sake of His body,*
> *which is the church. Colossians 1:24 niv*

The groan of Gethsemane and the cross is carried on by the church, each one bearing some part of it. *For a purpose!* When we suffer for Christ's sake, it is producing an eternal weight of glory (2 Corinthians 4:17 nasb).

A few verses before this one, Paul said that death in us is producing life for others (2 Corinth. 4:7-12). Some of you are suffering in various ways. Whatever way it is, God takes your pain for gain for the kingdom of God, if you are walking with Him.

When Jesus drew His last breath on the cross, the sky was dark, a huge earthquake took place, and the veil in the temple that separated people from God was torn from top to bottom. The way was made for us to *know God* face to face. Intimately. His message to us was, "Come! Now you can know Me! I have forgiven your sins. My blood cleanses you from all unrighteousness. Come to Me. I love you and want you to be with Me where I am for all eternity."

He *wanted* us, so He made it possible for us to come to Him. Salvation was made possible—a supernatural experience where God comes to live inside a person's spirit *if* one says YES to this invitation. If we say "yes" to Jesus, the weight of sin lifts off us and we feel inexpressible joy and peace. We feel loved and accepted. We now belong to a family, God's family, cherished and loved by Him and He lets us feel His loving embrace.

However, to be a disciple of Jesus (one who is a student and follower of Jesus, applying what he has learned), we must give up our own way. Jesus said, "If any of you wants to be My follower, you must give up your own way, take up your cross, and follow Me. If you try to hang onto your life, you will lose it. But if you give up your life for My sake, you will save it." (Matthew 16:24-25 nlt)

What does this mean? Do we need to be crucified on a cross? Not literally*, but there are many areas of our lives God brings a death to.

It means: this same process of death that Jesus went through works over and over in our lives, too. It is the breaking of the alabaster vase so the perfume of Christ begins to emanate from our lives. It is a tearing of our outer person, the soul, through painful situations like being rejected,

---

* though some are called to be a martyr

misunderstood, slandered, ignored, belittled, insulted, blamed unjustly, or being persecuted. We may experience these death blows through losses in our life: of a loved one, a marriage, a job, or a business. It can come through health situations, physical pain, prodigal children and grandchildren we are aching and praying for, time pressures and demands that seem overwhelming.

If we walk through these kinds of things the way Jesus did, the life of Christ begins to emanate from us like a fragrance. If you are new in your walk with Jesus, don't despair. God is a patient, loving father, and will teach you how to walk this walk a step at a time. When a baby learns to walk, he falls many times. Parents cheer him on to try again. That is how our heavenly Father is. "The godly may trip seven times, but they will get up again." (Prov. 24:16 nlt)

Through suffering, we come to know Him more intimately, and we walk in new levels of authority in the work of the Kingdom

Depending on how we respond to these death blows, they can either harden us into "justified" bitterness, or open the way to new levels of supernatural encounter with God, to know His love more deeply and to walk in new levels of authority and power in the spirit realm.

> *That I may* **know Him** *and the power of His resurrection*
> *and the fellowship of*
> *His sufferings, being conformed to His death.*
> *Philippians 3:10 nasb*

To truly know a friend intimately, we also suffer with them. Deeper intimacy with Jesus comes not only through the power of His resurrection, but also in the fellowship of His sufferings.

God's pathway for encountering more of His deep love and His power, is often through a crushed, torn heart.

At that point we have 2 options:

1. **Turn to Him and embrace Him** and His love in the midst of the pain, cling to Him, talk it out with Him, and hang on to Him. He in turn, embraces us and does a supernatural work in our hearts. Supernatural grace is given to us to bear the pain, and we are launched into another level of intimacy with Him and another level of destiny and authority, another level of glory.

Or…

2. **We try to cope on our**. At this point our hearts harden because we do not have supernatural grace from God to bear the pain and so we become bitter, cynical, and angry with God and people.

We have this choice. He doesn't force us. He invites, woos, and compels us, but does not force us. We've been given the freedom to choose.

Whatever pain you have gone through, God has already gone through that same pain and the same emotions. He gets it. He understands. He's been there.

Has family rejected you?

Jesus says, "My family, Israel, still rejects me. I came to them, to My own, and they did not receive me. Though I loved them, they rejected Me. I am still waiting for them to come and be restored to Me."

Has a spouse left you?

God says, "Read the Old Testament! I loved Israel like a husband loves a wife, but she went after other lovers."

> *How **I have been hurt** by their adulterous hearts*
> *which turned away from Me. Ezekiel 6:9 nasb*

He *knows* what that pain feels like!

Do you ache for a prodigal, wayward child?

God says, "Read what Hosea says about Ephraim" (another name for Israel). It says in Hosea 11:1-4, 8-11 that God's heart is *"turned over"* in longing for him, even though Ephraim continues to do his own thing.

Have you given of yourself, your heart, your help, a gift, and it was refused in a nasty way?

God says, "Millions spurn My gift every day: My gift to them—My precious Son, Jesus—who became the sacrifice for their sin. The very thing they need. I know what it feels like to have a gift rejected."

He fully relates to wrenching heart pain.

Through this pain you are going through, He is letting you know *His* heart and asking you to lean into Him as your Friend. He gets it. He understands. He's been there.

In all their affliction, He was afflicted. Isaiah 63:12

Keep talking to God and embracing Him in your pain

The Bible characters all had some crushing in their lives that was almost unbearable. The Psalms and Job are a great comfort and encouragement because David and Job were real with God, bringing their despair and complaints to Him. They kept talking with God. David, though he felt overwhelmed and fearful many times, always ended his Psalm with thanksgiving and trust in the Lord. If God came through for David and Job, He will come through for us, too.

In Hebrews 4:16 it says to come boldly before the throne of grace. Come to God and articulate your pain and your anguish. Something happens in our heart that enhances our ability to endure the pressure of what we are going through when we talk to Him. God gives grace, divine help.

We know that Joseph's end turned out well. He was elevated to reign as second in command under Pharaoh, and used by God to save nations during a seven year famine, including his own family who carried the Messianic seed. David became King over Israel and God called him "a man after God's heart". He promised that David's throne would be established forever.

If God did that for Joseph and David, He will do it for you. He is outworking a wonderful plan for your life through this painful process. Whatever you are going through, He has been there, feels your pain, and has future plans for you to reign.

There is a crown for those who persevere under trial

He says, "Through the cross, I gained an inheritance. You will also gain an inheritance through the cross you are called to carry."

> *For this finds favor with God, if for the sake of conscience*
> *toward God a person bears up under sorrows when*
> *suffering unjustly…if you do what is right and suffer for*
> *it, and you patiently endure it, this finds favor with God.*
> *For you have been called for this purpose since Christ also*
> *suffered for you, leaving you an example for you to follow*
> *in His steps, who committed no sin, nor was any deceit*
> *found in His mouth, and while being reviled, He did not*
> *revile in return; while suffering,* **He uttered no threats,**
> **but kept entrusting Himself to Him who judges**
> **righteously.** *1 Peter 2:19-23 nasb*

On the cross Jesus prayed: "Father forgive them, for they don't know what they are doing." (Luke 23:24 nlt). He wants us to pray this way also for our enemies, to bless them and to do good to them.

> *Blessed is the man who perseveres under trial, for once*
> *he has been approved he will receive the crown of life.*
> *James 1:12 nasb*

Many people give up and walk away from a marriage, a church, a job, etc. They may sometimes be insane situations, yes, no doubt, but we need to seek if *He* wants us to walk away (sometimes it is His will). If we haven't waited on God to know His will, we often walk away based on our feelings of being justified and convinced, and with others affirming us saying, "You don't have to put up with *that!*"

Perhaps God is calling us to a higher calling, a Gethsemane experience, a death, a cross, to come out the other end a deeper friend of God because we walked His walk and gained resurrection power.

> *"All of a sudden these afflictions are eclipsed by Your glory*
> *and I realize how beautiful and how great Your affections*
> *are for me."[6]*

As we come out the other end, our death experience brings life to others. God uses us to touch lives in a way He couldn't before.

The crushing, if we embrace Him and His way through it, will produce sweet wine in our lives that others can taste and drink.

> *Whoever believes in Me...out of his heart will flow rivers*
> *of living water. John 7:38 esv*

Chapter Sixteen

In This Painful Process Self Dies

Not only is God birthing something in and through our lives, or preparing an eternal weight of glory, He is also bringing death to "self" in us. Whom the Lord uses greatly, He prepares thoroughly.

"A disciple is not above his teacher." (Matt. 20:24 nasb). We cannot bypass the way of the cross to bring to fulfillment and to resurrection power the call of God in our lives. The way of the cross is death to self. Our own opinions, rights, and understanding of what should be said or done, must die. Even a good thing may need to be put to death if it is in the way of the best that God is calling us to. For example, fellowshipping with friends, though a good thing, can be a bad thing if it is keeping us from our time with the Lord. Even family can be more important than Jesus.

> *He who loves father or mother more than Me, is not*
> *worthy of Me; and he who loves son or daughter more*
> *than Me is not worthy of Me. And he who does not take*
> *his cross and follow after Me is not worthy of Me. He who*
> *has found his life shall lose it, and he who has lost his life*
> *for My sake shall find it.*
> *Matthew 10:37-39 nasb*

Satan tries to prevent us from taking up our cross

Satan knows that whenever we yield and submit to God, we gain authority over him and he loses territory not only in our lives but in the lives of many others as well, because death in us works life for others (1 Corinth. 4:12)

The "tool" that brings death to self may vary

The Lord may be allowing the next person to do things you are not permitted to do. It may seem unfair, but we are not to compare ourselves. "But when they… compare themselves with one another, they are without understanding" (2 Corinth. 10:12 esv).

We were created for different assignments in God's kingdom. Our weaknesses and strengths vary from person to person, so His methods of forming and honing us differs. In my life, one of my "deaths" was as follows. I asked God to show me my priorities when I was a 21 year old mom with 3 kids in tow, and a husband who was trying his hand at various businesses. It became clear God was calling me to sacrifice hobbies for a season, and especially super-orderliness, which was important to me. I had been raised that way so it wasn't easy to sacrifice. But to do God's will in my life—an hour a day in prayer and the word, supporting my husband in his businesses, raising and home-schooling five children, leading prayer ministry in our church, and being available to people—I needed to let those go. My house was never super messy, but it wasn't as perfect as I felt it should be. Now years later, my house stays reasonably tidy though it takes very little to keep it up with all the kids grown up and gone.

The reward of yielding to the cross

If we are called to give up anything for Jesus' sake, there is a great promise of returns.

> Jesus said, "Truly I say to you, there is no one who has left
> house or brothers or sisters of mother or father or children
> or farms for My sake and for the gospel's sake, but that
> **he will receive a hundred times as much now in the**
> **present age**, houses and brothers and sisters and mothers
> and children and farms, along with persecutions; and **in**
> **the age to come eternal life**.
> Mark 10:29-30 nasb

We may not have to literally give up these things, as it is their *hold on our heart* He is dealing with, but sometimes He does require it. There are other times God calls us to fight for something He has promised, like Caleb fought for his mountain which God had promised him (Joshua 14-15). In this case, He calls us to lay down something that is dear to us. A time for everything. "If you try to hang on to your life, you will lose it. But if you give up your life for my sake, you will save it." (Matt. 16:25). The promise of returns is there.

How to respond during the dying process

Perhaps you are in the middle of this dying process and are wondering what you are supposed to do.

> *Is any among you suffering? Then he must pray.*
> *James 5:13 nasb*

As I wrote earlier, David and Job continually talked to God, and He talked to them through all the affliction they went through. The Psalms are David's journal, a big part of them written by him.

What did David do?

He prayed and worshiped.

He kept talking to God. He was honest. He did not pretend.

God's secrets are given to those who keep trusting Him

Because he loved God and clung to Him, God revealed some of the deeper things of His heart to him. David was privileged to be a recipient of God's plans, purposes, and affections. He not only cried out for help for himself, but also cared about what was important to God, and fought for it.

That is why God loved him and called him a man after His heart. "The secret of the Lord is for those who fear (revere) Him." (Psalm 25:14 nasb).

At times David despaired of life, pouring out his complaint, but he also gave God thanks for the deliverance he was hoping for. The Psalmist didn't always seem to be able to praise God, but by faith said that he will praise Him again. The Psalms are down-to-earth and real.

*Why am I discouraged? Why is my heart so sad? I will put
my hope in God, for I will yet praise Him. Psalm 43:5 nlt*

David knew there was an end to the afflictions, in faith stating:

*Many are the afflictions of the righteous,
But the Lord delivers him out of them all.
Psalm 34:19 nasb*

If we don't quit, we will reap a mighty breakthrough. "We will reap, if we faint not." (Galatians 6:9 kjv)

He unveils His beauty to us

This is what God brought me to. To prayer. And He knew how to keep me in the fire until He forged the walk of prayer in my life. My desperation kept me praying. He didn't bring immediate breakthroughs, but in this process He began to unveil a part of Himself that I had not known. I discovered Him to be a God who not only answers prayer, but who delights in me like a bridegroom who rejoices over his bride. I write about in in Part Five, *Sweet Intimacy with Jesus.*

Chapter Seventeen

After the Dungeon Years The Doors Opened to the Nations

Remember how in the story of Joseph he spent years in the dungeon and suddenly the tables turned—they completely flipped! He was brought out of jail to a King's palace and was given a surprising assignment.

Those years the ravens fed us were the preparation to a sudden turn-around and years of ministry travel.

For many years we didn't travel much due to finances. Even the annual family Bible camp we enjoyed many years in a row, became a financial burden. Instead of staying in a cabin as we had over the years, we tented. Instead of eating meals in the dining room, we cooked our own food. In fact, Tuomo didn't even come to camp the last year because he had to work.

This leanness in travel lasted about ten years.

Then in 1992, the tide began to turn. God provided for us to attend a conference in New Westminster were Cindy and Mike Jacobs (Generals of Intercession) were speaking. Cindy has a prophetic call to the nations, teaching about prophetic intercession and praying for revival for cities and nations. There had been very little teaching at conferences on the subject of prayer up until that time, so this was a conference I really wanted to attend.

At the same time, there was an event in the Vancouver area for which three students from our Christian School were chosen to participate. The school paid our expenses to drive them. It was perfect because the dates of the school event and the conference coincided. God provided!

How brilliant God is! If He wants you somewhere, He makes a way. And He loves doing it this way, so we know *He* is behind it. And there was a bonus on top of everything: I noticed in the newspaper classified ads that someone was selling two tickets to the Swan Lake Ballet at the Orpheum in Vancouver at a bargain price. This date also coincided with our trip. God was blessing us after many years of hardship.

From that day forward God began to open doors to prayer conferences and ministry travel. I began teaching about prayer. I heard God speak in a dream that I would travel from my city nine or ten times a year. This became a reality for many years: attending conferences and gatherings, taking teams, or teaching. There was an annual apostolic/prophetic conference in Red Deer, Alberta, especially for equipping prophetic intercessors. It grew to over a thousand people attending. The first year Tuomo and I attended, we were billeted with a family. For many years following, I organized a group to travel there. We shared vehicles and hotel rooms. One year we had almost 30 people from Prince George.

In 1995, God led me to be a part of the Watchmen for the Nations journey. This took me to many prophetic prayer gatherings in Canada, most of the time taking a few intercessors with me: Whistler, Vancouver, Victoria, Harrison Hot Springs, Kelowna, Hope, Edmonton, Calgary, Montreal, Quebec City, Ottawa, Lethbridge, Langley, and Canmore. I also traveled to Israel in 2001 with the Journey of Hope Watchmen Gathering. These were prayer journeys, where we, as a company of people, worshiped and prayed prophetically for our nation, for Israel, and the nations.

In 1996 God shifted me into international travel, beginning with a dance team from our church in Prince George going to the ICEJ Feast of Tabernacles in Israel. I went ahead of this team to attend the All Nations Prayer Convocation in Jerusalem that took place some days earlier. Later in 1998, I attended both these events in Israel again, on my way to Africa.

These were amazing events of worship and prayer for the nations, with the nations praying *together*. Both the Feast of Tabernacles and the All Nations Prayer Convocation had delegates from all over the world. In the halls I heard many languages spoken. It was a foretaste of Revelation 7:9-12 where it speaks of countless multitudes from every nation, tribe, peoples, and tongues, standing before the throne, worshiping.

God led me to travel to Asia twice with a team who ministered to missionaries in Japan, China, Thailand, and Hong Kong, and to speak at a Bible School and several churches. I flew to Africa twice, visiting my son, Steve, who was doing mission work in Malawi, Zimbabwe and Zambia. My second trip was to teach about prayer, the *Power Perfected in Weakness* course, in each of these countries.

In 1997 I started working at our church as prayer pastor, leading prayer ministry and teaching about prayer. I also attended regional and national, denominational conferences. Pastors and their wives I met at these events invited me to speak and teach seminars about prayer at their churches.

In 2004, my church board released me to go to the International House of Prayer in Kansas City (IHOPKC) for a sabbatical. There I took a 3 month training course which led to the establishing of the Prince George House of Prayer. Since then I have made 11 trips, taking groups of people to spend time in the IHOPKC Prayer Room and for equipping at various conferences and other training events hosted there. (Please read the last chapter, titled *The Mystery of God's Grace*, if you have questions about IHOPKC).

In 2006 the Lord spoke to me to take a team from Prince George to the National House of Prayer in Ottawa for a week of prayer at the Parliament Building, in the House of Commons. When I announced it, 10 people from various churches responded to make up the team.

I have been to Israel on prayer journeys, taking people with me on some of these trips, being there a total of six times. It has been a great privilege to see the places where Jesus walked, taught, and healed, and to pray for the fulfillment of God's prophetic purposes for Israel.

I have also travelled to summits and conferences in Canada, having been part of a national team of prophetic intercessory leaders who regularly met for prayer conference calls.

I write this testimony to show how the years of trial opened up to years of open doors of ministry. I had no idea when I started praying an hour a day as a 21 year old mother on the brink of a nervous breakdown that these things would happen. I just desperately needed help from God. He has so much more planned for us than we ask, think, or imagine—if we start pursuing Him and never give up on that fascinating journey.

So don't give up! Your dark night of the soul has a purpose. Hang in there, and keep up that conversation with the Lord. Don't stop praying.

Part Four

The Call to Ministry
A Journey of Hearing
and Obeying

Your most effective ministry
will come out of your deepest hurts.
~Anonymous

Chapter Eightteen

A Widow gave Me a Jar of Loonies for Bible School

She plunked a glass jar into my hands—full of golden loonies. *"This is for you to go to Bible School."* With these firm but unaffected words, a senior First Nations woman handed me this gift. The loonies ($1 coins: an explanation for those who are not Canadians) added up to $101, a generous gift from a woman who lived on social services. She was a diligent woman who kept her small, simple home neat and orderly and continually gave from her meager resources to her children, grandchildren and others in need. She was not one for dishing out thanks or compliments, but I knew this was an expression of appreciation from her heart for the time I had spent with her, visiting and praying for her and her family when one of her sons committed suicide. She worked in a second hand clothing distribution center on a volunteer basis, and during her many hours a week, kept her keen eyes open, choosing very suitable clothes in good condition for family and friends. During our painful and financially barren years, this woman provided bags full of good quality clothing for the seven members of our family. We were dressed well in spite of everything.

I had sensed a drawing to participate in the fulltime Bible School that had started at our church, but I had resisted. Finances were certainly an obstacle. There wasn't enough to cover the registration, never mind the tuitions. Now that excuse was gone. This amount covered a lifetime registration fee of $100. I was now officially registered as a student. Done. I was headed forward on this path, a destiny I had not charted for myself. Someone bigger was at work in my life...

Call to Ministry—Hearing and Obeying

One day while doing errands downtown, I saw a woman pastor across the street. As I glanced at her, I heard the Lord say, *"I have called you to be a pastor. Prepare for the ministry."*

I told my husband what the Lord had spoken to me. He agreed. That Christmas he bought a *Vine's Expository* and presented it to me in the presence of our children, announcing that God had called me to the ministry. Our pastor affirmed it also, so there was a sense of confirmation.

This was not something out of left field. I had functioned in ministry for many years at our church, co-leading home groups with my husband, leading intercessory prayer, being an elder, praying with and counselling many people, teaching Sunday school, and speaking at times at various events.

In fact, both my husband and I had a strong call to minister. Tuomo had lead youth and children's camps earlier in his life. He was a Sunday school superintendent for 5 years. He led home groups, was an elder and board member, and enjoyed studying the Bible.

We both loved to hear the teaching of the word right from a young age. As a young couple, we ordered a weekly teaching tape from St. Margaret's Church in Burnaby, British Columbia. We wanted to hear more of the word than just going to church on Sundays. There was a revival happening at St. Margaret's and we were hungry so receiving their weekly audio tape was a great blessing.

I remember being frustrated about something and began to pray intentionally and persistently for wisdom and revelation in that specific area. It didn't take long that the pastor of St. Margaret's began a whole series on that topic! On tape after tape, for many weeks, he expounded on that very subject. As a 20 year old I saw how God was attentive to my prayers. I believe it gives Him great pleasure to answer and teach us when we ask Him.

For if you cry for discernment, lift your voice for understanding; if you seek her as silver and search for her as for hidden treasures; then you will discern the fear of the Lord and discover the knowledge of God. For the Lord gives wisdom; from His mouth come knowledge and understanding.
Prov. 2:3-4 nasb

He felt compassion for them because they were like a sheep without a shepherd; and He began to teach them many things. Mark 6:34 nasb

Our church offered a lay Bible school, so as soon as we started attending this church, we registered for these classes on Tuesday evenings. It was my favorite night of the week. We had assignments, tests, and book reports, all of which I thoroughly enjoyed. For many years we took courses covering many books of the Bible as well as many topics.

It wasn't the norm for a woman to be a pastor, so I thought maybe Tuomo had the call

From time to time I felt a call to ministry, but it was not the norm for a woman to be a pastor, so I thought maybe Tuomo had the call. He had always loved learning and teaching the Bible. I thought God was letting me sense the call so I would be ready if he felt to step forward in it.

In fact, at one time we almost went to Bible school, having found out about a specific one in the United States. Tuomo's work, which had gone quite well, took a serious turn in 1982. It was the beginning of our long, lean time. It became unbearable and we cried out to God, something which pressure really helps you do. We seriously pondered that perhaps God *had* called Tuomo. Were we to poise ourselves for that, to just let go and press into it? The sense of "calling" was definitely hovering over us. We continued to pray earnestly, wanting to hear from God.

A missionary-prophet came to minister at our church. We had previous knowledge of this man's ministry—that he was a prophet who heard from

God—because years before he had lived in Prince George. Back then, when we started attending the church, he took a shine to Tuomo and would at times unexpectedly drop by for visits when my husband was doing some extra-income building projects in our basement. At that time he built furniture, displayed them upstairs, and sold them through newspaper ads. Pastor Steve would come by and watch him build and talk with him. I made sandwiches and invited him to join us for lunch. He would tell me, "Your husband is a 'can-do' man. He gets things done!"

I was embarrassed because my home never looked like the homes of the other women in the church. For instance, this very time we had a long table in the kitchen made from a door, a couple of mismatched chairs on one side, and on the other side was a couch that Tuomo had built. One of the three of us had to sit on the couch during lunch. The couch was lower than kitchen chairs so it wasn't a normal set up. It was embarrassing for me that I did not have six or eight perfectly matched chairs that also matched a fancy buffet full of fine-bone china and crystal that a lot of the church women had. We always had something different and unusual going on at our house, which made us stick out. I wanted to blend in and be normal, but that was not the call on my life.

Pastor Steve would pray for us. Later when I began to understand the power of prayer and see amazing answers, I realized how much this man had prayed for us. I believe his prayers had significant impact on our lives.

That week Pastor Steve was back in town and was ministering to our church leaders on a Monday night. Tuomo and I decided to call him to see if he would counsel us, because we didn't know if Tuomo should carry on with his work or go to Bible school. We called, asking if we could meet with him but did not tell him what it was about. He said he needed time to prepare for the evening meeting, but perhaps we could talk after. That evening he preached for about two hours, and then suddenly shouted that the anointing had come on him, and asked who wanted prayer. One woman immediately jumped up. Within seconds she fell down under the power of the Spirit. He then went around the room and started prophesying over each person. The atmosphere was electric. When he came to us, he shouted to Tuomo, "Do not leave your vocation! Do not leave your vocation!" Stunning. Well, we certainly heard from God. One little repeated sentence was a clear answer. He was not to go into full time ministry. Well, that was puzzling because the sense of "call" still hovered over us.

With fear and trembling I moved forward

That fall day when I'd heard God's voice downtown, and then had begun to prepare for ministry, I finally understood the "call" to fivefold ministry was for me. Tuomo's call was to marketplace ministry in the area of business. Our paradigm of thinking had been hindering us from seeing this previously. It was not the norm for women to be called into ministry in that generation, though there were some. There were stereotypes of thinking that had to be shifted. With fear and trembling I moved forward, knowing other people also had paradigms I would most likely face. However, I knew I needed to obey God, fearing Him rather than man.

Soon after, at a conference hosted at our church, one of the speakers gave an altar call for those sensing a call to ministry. I wrestled with whether I should go forward as I knew people may question a woman standing up there while her husband stayed seated. But I had to put all that aside and respond. I walked to the front. There were a number of men lined up and I was one woman among them (there may have been some wives with their husbands). I stood there feeling I stuck out like a sore thumb. However, the pastors who were ministering almost immediately bee-lined to me and prayed with anointing, confirming this call.

Trusting God to make a way

This call came in the middle of our financial crisis. Tuomo was learning a new, commission-based business, so his income was small while on a learning curve. I worked in housekeeping at Holiday Inn 3-4 days a week, helping support our family. I homeschooled our kids 3 days a week (the other 2 days they attended the Christian school). Working on weekends, Tuesdays, and at times Thursday evenings, I was able to continue leading prayer on Thursday mornings and attend church Saturday evenings.

All right, how does one proceed in the middle of all of this? I knew (because God had trained me) that it was about hearing and obeying. It was not about circumstances. It was about the voice of God, so if He was leading me to do this, then I needed to align and trust Him to make a way.

Looking ahead, I aimed at starting Bible school the following year. The tuition was modest, but still a great stretch for us—much too much. However, I prayed intentionally, asking God to direct me. He began to bless me with extras, like getting stat holiday shifts at work. My income increased and I put aside everything I possibly could to save up for tuition.

Also, over the previous 15 years I had taken many evening Bible courses at our church's lay Bible school (College in the Word) so I had already completed almost one full Bible school year. During the year of preparation, while I worked to save up money, I completed 4 more courses.

Prayer is not a one way street. It is a conversation with God. So we need to have our "ears" open to listen to His voice, to hear what He is saying and do what He tells us.

Chapter Nineteen

The Test Came

After some months of grace in preparing—working hard and continuing to homeschool my children—we suddenly found ourselves in a storm. Just like in the ocean, a squall comes up, making visibility very poor. The morning may start with sunshine with a beautiful, blue sky, and then, almost from nowhere, dark, stormy clouds move in with cold, miserable, spitting rain. Truly in those squalls visibility is poor. What we saw with clarity a little while ago was suddenly blurred.

It seemed like a miserable cloud of frustration settled on me for two weeks. Everyone annoyed me. I was constantly irritated with either my husband or the kids. And then I was upset with myself for having so little grace. I began to doubt myself. Did I really have a call to ministry? How can I be called when I don't respond with patience and kindness? It seemed I hadn't even passed grade one! I felt overwhelmed with our schedule. It was exhausting and required everything. God *did* require everything. We had to be fully surrendered as the schedule was incredibly demanding and needed moment by moment discipline to stay steady. But during these two weeks, it felt as if grace was lifted and I was annoyed and irritated with everyone. Consequently I began to doubt my call.

Finally, since it did not ease up and no breakthrough was anywhere near the horizon, I knew I had to press in deeper with God. I decided to pray all day for several days in the middle of homeschooling, cooking, etc. In the morning I got everyone working on their assignments and then withdrew into my bedroom. I got on my knees and prayed fervently. We had just had a weekend seminar at our church, hosting Leonard Fox, a visiting speaker. He had spoken about how much we are loved by God. I am an avid note taker, so I took out my notebook and read over the points from Pastor Fox's messages. I turned the points into prayer. Knowing how much I am loved by God gave me confidence to come to His throne about this persistent difficult situation and ask for help.

I asked for more revelation of His love as well, for a fresh anointing of this love. When I ran out of words, I just waited in His presence. From time to time I came out to check on the children's progress, but then withdrew again to pray. I thought I will do this UNTIL HE SPEAKS. It says in the Bible that "He is a rewarder of those who diligently seek Him" (Heb. 11:6 nkjv). I had experienced this many times in my life already, so I knew what to do. Wait until He speaks.

This went on for about three days. The pressure persisted.
It did not let up, but scripture says, "We shall reap if we
faint not" (Gal. 6:9 kjv). I waited.

The next morning I woke up around 5 am. Something had shifted! I was amazed because God's presence was all around me in our bedroom. All the intense spiritual warfare had completely evaporated and in its place I was surrounded by the love of God. It felt like angels had invaded my space. The peace was tangible. The contrast was like having been in hell and now heaven; like the sun was shining and birds were singing again after a turbulent storm. All that day I marveled and gloried, and in this beautiful feeling of peace and blessing it was easy to give God thanks and rejoice. I knew something significant had happened in the spirit realm. Yes, something had shifted! *Someone is praying for me. I know it!*

That evening when I was cooking supper, the phone rang. I was surprised to get a call from Wichita, Kansas from one of the pastors who had been on staff at our church. His family had moved away about six months earlier. We had not talked with them since then, so I knew there must be a significant reason for this call. He told me he had woken up to a frightening dream about me in the early morning hours. He had jolted up in bed. He fell back asleep but the dream continued. Jolting awake again, he knew he had to pray for me, so he prayed for an hour.

He had my attention! This pastor moved in the prophetic. I sensed God was giving me a message and I was all ears.

His dream was this: he had been climbing up a giant "monkey bar" contrivance, being about 100 feet up. Other people were also climbing on parallel monkey bars at various levels. He noticed that I was climbing up a bit further down on a nearby contrivance. He was very concerned because I was slowing down to stop, so he whispered as loud as he could, *"Don't stop! Keep going forward! Do not stop! Keep going forward even if you go slowly!"* He was whispering so "they" would not hear—whoever "they" were. I answered back, *"I am too tired. I need to rest."* And I stopped. With urgency he whispered, *"NO! Keep going, even if you go slowly! Do not stop!"* Suddenly, to his horror, he saw the monkey bar I was on, collapse. I flew off, hurtling toward the concrete floor below. He jolted awake, horrified.

Realizing it was a dream, he lay back down and fell asleep. The dream continued. He saw me fallen on the floor and people running to me. Since the people didn't know me, he began backing down as fast as he could to get to me. As soon as he took one step backwards, the mechanism of his monkey bar gave way and he found himself falling backwards into open space. In that moment of terror, he realized, too late, that the mechanism was set in such a way that it only held together if a person was going forward. If you stopped or went backward, it fell apart.

As he told me this dream, I knew exactly what the message was: *"Do not quit. Keep going forward. Even if you go slowly, go forward. If you pull back, it will not go well with you."* I felt overwhelming joy that God had again heard my prayers and cries and answered me in such a profound way. At this point he didn't yet comprehend the meaning of the dream, not knowing what had been going on. I told him about my call to ministry and how I had seriously considered pulling back, feeling unqualified. I told him I had gone through two weeks of intense spiritual warfare and finally positioned myself to pray each day until I heard from God.

Then his phone call came. I told him I knew someone was praying for me because there was such an amazing breakthrough that morning, like a night and day difference. I thanked him from my heart for his prayers.

He immediately understood the significance of why God had given him such an alarming dream, and affirmed my calling, praying for me over the phone. He said, with great seriousness, *"No, you cannot withdraw"*.

I understood that the only way life would work for me, since God had called me, was that I needed to obey and press on in the "upward call of God" (Phil. 3.14). This was a test I needed to remember for life! God will come through no matter how big the storm. He will come through with GRACE! Grace to go on to fulfill His calling.

It was an uplifting moment for both of us. For me that God had brought help from heaven by answering my desperate cries. For him, that he had heard from God, responded in prayer, and called me. It always takes a risk and a step of faith to call someone when God has shown you something. When we obey God, though often with trepidation, His kingdom work is advanced. I *needed* that word—desperately! I was thankful beyond words that he did not brush it off, but obeyed God and followed through by prayer and a phone call.

I have never forgotten this moment. It is etched into my very being. When we position ourselves to hear from God, *He will answer*!

Chapter Twenty

My Plans Went Helter-Skelter

The miracle of multiplication

The next test was God messing up my numbers and coming through with His.

I began to see the Bible school fees coming together about three months before the fall semester started. It felt good! *If I continued to work through that summer, considering the number of days I would work, every penny would be in.* I had it all figured out.

Little did I know that God had plans that threw mine helter-skelter with a couple of unexpected whirlwinds.

I had carefully calculated the hours I needed to work that year to earn the tuition money. Life was busy—working, home-schooling part time, taking extra classes, leading prayer ministry, and overseeing three home groups with my husband. I had been promoted to the public cleaning job at the hotel, so I was making a little more than before. Also, through the summer and September, my cleaning days landed on stat holidays, so I earned double time and a half for those days, an added blessing.

Two unexpected things happened that summer, blowing up my neat and tidy calculations.

Our oldest son announced his engagement in early July. They planned to marry the following month in Kansas, where his fiancé's family lived. This was happy news indeed and we celebrated with an engagement party. We began to plan a trip to the United States for the wedding, knowing I would be dipping into my tuition savings to do so.

Two days later we received shocking news of my sister-in-law's sudden passing in an early morning phone call. I was up getting ready for work while everyone still slept. My 16 year old nephew was staying with us, waiting to get on a tree planting crew that our son was foreman for. It was one of the most difficult moments of my life to wake him up to receive this call from his dad about his mother. We made immediate arrangements for him to fly to Winnipeg and within three hours he was on his way. With aching hearts and prayers, we sent him off.

I was in charge of opening up the housekeeping department at Holiday Inn at 7 that morning. I called front desk to let them know the situation that caused my delay. Several hours later I was at the hotel cleaning, but found myself going in circles, repeating tasks as my mind was a thousand miles away. I called home and told my husband I felt I needed to go to be with my brother's family. My boss gave me time off for the week, and within an hour I was packed and on my way.

The funeral was a bittersweet time, celebrating the life of a precious wife, mother, sister, sister-in-law and aunt. God came with His great comfort as the body of Christ lovingly surrounded my brother's family and all of us in this time of grief.

Arriving home, I discovered my son's wedding could not take place in the United States due to paperwork requirements. It would take up to six months for processing to receive approval. However, he had been informed it would only take two weeks for paperwork to be processed in Canada. The plans changed to a Prince George wedding. In three weeks!

The bride's family would travel to Canada, so the planning for the wedding fell primarily on my shoulders. Each morning before work, I prayed and asked God to help and guide me, and He did! He showed me what to do and how to organize it. To cut costs, my daughters and I baked squares each evening after work, for a week. Every one worked together to set up the reception room and to decorate. My son, Ben, made up luncheon meat, cheese, and fruit trays. Finally, with cake and salads ordered, everything was in place, and God graced us with His presence at this momentous occasion, causing us to have tears of joy as we celebrated.

A month later, when Bible school was about to begin, I counted up my savings, and to my great astonishment found that I had reached my goal in spite of these two unexpected events. I had enough to pay the full tuition for the first year. What God calls us to do, He provides for.

Chapter Twenty-One

The Enemy Will Try to Stop You

At the beginning of the first Bible School year our pastor gave an opening talk. One heads-up warning was etched into my memory. He prepared us for the years of study ahead by saying there will most likely be a very big attack of the enemy at some point each semester, big enough to cause us to be tempted to quit. The enemy doesn't want us studying the word, nor preparing ourselves to be ministers of the word. He hates it because it equips more people through each of us, strengthening them in their faith and knowledge of God. The enemy does not want laborers in the harvest fields. Expect resistance.

I was very glad for this heads up. Since I had already been attacked severely six months earlier I understood this warning.

Sure enough, an attack came in the month of November during the first semester. I was feeling overwhelmed and tired with the level of work and responsibility I was carrying. One night I lay awake in the night, feeling stressed and oppressed. I couldn't feel the Lord's presence—only a sense of angst and hopelessness, wondering if I could keep going. I prayed that night, asking God to move on someone to pray for me. I needed extra prayer.

The following Sunday at church, a lady from our congregation approached me, telling me she had felt a strong burden to pray for me one night that week, in fact praying for an hour! She said, "I am not an intercessor, but I just had to pray for you". (She did not realize that we are all called to intercession, that she indeed is an intercessor). She stepped up to the task when God placed it before her.

Joy erupted in my spirit! Double joy because *I* had not asked any person to pray for me—just asked God to please have someone pray. He answered that prayer. And it felt all the more wonderful because this woman did not consider herself an intercessor, and here God had laid me on her heart and moved her forward in *her* prayer life. It was an encouragement to her that she was hearing from God when I told her how her obedience to God's prompting was an answer to my prayers.

God is brilliant! He multi-tasks in marvelous ways, doing much more than we ask, think, or imagine.

My faith and joy were renewed. When we have joy, we have new strength because "the joy of the Lord is our strength" (Nehemiah 8:10 niv). I was strengthened to carry on, seeing how God provided. This was a journey we were on together. He had called me and was making sure I received the help of heaven to complete it.

Chapter Twenty-Two

As I Moved Forward, Our Son Surrendered to the Lord

One concern I had about moving forward in ministry was 1 Timothy 3:4-5, which says those who are leaders in ministry need to manage their own household well, keeping their children under control with all dignity. It further states that if they don't know how to manage their own household, how will they take care of God's house?

One of our sons was not walking with the Lord. We had fasted and prayed fervently for him for many years. We loved him and ached for him to know the love of God—to discover what an amazing Person Jesus is, to walk and talk with Him, and to have a revelation of what God's plan was for his life.

My call was confirmed by my husband and spiritual leaders, but I still had a question in my heart. *What about this verse, God? Are You saying I am okay to move forward even though my son is not walking with You right now?*

I kept moving forward because God had called me and confirmed it in a clear way, but there was this niggling thought in the back of my mind.

Steve, who was 17, had gone on a North American trip with his beat up Toyota hatchback that summer. He went to the world's largest home-built airplane show in Wisconsin, and from there to Ottawa to visit cousins. Then he had headed to Florida to stay with my sister's family for a while, after which he drove west to see his newly-married brother and his bride in Wichita, Kansas. The final leg of his journey was to see his grandparents on Vancouver Island. With great trepidation I had released him on this trip. My husband was confident he needed this experience and it was time to let him go. Steve went through Hurricane Andrew in Florida, sleeping on Daytona Beach until the "all clear" came. In Wichita he watched a tornado touch down at a distance from his brother's porch, and on Vancouver Island he surfed too close to sea lions, turning back when he saw how *big* they were, realizing it might not be safe anymore. I prayed much all through his trip.

He wasn't going to be back until after my classes had begun.

Late one afternoon I was sitting on the couch in the living room, reading through one of my textbooks. I heard someone come in the house and head downstairs. Hearing male voices, I thought Tuomo had come home from work and was talking to Ben. I kept reading, not really paying attention to the world around me.

I heard someone come upstairs and around the corner to the living room. Looking up I was shocked to see Steve! He had not informed us of his exact return date, so it was a surprise. I stood up and he bee-lined to me giving me a big, long, bear hug. I sensed in the spirit that something had changed in him.

Soon it became evident. He'd had a personal encounter with God during his travels. Not long after, he was filled with the Holy Spirit. After graduating from high school, he was accepted at Southern Alberta Institute of Technology, Calgary, studying aeronautical engineering technology. Upon completion, though he had planned to begin work building airplanes, he responded to a call to missions. He served as a marketplace missionary in Malawi, Zimbabwe, and Zambia for five years. He built several churches, a Bible school dorm, a house, and developed farming and business projects, mentoring people in practical ways to prosper financially through them.

I realized God had looked after this, too. He saw that I honored His word so he honored me and moved on my son. I had gone forward based on Him calling me, but at the same time concerned that I live by His word. God saw the conundrum in my spirit and took care of it. Again it was God's brilliant multi-tasking. The big thing was that our son was back with the Lord! It was a great celebration in heaven and a great joy to us as parents, siblings, and church family who had interceded a lot for him. Secondly, I felt another level of confirmation that God had indeed called me to pursue this path I was on.

Chapter Twenty-Three

Jesus Melted Icy Hearts at Winter Camp

"Lord, I don't want to do this! I *don't* want to do this!"

I was on my knees in our basement family room crying out to God. He heard my desperate cry and sent a blast of -30 degree weather for a few weeks, which canceled the winter camp my husband and I were to lead. Temporarily canceled. It was postponed for 3 weeks. The three weeks gave me more prayer time. It was needed.

I was in second year of Bible School when Tuomo and I were asked by the principal of our church's Christian school to lead this camp for the senior highs. Why would that be so difficult? For a number of years, a spirit of rebellion, defiance, and utter indifference to the things of God had invaded the high school. There was a great spirit of resistance from the demonic realm. It was outright spiritual warfare! A few of the students loved the Lord and were walking with Him—praise God for them—but the majority were not. Parents, staff, intercessors, and these few students prayed fervently for spiritual breakthrough. We had pressed in and pressed in but no breakthrough had come. It was exhausting. We were all weary in the battle.

Now we had been asked to lead a winter camp?! With these hard-hearted students? It was like going into the lion's den. I felt like Gideon. I wasn't qualified for this job and I didn't have faith that anything would happen– just more of the same.

We asked two strong intercessors to join us, and before the camp we had a lot of prayer from the larger intercessory team as well as parents and staff.

Our son Steve, who was a grade 12 student, wanted to help. At that point, he hadn't told us yet about his encounter with God on his North America trip. Activities were planned for camp, which definitely needed his skill sets: activities like setting up a tent sauna on a frozen lake, cutting a hole in the ice for polar dipping, crazy hood rides (an old car hood being pulled behind a car, upside down), tobogganing and ice carving.

After all the preparations were completed, we were on our way to Baldy Hughes, a former military base about 40 minutes west of Prince George. The weather had let up, shifting into pleasant winter days.

When we arrived, there was the initial hullaballoo of getting everyone situated into their rooms, giving instructions regarding our schedule for the next three days, as well as dividing them into teams of four for meal setup and cleanup duties.

In the midst of it, right at the beginning, tension erupted between Tuomo, Steve, and myself. *Oh, I really needed this, didn't I, in the middle of this stressful event?* I knew it was warfare. I asked them to come to a side room. I asked forgiveness for my part and said we need to be in unity for this to work. We all agreed and renewed our purpose before God.

Our first main event was supper, which went well. My team of 4 young men was on duty for cleanup. After supper we had our first camp meeting upstairs in a large, open room. The boys and I were still busy in the kitchen, putting away the last washed and dried dishes and wiping counters, when the singing began upstairs. We could hear Terry leading worship on her guitar. I told the boys to head upstairs while I finished up. Lifting up prayers I looked around to see that everything was in order, and then headed upstairs, too—the last person.

As I stepped through the doorway, the presence of God hit me and I *knew*, just *knew* beyond the shadow of a doubt, *that God was about to do something big.* This was a sudden knowing. Up until that time it had been several years of slogging in mud. Now, in an instant, *I knew God was here!*

I "saw" as if a canopy was hanging from the ceiling, full of water, and it was *about to burst!*

I made my way to Tuomo, who was leading the meeting, and whispered in his ear what God had showed me. He waited until the song ended and then, with a microphone in his hand said, "Marja has something to say!" and thrust the mic to me.

"When I walked in the door," I began, "God showed me a canopy stretched across the ceiling and it was hanging, full of water, ready to burst.

God is about to show up!" I handed the mic back to Tuomo.

"Whoever wants prayer, come to the front," Tuomo said, and asked Terry to carry on leading worship.

We all waited and after a few minutes saw one young man step up to the front. He was one of the ones who *was* serving the Lord. Tuomo, Lee, and I went to him, asked him what he wanted prayer for, and prayed for him. As we were finishing, I noticed Steve had stepped up to the front as well, so we went to him. When we asked what he wanted prayer for, he said, "To be filled with the Holy Spirit." So we prayed for him and within minutes he was praying in tongues. Then we saw another person had come forward so we went to him. As the three of us prayed, I suddenly felt someone else praying with us. Steve had joined us and began to prophesy over him. I was amazed at what God was doing. Steve had not been walking with God for some years, but something was happening in his life. He was *back!*

…but that was only the beginning. Three young men standing together were crying. *Sixteen year old young men crying?* That was *definitely* the Holy Spirit moving on them! It's good to cry, but young guys often hold back. God was on the move.

One of the teachers had driven out that evening to join the meeting. He stood up and said, *"God showed me that some of you hate your fathers."* These three young men began to wail. This teacher went to them to pray for them.

Then Holy Spirit pandemonium broke out—everyone in the room was crying. I don't think there was a dry eye. All 20 senior high students had a powerful touch of God that night. God broke through. Icy hearts melted. At last!

We saw the glory of God—it was wonderful. Times of refreshing from the presence of the Lord.

A few weeks later we held a Junior High Camp. They had heard what had happened at the Senior High Camp and I am sure there were conflicting things going on in their hearts. Some were secretly hoping it would happen to them. Others held back. One emphatically said, "It won't happen to me!" He was not having anything to do with it.

God's Spirit fell on the Junior Highs, too! He let them have the same Holy Spirit downpour. The young man who resisted was in the middle of it all, crying, *"Jesus! Jesus! Jesus!"* When God comes, He is irresistible. He comes like an overwhelming wave of glory and everyone is swept in.

God was so good. I am writing this with tears. It still affects me because it was a sovereign act of God that the Holy Spirit fell on these students after many years of earnest prayer and fasting.

The kids had fun times: getting hot in the tent sauna and then dipping into the frozen lake, car hood rides, and other outdoor activities. We also watched a video, *China Cry* and I read letters from Carol Gray, our China missionary. Her stories were fascinating. I wanted them to get a vision beyond themselves, to see what is happening in the nations.

A report of this was written up in our church's newspaper:

> *"Twenty students and six staff braved the elements again this year and embarked on our third winter camp. Baldy Hughes was our base camp for food, sleep, fellowship, and hearing from God. Three days were spent learning and practicing the art of conquering. Fears were dispelled, peer pressure was turned for good, burdens for people and nations were laid. Some preached publicly for the first time, others moved in the gifts of the Spirit for the first time. All had opportunity, in such close quarters, to practice the fruits of the Spirit.*

Winter activities added to the challenge as we tobogganed, had crazy hood rides, built a sauna on the frozen lake, cut a hole through the ice for swimming and engaged in ice-carving. These activities are not that strange when you consider that our leaders were Tuomo and Marja Kostamo.

Thanks to all who helped to make this another memorable opportunity to get closer to God and to each other. Until next year, remember, the best way to prepare for the polar dip is to take only cold showers."

No name was attached but I think it was our principal who wrote it.

I am still moved in my heart remembering how God showed up. Thank You, Lord! You hear and answer our earnest cries. Every young person needs a sovereign encounter with God. You are never the same after God has touched you. After a touch like this, you *KNOW* there is a God and He becomes personal to you. That is what we need to continue to pray for, for this generation. Fresh encounter. Fresh outpourings. Undeniable moves of God's Spirit. It is these kinds of things that intercessors pray for, for this generation, because they have experienced these things in their own lives.

I love the story of the Hebrides revival. Two senior women, sisters who were housebound because of health issues, exercised one of the most powerful ministries there is, the ministry of intercessory prayer. They "prayed through". Other groups began to pray also and the glory of God came to that region in such power that unsaved people fell on their knees outdoors. The whole area was enveloped with a cloud of God's glory. Many people woke up in the night, feeling conviction of sin. They headed to the local police station, thinking they needed to confess there. The police realized this was a spiritual matter and Rev. Duncan Campbell was asked to come to do meetings. People congregated around the church, looking through windows because there was not enough room inside. The church was packed.

Let us keep praying for these sovereign breakthroughs of God's presence and power.

*Now will not God bring about justice for His elect who cry
to Him day and night, and will He delay long over them? I
tell you that He will bring about justice for them quickly.*
Luke 18:7, 8 nasb

Chapter Twenty-Four

Get In The Jet Stream!

I was exhausted. I had completed two full years of Bible School along with many family and ministry responsibilities. On top of that, we moved just days before the third year began. Moves are considered one of the top stressful events of life. I was dragging my feet.

One day our missionary-prophet, the same one who shouted to Tuomo, "Do not leave your vocation", talked to me. He was concerned about my health and began to prophesy with great gusto saying: "**Get in the jet stream! The jet stream! The jet stream!** You know what the jet stream is? It's the strong air current that flows from Japan to Alaska. Jets fly in it because there is less resistance and they are carried by air currents. If you don't get in the jet stream you are going to burn out!"

I knew this word was from God, but I didn't know how to get in the jet stream. How could I lessen my responsibilities? What could I change?

...Well, God's ways are above ours!

He does a play on words at times. Not long after this prophecy, something unexpected happened which broke up my demanding schedule and landed me in that literal jet stream.

Our senior pastor invited me to be a part of a small group of four to go to Asia for a month, to visit and encourage our missionaries in Japan, Hong Kong, China, and Thailand. All my expenses were covered. I was floored! I said "yes", but then thought I better ask Tuomo if he was okay with it. I was surprised with myself saying "yes" so quickly, not even thinking I should pray about it. I realized later that God had prepared me for this trip. We had faithfully prayed for these missionaries at our intercessory prayer meetings for a long time. And Tuomo was fine with me going.

Helena, who was 12 at the time, burst into tears, worried about me going to a communist country. It caused some trembling in *my* heart also, so I prayed fervently about that part of the trip. I wanted to be confident about crossing the border because I would be bringing Carol some books. I didn't want to cause problems for her, or for me.

God answered in a remarkable way.

I needed the word of the Lord—He gave it in a surprising way

One Saturday morning I drove to Fort George Park, a favorite prayer place of mine, taking my journal and Bible with me, to spend three hours seeking God about this trip. Because of the anxiety about going into China, knowing it was not a welcoming place for Christians, I needed to get "the word of the Lord" and I wanted my daughter to have peace.

When I opened my journal, I was disappointed because I had taken a fully completed one by mistake instead of a new, empty one (they had similar covers). There wasn't even one page to write on. I flipped it open and began reading what I had written. Before long I was captivated and read through most of it. I was awed with how much I had written and prayed about China over the past year. So many prayers for China!

My daughters and I had visited my son and his wife in their tiny basement suite in Vancouver. To keep my prayer time in the morning, I went for a prayer walk so I wouldn't disturb my sleeping family. As I walked and prayed in the early morning sunshine, everywhere I looked there were Chinese people. Many were doing morning exercises in the park.

At one point I sat on a stone wall to rest. A Chinese man came pushing his little girl in a stroller with another girl, slightly older, walking beside him. When he stopped near me to adjust something in the stroller, we began a conversation. He was a Christian. He told me about a team from the underground church in China that had spoken at their Chinese church in Vancouver recently, speaking about the persecution and trials they endured and continue to endure. This dad said it changed his life hearing what they go through—that in spite of the persecution their faith is strong. He and his wife had been greatly convicted as they "complained a lot".

The Lord often leads me to pray for the people who are around me when I am in other cities, so I prayed for these Asian people with heartfelt prayers written out in my journal, praying for believers and unbelievers alike.

I read further in my journal about the winter camps my husband and I had led earlier that year. At both camps, I told the students about China and about our missionary, Carol Gray, whom they knew. I had read to them some of her letters which were full of adventure. We also watched a movie called *China Cry*. I had a burden for these youth to see beyond themselves and get a global vision for the harvest. After challenging them with these things, we'd had a prayer time for China.

Carol had become my close friend over the years. She had been saved from a life of drugs and prostitution, had grown to deeply love Jesus, and learned how to pray and hear His voice. She went back to the streets of Prince George to preach the gospel to the street people, working with local street ministry groups. Her secret desire was to go as a missionary, either to the streets of New York or the ghettos of Hong Kong. This was impossible for her because she worked at cleaning jobs to provide for herself, never mind having money to put aside for a goal such as this. However, this did not deter her because she was a woman of faith. One day, the **impossible** happened! Her aunt passed away and left her a $25,000 inheritance. That was all she needed. She packed up and went to inland China after a short stay in Hong Kong, on an adventure that extended for 12 years. Her letters were read by our intercessors who prayed for her continually. I felt her story and letters were an adventure the high schoolers would enjoy and be challenged by, so I had shared about her at the winter camps.

I continued to read in my journal: one of the teachers of the academy, who was from Hong Kong, had acquired free tickets to the Chinese New Year celebration in our city, and offered them to whoever wanted them. I took some for our family. I wanted us to be more informed, to know how to pray for the Chinese people.

Now here I was at Fort George Park reading all these entries about China. I realized joyfully that God had been preparing me all year for this trip. God was smart, working it out that I took the "wrong" journal. I didn't have to write prayers about whether it was His will I go on this trip or not. Rather, God had me read my past prayers and experiences to clearly confirm He was indeed sending me.

God works in puns and riddles

I realized too, when I saw the itinerary, that we would be flying home in the *very jet stream* I had been prophesied about! God has a sense of humor and works in puns and riddles. *This* was His way of refreshing me. I wasn't to drop anything from my schedule. To deal with the exhaustion, He was taking me on this mission journey to refresh me.

The experienced suitcases

I fasted for nine days, wanting to be spiritually prepared.

I prayed for some money because I needed decent luggage (ours were so ragged they were out of question) and a few other items. $100 was given to me as a gift. *Thank You, Lord, for providing!* I shopped around for luggage but prices were much too steep for my budget, so I found a *Buy and Sell* paper (before the time of Face Book Marketplace and Kijiji). I saw three pieces of luggage for $5 each. Now *that* was my price! I called, inquiring about them, and part way through my sentence, the man on the other end of the call asked, "Is that Marja?" I was talking to Rob from our church! We had a good laugh. His family was heading to Hong Kong as missionaries for an indefinite period of time, planning to go into inland China ultimately. They would be leaving some weeks before us with their family of six. Their fourteen suitcases were all packed and these three were left over. In fact, he said, "You can have them at no charge." And further saying, "These suitcases have been to inland China and back." He got his wife on the phone, and she laughed, saying these suitcases were "experienced suitcases" having traveled to inland China on a previous trip they had made. *Unbelievable!* The chances of that happening was absolutely unbelievable!

Wow! I had experienced suitcases. They knew the way. Through a newspaper. God's ways are beyond finding out.

I was greatly strengthened and encouraged through this, realizing God *was truly* sending me there because He had gone out of his way to confirm it in this astounding way.

However, this is not the end of the story. One of the intercessors stopped by my house a week or so before we left, I think to give me something to bring to the missionaries. Many people had dropped off gifts for them. I told her the story of the prophet's word to me about "the jet stream", how within weeks I was asked to go on this journey, and was literally going to be flying in that very jet stream (though he meant it figuratively). I told her about the suitcases that had been to China and back, showing them to her. Suddenly she pointed and said, "Look!" I looked to where she was pointing: the logo on the suitcase said *JETSTREAM!* I hadn't even noticed. God was working out these wonders, bringing confirmation after confirmation.

Japan, Hong Kong, and China

We, the team of four, including our pastor and his wife, left in November and were away for about a month. Our first stop was Japan. It was wonderful to connect with my friend, Teresa, who had gone there as a missionary with her son, by faith. She'd heard God's call and responded, likewise going through many miracles that confirmed her journey. Teresa went as an English-as-a-Second Language (ESL) teacher, offering classes at a church as an evangelism outreach arm. When we arrived, she had been there for several years. We spent quality time with her, listened, prayed and prophesied over her. She was very encouraged. We also spoke at several churches and God gave me a prophetic word for the church where Teresa served. I was surprised when her pastor called me up to the front to prophesy to the church with no notice. He just told me to prophesy! God was faithful to give me a word, just like that. At the time of this writing, my precious friend, Teresa, has gone to heaven to be with Jesus. She served in Japan for 25 plus years, most of that time faithfully pastoring a small congregation as an ordained minister.

Teresa joined the rest of us for the next leg of the trip to Hong Kong and China. The skies were bright blue and clear as we descended into Hong Kong. Cliffs and skyscrapers were spread out in a panoramic vista and appeared to rise up out of the turquoise ocean. Beautiful! I thought of a prayer I had prayed on a hillside the summer before. I had asked God to let me see some of this beautiful earth He had created before it burns up. Here I was—my prayer being answered in such an unexpected way. We spoke briefly at a church in Hong Kong, and met with the missionary family from our church who had arrived before us.

Nervous

Then we flew into inland China. We descended into Chengdu, a city of 3.5 million people back then. A thick blanket of smog I had never seen the likes of, covered the city. I was nervous. I was worried about going through customs and security because I had a few *Power Perfected in Weakness* teaching manuals with me for Carol. This was the dreaded moment I had prepared myself for through fasting and prayer. However I needn't have worried because we were waved through without a hitch. It was a breeze. Whew! That fall Canada had made some kind of favorable step regarding China, so Canada was in good books with them. We wore Canadian flag pins on our lapels, which must have helped. God went before us, opening doors.

The unforgettable train ride

We needed to catch a train to Xichang, where Carol was—a 12-hour trip. From the airport we took a taxi to a place where we were to buy train tickets. No matter what our pastor said at the counter, they did not issue tickets. Teresa and I went aside, sat on a concrete half-wall, and prayed earnestly. I think the ticket sellers were hoping for a bribe. Eventually, suddenly, there were tickets available. Now we needed to get to the train, but no one gave clear instructions, partly because of the language barrier, but also a spirit of confusion operated in China. We finally made it to the station but still had to walk through endless halls before getting to the train.

We thought we could breathe a sigh of relief, but the next chapter of adventure unfolded. What a 12-hour experience—a memory not to be forgotten! The train cars consisted of first, second, and third class. We were second class. Guess what second class was? A train car of cubicles that were open to the hallway along one side of the car. Each cubicle had six bunks, three tiers high and quite narrow, barely wide enough for one skinny person. These folded down against the walls so people could sit on the bottom bunk until they were ready to sleep. Small, grey, folded blankets and tiny pillows, both of questionable cleanliness, were provided.

There were three Chinese people in our cubicle besides our four, so seven people crowded into a six-bunk cubicle. We took our shoes off, but carefully inspected the floor before we stepped anywhere, as one Chinese custom was hawking and spitting on the floor. We settled in and tried to sleep fully clothed and with our purses and other valuables tucked under us. The whole train car was in a thick cloud of cigarette smoke. People were up for hours talking, smoking, and playing card games. Finally the lights were out and I drifted off to sleep in the midst of thick smoke and the murmurings of a strange language in this lurching train.

I woke up in the middle of the night. All was quiet. What woke me? As I listened, I heard suppressed giggles. Someone was desperately trying not to laugh, but it kept bubbling up again and again. I recognized my pastor's wife's giggle, so I whispered, asking what was so funny in this strange setting in the middle of the night. In whispered giggles she said her husband was snoring in Chinese! This woman who was a meticulous housekeeper, and who had put a plastic bag over her filthy pillow before she laid her head on it, was finding joy in the middle of it all.

In the morning I found my shoes and tried to avoid those disgusting globs as I headed to the bathroom. After waiting in a lineup, I finally got in. I could not believe it—the tiny, square closet, which reeked or urine, consisted of a hole in the floor which opened to the railroad track!

That morning we watched the scenery as we chugged towards our destination. Chengdu had been a concrete jungle with heavy smog. Now we looked at rugged, green hillsides and terraced farmlands passing by our window. Poverty was evident everywhere. A little girl, maybe 8 years old, had a baby strapped to her back. Perhaps her parents were working in the fields. My heart went out to her—so young to be responsible for a baby.

How could I be so careless—my purse!

When we arrived in Xichang, we squeezed into a small, red, hatchback taxi with all our luggage, to head to the hotel our pastor and his wife had booked. Carol was to meet us there. Teresa and I were to stay at Carol's place. In the taxi, I dropped my purse to the floor so I could put my right arm across the back of the seat to hold back a suitcase from sliding onto the person next to me. At the hotel courtyard, we had an exciting and happy reunion with Carol.

When we went into the lobby to wait for our pastor and his wife to check in, I was horrified to realize I had left my purse, with passports, money, and all, in the taxi. The driver had sped off quickly after we had unloaded. How could I be so careless? I reluctantly told my team, kicking myself for bringing this frustration on everyone. I had heard that you had to hold tight to your valuables in China because they were very liable to disappear. What were we going to do now? I know Teresa probably kicked into praying and I tried to find a way to phone the taxi company. It was difficult to communicate as only some people spoke English, and not very well.

I was extremely stressed. It was a needle in a haystack type of thing to locate the right taxi in a city the size of Xichang (a population of close to half a million). For a dishonest person, the money and passport were a good catch. The hotel was not able to contact them. It was really hoping for a miracle to expect to recover my purse and passport.

Forty-five minutes into my dilemma, I was still kicking myself, when all of a sudden the little, red taxi drove into the courtyard. The driver came out and handed me my purse. Praise the Lord! Praise the Lord! Carol was very surprised. She said this does not happen in China—she was positive my purse was gone for good. After thanking the driver profusely, I checked to see if everything was there. Not a thing was missing. It truly was a miracle. God was covering us!

Too soon our time ended

After Carol helped our pastor and his wife settle into their hotel room, she took us to her apartment. It was a three-story, 12 unit apartment building with *one toilet*. Outside. Open air. A trough to squat over beside the pig pen in the back. And we had to walk past a vicious dog to get there. Aaagh! Well, we were on a mission trip.

We took quality time with Carol, to hear about her life and ministry, as well as ministry time with some of the ones Carol had led to the Lord and was discipling. A government official and his family, who were also her converts and English students, invited us to their home for a feast.

Too soon our time there ended. We took the train back to Chengdu and flew to Hong Kong. From there, Teresa headed back to Japan and the rest of us flew to Thailand. We spent this last part of our trip with our Thailand missionary and his congregation in Chiang Mai. He had recently married, so we celebrated with them, eating a beautiful dinner at a fancy restaurant with live music with stringed instruments.

A rude awakening

Every security check went without a hitch, a breeze really. Amazed, I felt I could relax now as we flew back *in the jet stream* to Canada.

It had been a wonderful trip with lots of answered prayers and experiences to last a lifetime, but it felt wonderful to arrive at Vancouver International Airport. We were home!

My sense of ease was abruptly jolted at Canadian customs. I was thoroughly interrogated because they found a strange, metal pipe in my suitcase. I had a lot of explaining to do regarding this. In Hong Kong, Rob had asked me if I would take a bicycle pump back to Canada for him. It belonged to a friend of his, had been on loan, or some such thing, and had ended up travelling with them all the way to Hong Kong.

It was funny, really. Every single security point went smoothly except for Canada, the one we had not covered in prayer! It was God's sense of humor to show us how much He was involved throughout the whole journey, taking care of everything with His presence and His angels.

God answers prayer in such profound, specific, and delightful ways, showing us His wonders and marvels all along the journey of life, if we just care to ask Him. When we really pray, meaning business in our prayers, He answers: I literally flew in the actual jet stream from Japan to Alaska! I had been invited to be a part of a team that went from our church to visit our missionaries in Japan, Hong Kong, Thailand, and China—all expenses paid!

God knew how to refresh me. The prophet prophesied to *get in the jet stream* hypothetically, but God meant it literally. God's word play is fascinating—those hints, clues, and riddles that color our journey of life.

This prophecy and trip was the Lord reaching down, picking me up, and carrying me. He was continually helping me through these years to complete this Bible School assignment.

These following verses are an amazing picture of flying in the jet stream:

> *There is none like the God of Israel.* **He rides across the heavens to help you, across the skies in majestic splendor...** *Deut. 33:26-27 nlt*

> **Like an eagle...He spread his wings and caught them, He carried them on His pinions.** *Deut. 32:11 nasb*

Chapter Twenty-Five

What Kind of Pastor Am I Called to Be?

Finally the third year rolled to an end. This time I was behind in tuitions, so after graduation I found a morning job working at a motel to pay everything off. I knew that in a couple of months of work this debt would be cleared. I had done what God had told me to do. I had prepared myself for ministry.

Having taken time to think about my call, I didn't feel I was to be a traditional pastor—it was not my mantle to wear. So I asked myself the question, "What is my passion in ministry? Where do I find myself anointed the most?" I knew immediately. It wasn't rocket science. I loved prayer ministry and the prophetic. I seemed to be drawn to budding prophetic intercessors, who didn't know they were that. Often they were going through rough times and a lot of brokenness. God would bring me alongside them to mentor them, though it wasn't official that I was doing it. It was more like a friendship. I loved to teach about prayer and the prophetic, having done that for a while already. And I had a heart for missions, missionaries, Canada, Israel, the nations, the church, spiritual leaders, five-fold ministry, and for the unity of the body of Christ. I prayed much for all these things and led groups praying for these. I wondered though, how that would all fit into a "pastor" ministry role.

Though in the natural I did not see how the next step would unfold, I had confidence God was on the move and would open a door for me since He was the one who had called me. I did not want to open any doors myself. I would wait for the Lord.

In the meantime, God gave me an assignment: a trip to Israel with our church's dance team, for which I was the intercessory leader and fund raising facilitator. *The Hannah Cry* chapter chronicles the adventures of that story.

God dropped a big hint

During the year of preparing for the trip to Israel, God dropped a big hint about things that would follow the Israel assignment.

That spring I organized a group of intercessors from our church to travel to an Apostolic/Prophetic/Intercessors conference in Red Deer, Alberta. These annual conferences were excellent equipping times: the intercessory team always came back greatly encouraged. Our senior pastor also attended, since he was part of the leadership team for these events.

Dr. Peter Wagner, who is in heaven now, was a yearly, greatly-loved speaker. He had an international teaching mantle and left a legacy of many books through which the body of Christ continues to be equipped regarding apostles, prophets, prophetic intercession, signs, wonders, healing and deliverance.

If you are serious about revival, you need a prayer pastor on staff

Prophetic intercessors especially were very grateful for Peter's ministry because he was a forerunner in bringing teaching about the importance of prayer to the body of Christ. He explained "prophetic intercessors" to the rest of the body, a calling often misunderstood—both wanted but not wanted. These ones were often misfits. Now through teaching, they were finding their place, and pastors began to understand more clearly how to receive the blessing of their gift.

In one of his sessions, Peter made this statement to senior pastors in the gathering: "If you are serious about revival, you need to have a prayer pastor on staff. Most likely it will be a woman. You also need to have a budget for prayer ministry", going on to describe this in more detail.

I was fascinated. What he described, resonated loud and clear. *This is what I am called for! This is my job description stated and defined!*

I was in a God moment!

I didn't look around to see how my pastor was responding. I continued listening, sensing destiny unfolding. Later, at break, as we worked our way to the doors, one of our intercessors who was a board member, came to me. He, with no preamble, asked straight out, "Does that describe you—how do you feel about it?" I said, "Yes, it does." He said he would bring it up to the pastors and board.

Eight months passed. These months were filled with much work, excitement, and prayer, preparing for the trip to Israel. This occupied me along with the other prayer and leadership ministry I carried.

After we returned home from Israel (I tell that story in the next chapter) and settled into the more normal rhythm of life, my pastor asked me to come to his office. He said the staff and board would like me to be the prayer director of the church. I was given a budget to run a prayer room starting January 1, 1997, as well as an honorarium. I became the official paid prayer pastor on staff.

Here it was!

Six years earlier God had spoken to me as I walked downtown, that I was called to the ministry. Financially, time-wise, and in many other ways it had seemed like an insurmountable mountain. But God had backed me up, giving me grace and strength in supernatural ways as I stepped into this journey of faith. I had run into intense warfare where the enemy tried to divert me. By God's grace and the prayers of many, He carried me through all these hurdles, always showing His hand and confirming His call.

What He calls you to, He empowers you to do

This is the beautiful God we have, who has a "scarlet chord of destiny" for each one of us. What He calls you to do, He makes a way for, He provides for, and He strengthens and empowers you to do. The whole journey is an ongoing treasure hunt with hints and clues, and unfolding, unexpected surprises along the way. It's not without difficulties—He makes that clear in His word—but it is an abundant life worth living. An adventure beyond our expectations!

Chapter Twenty-Six

The Hannah Cry and an Unexpected Outcome

I'd had enough!

In the spring of 1995 I had had enough! Something *had* to shift. Fourteen years of this was *too much.*

We made an appointment with one of our pastors and his wife to ask for prayer regarding our endless, stressful, financial trial. I had already decided to go on a 40 day fast to pray for Canada, so I determined also to pray daily for financial breakthrough. Enough was enough!

After completing Bible school, I had a part time housekeeping job at a motel to finish paying off my tuition. Since cleaning rooms is heavy work, I went on a partial fast. Daniel and his three friends ate no "pleasant" foods during their fast, so I ate porridge each morning, something I didn't like. I only worked mornings, so for the rest of the day I didn't eat. I was desperate like Hannah in the Bible.

As I said, there were two things I was fasting for: the first was for Canada to experience an open heaven, an awakening, a revival. I had been gripped by the shedding of innocent blood (abortion) for many years. I had prayed, cried, fasted, and lost sleep over it. I wrote in Chapter 12, that I saw from scriptures that God brought judgments on Israel on account of idolatry and the accompanying killing of their babies (Psalm 106). I knew how God viewed this bloodshed, and knew there was pending judgment over our nation. I wanted my children to have a future and a hope. Secondly I fasted for financial breakthrough.

I timed this fast to end at the first Watchmen Gathering to be held in Whistler, BC, June 28 - July 5, 1995. It was a gathering to seek the Lord, to pray and ask Him what was hindering Canada from experiencing an open heaven. There were no named speakers or worship leaders, but rather a faceless group of people seeking the Lord together. Tuomo and I were registered to attend. A group of 14 of us had rented a large vacation home which cut costs to a minimum.

At that time Tuomo had been working in his financial services business for six years. He needed to add a mutual funds licence to his portfolio to better serve his clients, and which would also raise our income level. He was diligently studying to attempt the exam a third time. Back in those days, this exam was in essay form. Tuomo is dyslexic, and to further complicate things, English is not his first language, so it was not an easy hurdle to jump.

God sent help!

One beautiful, spring evening I was cleaning up branches after our landlord had trimmed the hedge. Friends of ours happened to drive by, and seeing me outside, they stopped to talk. It was the missionary-prophet and his wife. They had prayed faithfully for our family for several decades. I invited them in for tea. Asking how we were doing, I told them Tuomo was writing the exam the next day, his third try. They immediately began to pray for God's help, grace, and favor to be on him. It was a divine appointment. Help had come!

When Tuomo came home from the office, I told him the "prophets" had come by and had prayed for him. He was encouraged. The next day he wrote the exam and then settled in for several weeks of waiting for his results.

The battle before a word from God

A few days before we were to leave for Whistler, Tuomo suddenly announced he wasn't going. I was sitting on the back steps enjoying the late afternoon sun until he dropped this bomb. I was upset and asked why. He said he wasn't going anywhere until this financial trial turned around.

Tuomo was mostly a positive person, but this time I saw discouragement on him. I tried to encourage him to attend since our accommodation, registration, and travel were taken care of, saying it would be better to wait for the results at this gathering than at home. But his mind was made up.

I sat there for half an hour, stewing in silence. I was angry at this ongoing situation. I didn't pray. I wouldn't pray. Hadn't I prayed and fasted and done everything I could? I was at the end my rope. As I sat in heavy silence, I began to hear in my spirit, *Take Helena in Tuomo's place*. Both Tuomo and Helena thought it was a good idea, and she was an excited 13 year old, ready for this adventure. Her ballet teacher and husband were going and since she had a very warm place in her heart for them, it was an added bonus for her.

The Whistler Gathering was amazing with 2300 people attending from all over Canada. Long lines formed at the doors an hour or more before each meeting. The presence of the Lord was very strong. Many sat on the floor as that was the only way to fit everyone into the auditorium. The days went by quickly as we worshiped, waited and prayed with prophetic direction. It was wonderful to be with so many, like-minded intercessors who had been praying earnestly for Canada.

I tried to fight the "distraction"

I am going to explain something which is important to understand—what happened next at the Gathering is significant: Sonja and Leon, the ballet instructors from our church (Helena's friends), had been talking about taking a dance team to Israel to the Feast of Tabernacles. Sonja had mentioned it several times asking if I would go with them, meaning the girls and I. I had not given it too much thought, though I would have *loved* to go. It was too much out of reach for us financially. So I thought.

At one of the final meetings the leaders sensed that we had ministered to God's heart and now He wanted to minister back to us, to deposit something into each of our hearts. We were encouraged to sit in quietness and wait. As I sat there, ideas for fundraising for this trip to Israel began to swirl in my mind. *I should be waiting on God!* Frustrated with myself for getting on rabbit trails, I worked at focusing my thoughts. But within a few moments I was thinking about fundraising again. Though I chastised myself, the whole time went like this and I was disappointed with myself for losing the moment.

That evening when the doors opened, I found a spot near the front beside a couple. Within minutes they told me about their recent trip to Israel to the Feast of Tabernacles, which had been an overwhelming blessing. Because of it they wanted to help others experience it by providing funds. I was astounded by this conversation with them. I suddenly realized that God wanted me to go, and that it had been *HIM* talking to me during the waiting on God time. I had *not* been distracted. That had been the voice of God.

A happy husband

When we came home, I found a very happy husband. He had received his exam results and *passed!* A mountain was conquered, and a whole new season began. God had heard our prayers, cries, and fasts. Our financial situation did not change immediately, but gradually the tide turned from that time forward. Also, while we were at the conference, he built a cedar-strip canoe which he sold and it paid some of our bills.

We were committed to go to Israel

I talked to Tuomo about the girls and I going to Israel and he was supportive of it if we were able to raise the funds. I acquired a number of house cleaning jobs. Also, we had a Free Press Newspaper route of about 500 papers, and both girls had their own daily PG Citizen Newspaper routes.

I let Sonja know the girls and I were committed, and became the fundraiser and intercessory leader for the team. God gave me many creative ideas for raising money as a group. Each person received a portion of the funds according to how much work they put in, having to come up with the balance themselves. We raised almost $12,000.

A divine and unexpected assignment

I found a research job in a newspaper ad which helped raise funds for our family. The information was mailed to me, and after reading through the instructions, I proceeded. One night as I lay awake, I realized I had misread the instructions. I couldn't sleep until I got that settled so I got up. I found the instruction papers under a Prayer Canada newsletter, which I picked up and began to read through first. As I flipped pages, a small announcement caught my attention: a 10 day All Nations Prayer Convocation in Jerusalem just before the Feast of Tabernacles. As I read, I felt an undeniable call to attend this convocation. I just knew I was to be there. At that point, airline tickets had not been purchased, so it would work. I could fly to Israel with my girls before the rest of the team arrived, and since we have family in Israel, the girls could stay with them while I attended the convocation.

I called Arnie Bryan, the leader of Prayer Canada, and inquired about this convocation, asking how I could register. He informed me that it was by invitation only, but he would arrange for me to attend. Apparently there were six or so Canadians going to join delegates from most of the nations of the world.

A few months before the trip I received a call from Arnie Bryan. He wasn't able to go after all, and wanted me to take his place to present Canada at the convocation. One delegate per country was to present their nation. I was overwhelmed and surprised by this honor, and wondered if I could do it. He explained that each country was given ten minutes. In that time the delegate was to share the 7 main prayer needs of their country and lead in prayer for those areas with the other nations joining to pray in agreement. I accepted this, sensing the Lord in it.

A sign—a double rainbow

Weeks later Tuomo drove the girls and I to Vancouver, the departure city of our flight. On our way, a beautiful double rainbow crossed the highway. It was spectacular, brilliantly contrasting against the dark canopy of rain clouds. I had an inkling it was for a reason—a promise—but had no idea of the danger we would encounter a few weeks later.

I did research on Canada to be more knowledgeable of the seven most important prayer points. I borrowed some magazines from a friend, and also a thick book about our nation from one of our pastors. These added weight to my luggage, unfortunately, but I wanted to be properly prepared. I read during the long flights, and prayed incessantly for anointing, the presence of the Lord, and that I would do the presentation honorably.

Nervous, but also knowing God had prepared me for years

Arriving in Israel is always wonderful. The passengers, as one, jubilantly clap and cheer when the wheels touch down—such an uplifting sense of shared joy for landing in Israel and gratefulness for a safe arrival.

We were spoiled by Tuomo's sisters' families, thoroughly enjoying our time with them, and the girls were happy to spend time with their Israeli cousins. After a few days I left them in the care of their aunties and took the bus to Jerusalem from Tel Aviv to get to the convocation.

It was common to see soldiers in uniform carrying guns among the milling crowds at the busy bus stations, as well as *on* the buses. After transferring in Jerusalem, I finally reached Ramat Rachel Hotel where the convocation was to take place. Delegates from many nations were milling about, speaking many different languages. At the registration desk, after a long line up, I was directed to another hotel many kilometers back towards the center of Jerusalem. I was quite exhausted from having hauled my luggage on two buses already, so it was difficult to process that I would have to figure out another bus to get to Mt. Zion Hotel. But before I had a chance to get too frustrated, a young Estonian man, also a conference delegate, said he would help me get a ride in a car. Before long, I had my luggage in the back of a car and travelled to the other hotel with several other people.

When I entered my clean and cool hotel room, I felt a sense of rest and peace begin to wash away the tension of the journey. I had signed up for a shared room to save money. Soon a woman from Palau arrived. She was a governmental leader from this small island nation in the Western Pacific.

We listened to each other's stories and prayed for one another, and she gave me a traditional dress from her island as a gift.

I loved the meetings! As we worshiped, I thought of the scripture in Revelation where it talks about every tribe and nation worshiping around His throne. This was a *foretaste of heaven!* I loved the idea of hearing about each nation and then praying together for one another's nations. I was doing what I had been created for!

At one point, the "Americas" were asked to meet with Rick Ridings, who was overseeing the Western Hemisphere. He gave us the schedule and told us how to proceed. I felt nervous, wondering if I was adequate to present Canada to all these nations. But a fleeting thought which had come and gone over the months, came again. Yes, God had prepared me for this. I had wept and prayed for Canada for almost 20 years. My husband and I had led Prayer for Canada, a monthly prayer meeting for most of that time. That is why He connected us with Watchmen for the Nation. That is why He led me to fast for 40 days. I had been carrying Canada on my heart for a long, long time, and that is why He had led me to this moment to represent Canada.

Finally the moment came for Canada to be presented. I shared the main points. Then—with deep regret about Canada pushing abortion on third world countries, influencing them with this atrocity—I got on my knees and asked the nations for forgiveness. I led in prayer for Canada to turn from these kinds of things and to enter her calling to be a healing to the nations, something that has often been prophesied. It was wonderful to have prophetic intercessors from all over the world join with me to call on God for our nation. It was a moment of a lifetime. It wasn't just a gathering in Canada of fellow Canadians praying together for our country. It was the nations praying with one heart for us—what a blessed moment! I somehow sensed the deep spiritual significance of this before God's throne in heaven. I felt Him saying, "*This* is what I created the nations for. When they come together as brothers and sisters, praying for one another, I *will send* My commanded blessing."

Now I understood why God had given us the double rainbow

When the conference came to an end, I travelled to meet up with my people, the Shoshannim Dance troupe from Prince George. We travelled for a few days to see Caesarea and the Galilee. This troupe had seven adults and six young women ages 12–15. Three of us travelled as intercessors/

chaperones. Four adults were dancers, including Sonja and Leon, the leaders of the team.

We finally arrived in Jerusalem and settled into the New Imperial Hotel, a vinitage hotel built in 1884, just inside the Jaffa Gate of the Old City. The walls of the Old City fascinated me, and I never seem to get enough of them. Every time I returned to Israel, I sought out the ramparts on the walls, to walk and pray there. These scriptures became real to me:

Walk about Zion and go around her; count her towers;
consider her ramparts; go through her palaces that you
may tell it to the next generation.
Psalm 48:12-13 nasb

On your walls, O Jerusalem, I have appointed watchmen;
all day and all night they will never keep silent. You who
remind the Lord, take no rest for yourselves; and give Him
no rest until He establishes and makes Jerusalem a praise
in the earth. Isaiah 62:6-7 nasb

A brooding and escalating tension was tangibly present in the air and we were informed of rising unrest between Palestinians and Jews. Our team took the bus daily to the Binyanei Ha'uma, now known as the Jerusalem International Convention Center (ICC), to practice the dance in the days leading up to the conference. Security was very high. Soldiers carrying guns were everywhere. They traveled on buses to guard against terrorists because there had been recent, deadly bus bombings. Our bags were checked before we boarded. It was unnerving, but the Israelis seemed to take it in stride and carry on with their lives. Not only was there tension in the city, it affected our team and we had several days of tension and conflict among us as well (God lets prophetic intercessors feel what is going on in the spiritual atmosphere), leading us to pray more.

While the team practiced on stage, I paced and prayed on the top floor concourse behind the balcony. There were tall, ceiling-to-floor windows providing a grand view of east, north and west Jerusalem. Spectacular! A joyful burden of prayer flowed effortlessly and endlessly from my heart. I was delighted to have this top floor to myself, to pray like a watchman on the wall for Jerusalem.

Gun-carrying soldiers were everywhere

One afternoon we got on a bus to travel to the Dead Sea and Masada, the impenetrable mountain fortress where a remnant of Jews held off the Romans for a long time. We noticed increased security on buses. As we traveled through the desert, the driver suddenly and unexpectedly slowed to a stop and announced that we were to get off and take our belongings with us. Gun-carrying soldiers were everywhere. Some of them got on the bus, did an inspection, and then released us back on. Carrying on, we toured Masada, after which the dancers headed back to Jerusalem for practices while we three intercessors stayed back to enjoy a swim in the salty waters of the Dead Sea. My sister- and brother-in-law, who live in Israel, joined us.

Night falls quickly in Israel. There is no gradual twilight like in Canada; it just goes from light to dark very fast. The five of us traveled back on a bus in the dark, along winding roads. It was relaxing as the bus wound around the bends and rumbled on in the evening quietness of the desert. We were feeling pleasantly drowsy having experienced a very hot day and then a soak in the Dead Sea. There were only a few people on the bus. The radio was on but the commentary was in Hebrew so I didn't understand what was being said. However, I was alerted by the tone of the newscaster and by how my relatives where listening intently and talking to each other. I asked my sister-in-law what was being said. "Something is going on in Jerusalem, something not good!"

I felt a chill run through me, wondering how my girls and the dance troupe were doing. We finally arrived after 9 pm. My youngest daughter, who was 12, ran to me and told of the trouble brewing nearby. She was afraid. Sonja and Leon brought us up-to-speed on the details they knew.

We slept a troubled night. In the morning we awoke to find the market square below the hotel profuse with police and soldiers, maybe sixty of them, waiting and alert. We sensed something serious was about to happen because even in Israel it was not normal to have this much security. The tension and strife were tangible. We all felt it as we boarded the bus outside the Old City wall. While the troupe practiced, I paced and prayed at my post on the third floor gazing out over Jerusalem. Sirens blared, emergency vehicles raced to unknown places, and from the east I saw a pillar of smoke rising *right where the Old City was!*

Later we learned there had been a violent riot and 4 people had died in the clash, just one quarter of a mile or so from our hotel. That is why we had felt so much tension in the air! Spirits of strife, anger, rage, violence, and murder had been rampant all around us.

All in all, 16 Israeli soldiers and 69 Palestinians died, and hundreds were injured during those days of clashes.

I understood then why God had given us the double rainbow.

He is my defense, I shall not be moved!

A few days later the Feast of Tabernacles began. Prime Minister Benyamin Netanyahu came to officially open the conference. He arrived, preceded by body guards who positioned themselves in strategic points around the auditorium. He welcomed all the guests from many nations. The meeting host called for us to stand and reach our hands toward him, to pray for him. It was a powerful moment as 5–6000 believers from all over the world prayed a blessing over the Prime Minister.

Tension was escalating in Jerusalem and we could feel the fear and anxiety people were experiencing. Into the middle of this the Lord had called a great company from the nations to worship and pray at two convocations back to back. First the 10 day All Nations Prayer Convocation, followed by the Feast of Tabernacles, an 8 day event of worship led by an orchestra of anointed and highly-skilled musicians, gifted singers, and a troupe of exceptionally-trained ballet dancers from all over the world. I thought of Chronicles where it records how David set up 4000 day-and-night singers who prophesied on stringed instruments. It says in the scriptures they were highly skilled. Night after night we declared the praises of God. It was a glorious foretaste of Heaven as the nations worshiped together. Even a queen—the Queen of Botswana was present in the audience. She had come to worship the King of kings in the city of the Great King! God knew how to order things. He brought His worshipers from all over the world to quell the escalating rage, though they did not realize they were being sent there for such an assignment, at such a time as this.

Sonja had prepared our troupe, saying they might not be invited on stage, but as the week of training progressed, the event organizers extended an invitation. One night, in the middle of this strife and anger that raged through the city, our dance troupe stepped up on stage as the orchestra played and the singers sang Psalm 62 (nkjv), *"He is my defense, I shall not be moved! He is my defense, I shall not be moved!"* The house came down, and the Lord and the troupe received a standing ovation. This prophetic song, danced and sang with such vigor and grace, resonated and echoed through the hearts of everyone there. It was a mighty faith statement in the midst of the storm that had hit Israel. Power is perfected in weakness: this troupe of young people, along with 4 adults, brought the prophetic dance at just the right moment, in the hour of distress.

We understood then why we also had experienced strife and tension in our group…the battle before the outpouring.

He adds much more to the answer than we ask for—the bonuses

Out of desperation I had fasted for 40 days for an end to our desperate, financial trial, and for Canada. Tuomo passed his exam, which opened the door to financial breakthrough, and God sent me to Israel to present Canada at a global prayer convocation. When I began the fast, I had no idea I would end up in Israel with my daughters and this harmless company of "hobbits"—these young girls who made a difference for Israel and the nations—and in the course of that, to end up presenting Canada to the nations for prayer.

That is how God works. If we seek Him, we will find Him, and He will add much more to the answer than we asked for. The bonuses.

> *Now to Him who is able to do far more abundantly*
> *beyond all that we ask or think.*
> *Ephesians 3:20 nasb*

Chapter Twenty-Seven

The Miracle—Only God Could Do This!

One evening I came home to find a new family member.

Ben, our son who was a youth leader at the church, had brought home a lost puppy—a young man with no place to go. Two girls, who played "hooky" from youth group, had met him and brought him to youth group. The girls' parents had dropped them off at youth church but they'd gone to the mall instead, once their parents had driven off. The mall was closed so they wandered back and along the way met Jake*. He had just arrived in Prince George and didn't know anyone or where anything was. He seemed quite lost so they invited him to youth church. He accepted the invitation and the girls brought him to Ben.

Hearing Jake's story, Ben sensed he was quite open to the Lord. He didn't feel right about leaving him with no place to go, so he talked to his dad, asking if Jake could stay at our place for the night.

That one night turned into nine months

Jake had lived a rough life and had FAS (fetal alcohol syndrome). He was high maintenance, but somehow we grew to love and care for him a lot. He didn't have basic life skills, having lived a street life for some time.

---

* *name changed*

He told us his story

Having been given up for adoption at 18 months of age because his father was violent and abusive, he had now come to Prince George to find his mother. Somehow he knew that much about his infancy and knew his mom lived there. A family near Salmon Arm had adopted him, but due to his out-of-control behavior at times, they could no longer keep him. He had ended up on the streets of Vancouver.

A sore developed on his foot and began to fester, worrying him that he might die. It woke him up, resulting in him wanting to leave Vancouver. He went to a rehabilitation center and they recommended a move to one of two cities. He chose Prince George because he knew his mother lived there and he hoped to find her.

Finding Jesus

Tuomo and Ben spent quality time with him, and he soon accepted Jesus as his personal savior.

Revival hit Prince George. The nightly meetings at Gateway Christian Fellowship were so packed that people had to sit on the floor because there were no more seats left. The presence of the Lord was strong and sweet, and people worshiped with abandonment. God touched us in profound ways, reawakening love for Him. Jake flourished in this atmosphere, experiencing God's amazing love. His favorite song, which he loved, was *Light the Fire Again*. His heart was ablaze with love for Jesus.

The girls and I were fund-raising for the trip to Israel which was to take place the following year. One of the jobs was delivering the Free Press paper to 500+ homes twice a week. We asked Jake to help to keep him busy. He wanted to use roller blades so I assigned him a few streets with no apartment buildings. He practically flew down those streets going from mailbox to mailbox.

At Christmas time our family made a trip to Kansas to visit our oldest son's family. We asked Jake if he would consider staying with his adoptive family while we were away. We had spoken to his parents, telling them about the change in his life. They were open to have him stay for that time.

When we returned, Jake was nowhere to be found. He had stayed with his adoptive parents for a few days but had gotten offended about something and left. It was a deep blow as we had witnessed the beautiful work of God in his life, and now he was back on the streets. We were disappointed, but continued praying for him.

One spring day he walked up our driveway! He had lost a lot of weight. We took him back to live with us and Tuomo arranged for him to work with a Christian landscaper.

He attended youth group but was a handful at times, not knowing how to fit in with kids who had grown up differently from him. There wasn't anyone like him who had lived on the streets. He had a strong, forceful personality and would get aggressive if things didn't go his way, so Ben had to confront him at times. He did not like that.

His deep pain

After one very volatile incident, Tuomo stepped in and took him for a walk up to Connaught Hill Park. He asked Jake what caused the most pain in his life. With tears in his eyes and choking back the pain, he said his mom had given him away. He desperately wanted to find her, but at the same time worried that she might be dead, in jail, or a prostitute.

Tuomo said, "We don't know that, but if she is alive, God has promised that if you receive Jesus, that you and your household will be saved (Acts 16:31). Let's now pray that if she is alive, and if she isn't already a believer, that she will turn to Christ, and that you will find her." Sitting up on that hill, they prayed together that summer evening.

The miracle

Jake had a birthday coming up a few weeks later. He was turning 21. I thought we needed to do an extra special birthday party because he needed to know he was cared for and loved.

In the meantime, our church hosted an evangelistic worship event at the CN Centre where some people received Christ into their lives. After this I noticed a new lady attending church and greeted her. She told me she had received Jesus at that event. I told her about our home group, inviting her to join us.

Lorraine* came that Friday. After the meeting we sat around the kitchen table having coffee and talking, each sharing a bit about ourselves so Lorraine would get to know us and we would get to know her. I mentioned we have five children. She said she also has five, but had to give up the oldest one at 18 months of age due to a violent father. I felt a stir in my spirit! *No, no, it can't be, just settle down.* I casually asked how old this child was now. She said he was going to turn 21 on July 11. I was shocked. *That was Jake's birthday – he was turning 21, and he had been given up at 18 months of age. Can it be possible that there was another situation so similar?* I carefully asked her what his name was. She said, "Allen**". I excused myself, ran upstairs to find my daughter Helena and asked her what Jake's middle name was, thinking she might remember. She said, "Allen".

I came back down stairs and sat down. I looked at my husband and he knew what I had found out. We carefully told her we had Allen living with us, saying he was going by the name Jake, but his middle name was Allen. We told her he had been given up for adoption at 18 months and we were planning a birthday party to celebrate his 21st birthday on July 11. She began to shake uncontrollably. Tuomo said he would make some phone calls to verify this before we reveal it to him. Our group was in awe of what was taking place right before their eyes at the kitchen table! I knew they would all be praying.

She continued to shake as I drove her home. It was overwhelming her that she may be meeting her son very soon.

Back at home, Tuomo told our family not to say anything to Jake until this was confirmed. He contacted his adoptive parents and found out Lorraine *was* his birth mother. Usually adoptive parents don't know who the mother is, but somehow they had a document with this information. Tuomo called Lorraine, letting her know and asked if she was ready to meet him that evening. She was!

---

* *name changed*

** *name changed*

When Jake came home from work, Tuomo said to him, "Jake, you and I need to go for a drive."

Jake had a unique way of dropping his jaw and moving it up and down as if he was going to say something, but nothing would come out. He did that jaw drop and finally said, "What's wrong? Is something wrong?" Tuomo assured him nothing was wrong.

The rest of us waited with bated breath at home. It was just too exciting!

When Tuomo returned shortly without Jake, we bombarded him with questions, wanting to know everything. He had first driven to a house on a street near the church and asked him if he knew this house. Jake said no.

Tuomo said, "This was the first house you lived in. Are you ready to meet your mom?"

Jake dropped his jaw, wagging his chin. He was astounded. Finally he said,

"Does she live here?"

Tuomo said, "No, but I know where she lives. I can take you there."

"Now??"

"Yes."

So they drove to Lorraine's house, *a house Jake had been delivering Free Press papers to on roller blades!*

When she came to the door, he introduced them, saying, "Jake, this is your mom. Lorraine, this is your son, Allen." They fell into each other's arms in a heartfelt embrace, and sat down to talk. Lorraine pulled out photo albums. Tuomo said to call when he's ready to come home, but to take as long as he wanted. When he left, they were deep in conversation looking through photos.

We were too excited to sleep even though it was late. Finally, after one in the morning, Jake phoned saying he was ready to come home. When he came in he was smiling from ear to ear. He headed for the fridge, loaded up a plate of food, and sat down at the dining room table. Pointing at Ben, he said, "Ben, you have a mom!" Then pointed at himself saying, "I have a mom!" He kept saying this over and over with a silly grin on his face, "Ben, you have a mom! I have a mom!"

We were all giddy with joy.

This was a MIRACLE!

How could God orchestrate this? It was beyond our wildest dreams. God loved that boy and wanted him to know he was loved. He went out of His way to co-ordinate this. What amount of planning and designing took place in Heaven to bring this about in such a marvelous way? It says in Psalms that we are to tell of his marvels and his wonders. This definitely took the cake.

It stunned us that Jake had been delivering papers to his mom's house. I could have given him any other street, but since he insisted on roller blades, *that* street was the only one that could be done on roller blades.

That God ordered Lorraine's steps to be at the CN event where she accepted Christ into her life around the same time as Jake poured out his heart pain to Tuomo—desperately wanting to find his mom—was amazing.

That God directed me to notice her at church, talk to her and invite her to *our house* for home group—the *very house* where Jake lived—was head spinning!

One more step had to happen, or this reunion may not have happened. If we did not have the type of conversation we had around the kitchen table, Lorraine and Jake may never have realized who each other were. They may have walked past each other at church often, without ever discovering they were mother and son. BUT GOD directed us to share about our lives and specifically about our children, the number of kids and so forth. It opened it up to the next step, and the next!

What a breath-taking moment it was when we all realized that a MIRACLE was unfolding at our kitchen table, at our ordinary little home group.

How unsearchable are His judgments and
His ways past finding out!
Romans 11:33b nkjv

Part Five

Sweet Intimacy with Jesus

Draw me after you and let us run together!
Song of Solomon 1:4 nasb

My beloved is mine and I am his.
Song of Solomon 2:16 nasb

Make my Garden Breathe out Fragrance

God not only takes us through death processes to form us, but He also reveals to us His sweetness, love, and intimacy. The depth of suffering equals the height of glory. Whenever we go through death experiences, there are corresponding experiences of His love and glory that follow... *if* we continue to trust Him through the storms. These together are the north and south winds that must blow upon the garden of our hearts to release the fragrance of what God is forming to waft from our lives.

Awake, O north wind, and come, wind of the south;
Make my garden breathe out fragrance, let its spices be
wafted abroad.
May My Beloved come into His garden and eat its
choice fruits!
Song of Solomon 4:16 nasb

Chapter Twenty-Eight: Sweet Intimacy with Jesus

Who is This Coming Out of the Wilderness Leaning on Her Beloved?

In my early years of praying I did it with deep conviction, commitment and earnestness. I did it because I understood from the scriptures and also from the biographies and writings of a few people like Rees Howells and Paul Yonggi Cho, that it is the main and first thing God has called us to do—to pray—to talk with Him. And I began to see awe-inspiring answers to prayer.

However, I did not realize He was going to reveal more of Himself to me in this process: revealing His heart, emotions and thoughts, showing and stunning me with what He is like.

A scripture I had memorized fascinated me, but I have understood it more and more as my relationship with the Lord has grown.

The secret of the Lord is with those that fear Him.
Psalm 25:14 nasb

We don't share our secrets with just anybody, for goodness sakes!

I began to see that God is *like us.* The closer the relationship, the greater the trust, and greater our freedom to be ourselves with that person.

God is the same. He waits for the relationship to grow and mature. As He sees that He can trust us, He reveals more of Himself to us. Selah.

He is a God who wants to be loved!

The valley of trouble that we walk through, sometimes for a long season—and if we keep clinging to Him through it—is the very pathway He brings us through to reveal His bridegroom love to us. He unveils more of His heart to us.

> *Therefore, behold I will allure her, bring her into the*
> *wilderness and speak kindly to her. Then I will give*
> *her her vineyards from there, And the Valley of Achor*
> *(trouble) as a door of hope…it will come about in that day,"*
> *declares the Lord, "That you will call Me Ishi*
> *(my husband) and no longer call Me*
> *Baali (my master). Hosea 2:14-16 nasb*

I heard a preacher once say that all kings in history make serving them the most important thing. *This* King makes *loving* Him the most important thing.

He is a King who desires to be loved! This is what God wants most, our voluntary love. And He longs to reveal to us His tender affection and love for us (Isaiah 30:18).

It's not just about us working for Him, praying, and serving Him faithfully. He wants relationship. He wants love.

I recall one of the first instances when I was overwhelmed with His love:

Drumming up courage to speak it out

This story is from early in my walk of stepping out in the prophetic. I knew God was moving on me with this gift, but I was afraid to speak out, fearing it might be my own thoughts and not God at all. I would hold back and hold back until I was almost bursting because He increased His anointing on me, and I wouldn't let it out.

Our pastor was to travel to some communist countries with my brother-in-law, who regularly travelled to these as a missionary. Our church prayed earnestly for this mission trip, myself included, as travelling into communist countries was dangerous. One night I awakened from a dream. I had dreamt that my pastor had a strange pair of shoes on. One shoe was normal but the other had a huge sole that spread out many inches in all directions. It was like a normal shoe with a giant-sized sole attached to it. I knew this dream was from God, but what could it mean? Praying for understanding, I took my big Strong's Concordance (before internet) and looked up scriptures that might give it meaning. When I read Luke 10:19 (niv), I knew this was it!

I have given you authority to trample on snakes and scorpions
and to overcome
all the power of the enemy; nothing will harm you.

The next step was to drum up courage to speak it to my pastor. So I prayed much. The next Sunday, I waited until he had greeted everyone at the door after the service. Then timidly I went up to him and shared the dream and scripture. His face lit up and he exclaimed it was the very same scripture his cousin, who is a pastor, had shared with him. Confirmation!

I was overjoyed! I went for a prayer walk in the forest near our small acreage later that day. I thanked the Lord over and over. I felt the joy of the Lord, feeling His pleasure that I had taken this step of faith to speak out what He was speaking to me, and knowing that this word had encouraged my pastor as he was preparing for this dangerous mission.

He climbs walls over us
Some years ago, a young couple we knew were about to be married within a week. The bride-to-be lived in another country and was flying in to our city, arriving late on a Sunday afternoon. In the morning at church, I asked the parents of the groom how their son was doing in anticipation of her arrival. He had been separated from her for some time by an ocean of distance. His father, with a gleam in his eyes, said, "He is climbing walls!"

A few days later I was reading Isaiah 62. I stopped dead at verse 5:

...as a bridegroom rejoices over the bride, so your God will
rejoice over you.
Isaiah 62:5 nasb

I thought about the young groom "climbing walls" in anticipation. I asked God, "Do you climb walls over me?" I could only imagine a love that pities me because God is majestic, great, the King of the universe, perfect, and sinless. I am a sinner, often failing in many ways. To think Him actually crazy in love with me, like the young groom climbing walls waiting for his bride to arrive, could it be?!

"Do you really love me like this?"

I heard Him say an emphatic, "YES!"

I began to weep.

As a waistband clings to a man

One day I saw a verse in the Bible that brought me to another full stop. I memorized it and pondered it many times. It is another one revealing God's longing for close relationship.

"As a waistband clings to the waist of a man, so I made
the whole household of Israel and the whole household
of Judah cling to Me," declares the Lord,
"that they might be for Me a people for renown,
for praise and for glory,
but they did not listen." Jeremiah 13:11 nasb

He wants us to *cling* to Him. Selah.

I painted a picture of a child standing beside God, with her arm around His waist. Clinging. That is relationship. That is what God wants from us.

He was sick of His people because they kept all the outward rules but their hearts were far from Him.

"…this people draw near with their words and honor Me with their lip service but they remove their hearts far from Me, and their reverence for Me consists of tradition learned by rote." Isaiah 29:13 nasb

He is after our HEARTS! Selah.

Chapter Twenty-Nine: Sweet Intimacy with Jesus

God's Wonders and Marvels

He makes His delight known to those who diligently seek Him with all their heart.

> *"You will seek Me and find Me when you search for Me*
> *with all your heart.*
> *I will be found by you", declares the Lord.*
> *Jeremiah 29:13-14 nasb*

We will find Him if we seek with *all our heart*. He loves to make Himself known to those who pursue Him. I have found this true through many awe-inspiring experiences. He has actually "shown up" to let me know how pleased He was with my pursuit by showering me with surprising blessings beyond the answers I sought Him for.

God Played Tag with Me

In the fall of 2008, on one of my many trips to the International House of Prayer in Kansas City (IHOPKC), I had the most remarkable God encounter of my life. Every time I have gone there, I have fasted almost the whole time, praying about a specific focus. That time I was praying for a youth awakening in the province of British Columbia, and for Canada as a whole, but particularly BC. It was a part of a 40 day thrust happening across Canada, each province taking 10 days of the 40 days. I had a few other items on my fasting list, but that was the main one.

Each morning I started my day by first walking to Shiloh—a beautiful, nature lake park owned by IHOPKC—before going to the actual house of prayer. A friend and I were staying at a home near the park, so it was only a short walk to the lake. I took my Bible and a cup of coffee, and sat on a bench overlooking the lake early in the morning. Over the years I have found God's creation a place of encountering Him. Somehow in the stillness of the morning He speaks. Since my young teens, I loved the song *I Come to the Garden Alone*. I took pains to learn it on the piano.

> *I come to the garden alone*
> *While the dew is still on the roses*
> *And the voice I hear falling on my ear*
> *The Son of God discloses*
>
> *Chorus: And He walks with me and He talks with me*
> *And He tells me I am his own*
> *And the joy we share as we tarry there*
> *None other has ever known.*
>
> *He speaks, and the sound of His voice,*
> *Is so sweet the birds hush their singing,*
> *And the melody that He gave to me*
> *Within my heart is ringing.*[7]

So, here I was in Shiloh, my garden of encounter with Jesus.

There were a couple of big, grey squirrels with fluffy tails that scampered about noisily in the yellow, crackly autumn leaves that covered the ground. I got used to them and they got used to me, so they went about their business unperturbed, as did I. It became a pleasant background noise along with the morning songs of many birds. I breathed in God's beauty displayed in the sights and sounds around me.

It was only after these early morning vigils that I went to the "indoor" house of prayer for the rest of the day.

All week long I prayed for the youth and other things on my fasting list. A few days before the end of my time, I walked along a park pathway and saw deer tracks. I whispered a little prayer, just a little wish, "I would love to see a stag, Lord, a gazelle, as Song of Songs calls it. Because it represents You! You are the gazelle leaping on the mountains, calling me to follow."

> *Listen! My beloved! Behold He is coming, climbing on*
> *the mountains, leaping on the hills! My beloved is like a*
> *gazelle or a young stag…*
> *My beloved responded and said to me,*
> *'Arise, My darling, My beautiful one, and come along'…*
>
> *Turn My beloved, and be like a gazelle or a young stag*
> *on the mountains of Bether. Song of Songs 2:8-10, 17 nasb*

Two days passed. I had forgotten about my little prayer. I was at Shiloh again, enjoying the stillness of one of my last mornings there. I heard the familiar rustle and bustle of the squirrels. *So I thought.* Suddenly my senses were on full alert—I knew instinctively this was a completely different rustle of leaves. Something was slowly creeping up behind me. In a split second I whirled around. To my astonishment I saw a "stag", a "gazelle", slowly stepping toward me. He was about ten feet from me and had his beautifully antlered head bowed low in harmless curiosity. My quick motion startled it. In a flash, he leapt backwards and then stopped for a few seconds to gaze at me with his head held up majestically, his antlers a princely crown. Breathtaking! Astounding! Exhilarating! Then turning, he bounded up the slope, disappearing into the forest.

I was spellbound. Utterly undone. I remembered my little whisper of a prayer and realized God had just answered it. *What a God He is! What a God!* I felt as if He had played tag with me: "Tag—you're it!" Then laughed as He pranced away up the slope and disappeared into the trees.

This is my God, my Beloved, my King.

For many days I was in a glorious daze knowing Jesus had shown a wonderful part of Himself to me. He is a playful God, an intimate God. He heard that faint whisper. Psalm 139 had a whole new meaning for me:

O Lord, You have searched me and known me.
You know when I sit down and when I rise up;
You understand my thought from afar.
You scrutinize my path and my lying down,
And are intimately acquainted with all my ways.
Even before there is a word on my tongue,
Behold, O Lord, You know it all.
You have enclosed me behind and before,
And laid your hand upon me.
Such knowledge is too wonderful for me;
It is too high, I cannot attain to it.
Psalm 139:1-6 nasb

This encounter was too wonderful. I could not comprehend that God would do this for me, but I enjoyed it. And marveled with wonderment that He did.

I also realized, in a flash, even more of the weight of this: if He answered my little whisper that I had forgotten, that I didn't deeply labor in prayer about, then how much more had He heard all my earnest prayers with fasting. So even though I may not see immediate results, I knew *all* my prayers, tears and fastings were before Him, and they will be answered at the appointed time.

…and that is how it is for you also.

Turn, my Beloved, and be
like a gazelle or a young
stag on the mountains
of Bether
Song of Solomon 2:17

Chapter Thirty: Sweet Intimacy with Jesus

Fragrances

His fragrance came when I opened up the House of Prayer

When it was finally time to open up the Prince George House of Prayer after many years of preparation, this following happened.

Backing up, In 1995, God dropped a word into my heart that surprised me: *"My house shall be a house of prayer for all nations"*. In that moment I knew He wanted me to be a part of this and somehow be doing something about it. I had learned over the years not to rush off to make things happen when He speaks, but to pray about it and wait for His timing and instructions. Ten years passed, and now it was the day before the official opening. I was alone in the building setting up chairs and the sound system in the open area, with worship music playing in the background.

I began to smell a beautiful fragrance, like lilies. It would waft, ebbing and flowing. I was amazed and took in deep breaths, wondering where this lovely aroma came from. I went to different rooms in the building to check for the source. I could only smell it in the open area where I was setting up. Then I realized it was the Lord! He was present and giving His smile of approval for the opening of the house of prayer. My joy rose to a new level, knowing that all the struggle leading up to the birthing was worth it.

An aroma to seal a revelation

In March of 2008, I was at IHOPKC with a couple of friends. I took in a weekend seminar called the *Bridal Paradigm at the End of the Age*. The shakings of the end times had always frightened me, but during this course I felt God lifting that fear and giving me a new understanding.

Between the afternoon and evening sessions I hurried to the prayer room because I wanted to hold onto and meditate on what God was revealing to me. I felt His love and did not want to lose the moment. As I paced back and forth, I smelled a beautiful aroma.

I realized God was "sealing" this revelation to me, showing me that the end times was about the culmination of His love.

God's language is not always words

This book, Treasures of Darkness, is about prayer, which is an ongoing dialogue with God. His language is not always words, though the Bible, His written word, is to dwell in our hearts richly (Col 3:16). His word is truth (John 17:17).

He speaks back to us in many varied and delightful ways, like these fragrances, confirming He is with us, listening, loving, convicting, correcting us, and guiding us into those works He has prepared for us to do.

> *My sheep hear my voice, and I know them. John*
> *10:27 nasb*

> *Indeed, God speaks once, or twice…*
> **In a dream, a vision of the night…**
> *Then He opens the ears of men and seals their instruction.*
> *Job 33:14-16 nasb*

> *For ever since the world was created, people have seen the earth and sky.* **Through everything God made, they can clearly see His invisible qualities — His eternal power and divine nature.**
> *Romans 1:20 nlt*

> **The Helper, the Holy Spirit… He will teach you**
> **all things,** *and bring to your remembrance all that I*
> *said to you.*
> *John 14:26 nasb*

Chapter Thirty-One: Sweet Intimacy with Jesus

In The Wilderness We Discover Who God Really Is

I began to understand that God actually **on purpose** leads us *into* the wilderness and leads us *through* the wilderness, like He did the children of Israel from Egypt to the Promised Land. Yet He led them safely, so they did not fear.

> *He led forth His own people like sheep and guided them in*
> *the wilderness like a flock; He led them SAFELY, so that*
> *they did not fear! Psalm 78: 52-53 nasb*

He is the same Shepherd today, leading us through a wilderness at times, teaching us to lean on Him.

> *Who is this coming up from the wilderness leaning*
> *on her beloved?*
> *Song of Solomon 8:5 nasb*

So powerful!

We learn to lean on Him in the wilderness. Why does it have to be this way that we need a wilderness to learn to lean on Him? Why does He take us into this uncomfortable place?

He has a good plan He is working out: He wants to reveal His bridegroom love to us there.

He wants *all* out heart, not just part

We begin to seek God with all our heart. When Israel was falling away from God, He allowed troubles to come into their lives so they would turn back to Him with all their heart. He is a Bridegroom God who wants *all* our heart, not just a part.

> *Then you will call on Me and come and pray to Me, and I*
> *will listen to you. You will seek Me and find Me when you*
> *seek Me **with all your heart**.*
> *Jeremiah 29:12-13 niv*

God is a passionate God who loves us and yearns for our love in response. Paul Billheimer, in his book, *The Mystery of God's Providence*, says, "The Messiah came for one glorious purpose: to woo, win, and train the members of Christ's church *and prepare them to become His bride*. The world, and much of the Church, does not know this, but *the universe is romantic. It was created entirely for the purpose of romance.*"[8]

He longs for intimacy with us. He is a jealous God, wanting all of you and me, not just a part. He is waiting to reveal more of His love to us.

As we turn to Him with all our heart, we begin to experience intimacy with Jesus and abide in Him, to walk and talk with Him as our closest friend and lover.

Because of the way human nature is, it seems we must be separated into a wilderness, separated from the pleasures of life that distract us from Him—things like friends, financial security, sports, material things, position, fame, talents, etc.—before we venture into the fullness of the beautiful relationship we can have with God.

Often, when every door is finally solidly closed, only then do we yield to sitting still before the Lord, allowing Him to have His way in our lives. We finally learn to be still and know He is God.

He reveals His bridegroom love to us in the wilderness

> *Therefore, behold **I will allure her, bring her to the***
> ***wilderness***
> ***and speak kindly to her**...and I will betroth you to me*
> *in faithfulness.*
> *Then you will **know** the Lord." Hosea 2:14-16, 19-20 nasb*

He dines with us in the wilderness
He dines with us when we finally open the door and fully let Him in.

> *You prepare a table before me in the presence of my*
> *enemies. Psalm 23:5*

> *"Behold, I stand at the door and knock; **if anyone hears***
> ***my voice and opens the door, I will come in to him,***
> ***and will dine with him**, and he with Me."*
> *Revelation 3:20 nasb*

He calls us friends and shares His secrets with us

His secrets aren't for everyone—they are for the whole-hearted ones.

> *The secret of the Lord is with those who fear him. Psalm*
> *25:14 nasb*

> *You are my friends if you do what I command you. No*
> *longer do I call you slaves for the slave does not know*
> *what his master is doing; but I have called you friends, for*
> *all things that I have heard from my Father*
> *I have made known to you. John 15:14-15 nasb*

We bear fruit

Out of intimacy with God comes fruit. Out of intimacy between a husband and a wife, come children. It is the same in our relationship with God. If we abide in Him, we bear much fruit (John 15:5 nasb).

In the wilderness we learn to lean on Him

> *Who is this coming up from the wilderness leaning on*
> *her beloved?*
> Song of Songs 8:5 nasb

Love cannot be forced: we have been given the power to choose

God wants to speak intimately with us, but He has given us the power to choose. The choice is ours. He helps us along by allowing some shakings, some wilderness experiences to turn us to Him, but still, the ball is in our court. We can choose to go deeper into this relationship with God.

Or not.

The down side is, that if we do not choose to draw near to God in our pain, we don't have the grace to deal with it, and our heart becomes hardened through unforgiveness and bitterness.

If we say "YES" and surrender to His leadership, we begin to know His what is on His heart and bear His burdens, His griefs and joys. We don't just pray for a list of things, rather God moves and stirs our hearts to pray for the things on His heart. Is it wrong to pray through a list? No, but He wants to take us deeper.

Abraham, Jacob, Joseph and many other Bible people were led into the wilderness to know God

This is His way. All our Bible heroes were led by God into a wilderness of some form or another, and it was there He revealed Himself to them and spoke to them: Abraham, Jacob, Joseph, Job, Moses, David, Hagar, Hannah, Daniel, and John.

They became ones who truly **knew** their God and His voice, and became mighty oaks planted by the waters, bringing shade and comfort to others. Because of their encounters with God, and their response, they have touched lives throughout the centuries—even our lives are touched by them in this present time.

For example, Abraham. God tested him. Abraham was tested with a very severe test: asked by God to sacrifice his only son. He just obeyed; he didn't resist. God saw his heart and obedience and stopped him before he went through with it. Then He spoke to Abraham that because of his obedience all the nations of the earth will be blessed. What a promise! What a breakthrough. There is always a breakthrough after a test. And to think that even *my* blessing is on account of Abraham's obedience. That is wonderful.

Even Jesus was led into the wilderness by the Holy Spirit. Jesus modeled for us the walk of intimacy with the Father, showing us that we too will be called into a wilderness at some point in our walk with Him.

Don't despise your wilderness—it may be the best thing that happens to you

If God has separated you from friends and family, or things, you may be at the cusp of the best thing ever happening to you. When God takes something away, He is about to give you something much better instead. He wants you to *know Him*, and as a result, you will touch others' lives, bringing them hope and comfort.

It doesn't mean you will permanently be without friends, family, or things. Those are gifts He gives us as well, but they should not take the place of God Himself in our lives.

He allures us into the wilderness so distractions would go.

Then, when we are still before Him, He begins to speak.

Psalm 37:7 says, *"Rest in the Lord and wait patiently for Him."* In the NASB version margin it says the word *patiently* is actually *longingly*. So it says, *"Rest in the Lord and wait longingly for Him."* If you do, He will reveal His bridegroom love to you and speak to you. He has something to say. Your true destiny will begin to unfold.

The fall feasts are a picture of God returning to marry us and dwell with us

The fall feasts, (the Feast of Trumpets, the Day of Atonement, and the Feast of Tabernacles) that Leviticus 23 speaks of, are a prophetic picture of God coming to *dwell* among us. That is His ultimate plan. One day He will come and literally dwell with us (Revelation 21:2-3). We will see Him face to face. But for now, He wants to dwell with us by His presence though we don't see Him visibly. We are His temple. He comes to actually live *in us* (He desires to be *that* close) when we invite Him into our hearts (John 14:23).

The first feast is the Feast of Trumpets. In scriptures it is about blasting the trumpets to announce a time to stop and fully rest for a day. It is a picture of this very thing I have been talking about, to learn to rest in the Lord, be still, to cease from our own works and to lean on Him.

God is calling us individually and also calling the corporate global bride to lean on Him, our beloved, to know His love, His kindness, His tender voice, and the things He is carrying in His heart.

Before He returns to literally and physically dwell with us, He is teaching us to know Him and lean on Him.

Jesus' prayer to the Father for us is to know Him

> *This is eternal life, that they may **know** You, the only*
> *true God,*
> *and Jesus Christ whom You have sent.*
> *John 17:3 nasb*

God wants to be *known* by us. Jesus Christ wants to be *known* by us.

What an amazing privilege we have! They are available for that intimate relationship, waiting for us to take the step to pursue them.

They don't force it on us. It is voluntary love they are looking for. Our choice. Our choice to enter into the deep things of God's heart. Otherwise it would not be true love.

And that is what they are longing for. True love.

Chapter Thirty-Two: Sweet Intimacy with Jesus

Creation Reveals Jesus' Heart, His Delight, His Presence, His Mind, and His Words

But ask the animals, and they will teach you, or the birds in the sky,
and they will tell you; or speak to the earth, and it will teach you, or let the fish in the sea inform you.
Job 12:7-8 niv

When you have a prayer life, you become more aware of the continual thread of heaven and earth working together: signs, wonders, miracles, angels, rainbows, gusts of wind, storms, and animals that "speak". Yes, miracles. Some big ones but mostly little ones, those signs that He is there, showing the way.

In the following experiences, sometimes He was teaching me that He was doing it because He is my friend and enjoyed me. Just for Him and me, not for some ministry I was to do. I learned along the way, too, to enjoy Him because He enjoyed me. Just like earthly friendships. Not just for the things we are to accomplish, but simply to enjoy one another.

My purpose to write this is so you can see what happens from a life of prayer, weak as it is at times. If we pray faithfully, regularly, and with expectation, *God shows up!* I pray He shows up for you, as you persevere in seeking Him with all your heart.

God often lets me see unusual displays of animals, birds, and fish to confirm His intimacy, His presence, and that He has heard my prayers. These often happen on my prayer walks, or during seasons of seeking Him deeper. At times, unusual gusts of wind and thunder have been the voice, activity, and presence of God and angels. Not all winds and thunders are such, but when they are, there is something different about them. You *know*. Rainbows, too, have appeared in spectacular and timely ways to let me know His promise to be with me. It's like He is swirling around me in this spectacular heavenly and earthly dance. He is very near us, we just can't see Him.

I have pretty ordinary days too, but these ones interspersed in the mundane keep me aware and alert of the activity of heaven around me. I have learned to look for it.

Defying the current

I was sitting on a big log on the shore of the mighty Fraser River, having my time of prayer. The Fraser has a very strong current—nothing to take lightly as occasional drownings have taken place. Suddenly my attention was drawn to a mother duck swimming *upstream* with her brood of little ducklings. I marveled watching these little, yellow puff balls skittering on the surface, almost effortlessly, behind their mother, defying the relentless current. He made them that they could do this!? If they can, so can we! We can go upstream against the strong currents of life that come against us as we follow the leadership of our Good Shepherd, Jesus.

A momentary glimpse on a crisp winter day

One time in the middle of winter, when big banks of fluffy snow covered everything and made walking near to impossible, I parked my car in my regular spot by the Nechako River in Prince George. I often parked there, facing the river—spring, summer, and fall—to read my Bible, write in my journal, and then prayer-walk along the trail. If the trail was plowed, I walked in the winter also, but even if not, I was still drawn to park and pray in my car in this my regular spot. It seemed like the place where I could let go of pressing things and meet with God.

That day was a cold day, so I stayed in the car. There was a big snow-bank in front of me, so I couldn't see the river (which was frozen and covered with snow), but I could see across the river—a beautiful, wintery horizon. As I was journaling, I happened to lift my eyes and was startled as a beautiful fox—black, rust, and white in color—leapt up onto the snowbank. It suddenly appeared there—smack in front of my car at eye level. Gorgeous! I had seen rust colored foxes before, but never one with this combination of colors. It contrasted magnificently against the blue-white of winter. As quickly as it came, it scurried away, just giving me a momentary glimpse. Joy!

Eerie, high-pitched screeching woke me up

When we moved to Youbou, a tiny town on Vancouver Island, the wildlife encounters increased. We hadn't been there more than a few weeks when I awakened to ominous noise outside our house—an eerie, high-pitched screeching sound that made your blood run cold. I ran to the window and was shocked to see our house surrounded by *elk!* I counted. There were 17. They were all around our house and on the road in front of us. I quickly grabbed my cell phone to take pictures, quietly moving out onto the front deck. The females immediately started to slowly move away and a big bull elk moved into position to stand square in front of me, between me and the females. He let me know who was in charge of this harem in no uncertain terms. What a sight! The eerie sound was the bugling the males do during mating season, running chills up your spine, especially at night.

What I saw made no sense

One time I was typing on my computer, I think working on this book. I had my patio door wide open to enjoy the beautiful summer day. I paused at times to take in the pretty view of big green trees that framed the yard and the flowering potted plants on the edge of our wooden patio. My computer desk was right beside the door, so I had this vista to see when I looked up. While I typed, an odd movement in my peripheral vision alerted me. I turned to look. *What is that?* It didn't make sense. It looked like a bent stick waving back and forth close to the patio floor by the door, a few feet from me. I got up cautiously to look outside. An elk! Feasting on my geraniums!! The "stick" was one of his antlers moving back and forth while he munched. I told him to get a move on in no uncertain terms—"*those are out-of-bounds for you!*" He looked up and took his own good time to decide if he was going to move or not. Finally, on *his* terms, he slowly turned and meandered off.

We were delighted to have many sightings of elk during the two years we lived there. It felt like God's smile was on us regarding our move, a seal of some sort to let us know we were in His will. Even though the elk ate tree leaves and messed with my flowers at times, the novelty of having them visit far outweighed the negative. It felt like a blessing from God.

Later in this book I write about how God used the elk to prophesy what He was doing. Truly, the animals will teach you.

A distraction that diffused my anger

One of the most amazing things that happened to me was an encounter with a turtle. I drove to the parking lot of a lakeside park in Honeymoon Bay to pray. I was angry about something and headed to a quiet place to sort through it. This quiet, little town is 10 kilometers from where we lived in Lake Cowichan on Vancouver Island. I often drove there, walked in the apple orchard park across the street and along the quiet street bordering the lake. Then I would sit at one of the picnic tables or in my folding chair and pray.

This time as I drove in, I saw something slowly lumbering across the parking lot, moving inland from the lake. I got out of my car and saw it was a turtle about 14 inches in length. I wanted to make sure it got safely to the grassy area, so I stayed nearby in case I needed to alert an incoming car. She got through okay, so I went to the beach to pray.

After about an hour, I decided to look for the turtle before heading home. At first I couldn't locate it in the acre or so of open field. Then, to my surprise, I found her steadily digging a hole with her back legs in a completely open area close to the road. I realized this was a mother turtle preparing to lay eggs. She had chosen a sun-warmed place and had already dug quite deep. I thought, *I am going to see this mother turtle give birth! Incredible!*

Sure enough. I don't remember how long she still dug, maybe 15 minutes. Then she quieted down and an egg fell into the hole from her back end. She immediately began to pull some dirt she had dug, over the egg with her back legs. Then another egg, and the same procedure. Then another, and another. I think there were 6 or 7 eggs. Taking her time, she meticulously covered the eggs with her hind legs, never once turning back to check. Finishing the job, she even pulled some dead grass back on top to hide any vestiges of a hole having been dug there. Then she began her slow walk back to the lake. I recorded this rare experience with pictures and videos. I don't remember anyone ever telling me they had seen something like this happen in nature.

I felt blessed and favored to be given this privilege. In fact, God distracted me from what I was seething about. On purpose, I believe. God's ways with us are so unique and clever.

The Creator of the universe, who has designed this marvelous complexity *of nature, the One who made it all, wants to have intimacy with us. God wanted to share this with me!*

In close relationships we humans want to share what we have created, what we are into, what we enjoy—with a friend. Like artwork, or a piece of furniture or boat we have built. God wanted me to see His artwork. *Thank you for sharing with me, Lord! I love seeing these things You have made. And You timed it perfectly to distract me and help ease my heart from what I was angry about. I didn't feel you disvalued what had upset me, but rather helped me. Thank you.*

Creation is a reflection, a shadow of God

I think about this often. This is an excerpt from my journal:

Creation. You spoke the word and brought into existence myriads of kinds of animals, birds, and fish. Watching videos about nature is incredible, realizing You thought it all up. The migrations of millions of animals: caribou, antelope, fish. Grey whales travel a 12,000 km round trip from Mexico to the Arctic and back yearly. Not to mention birds. How do they know where to go and when to go? You wired them with Your instructions in their DNA. The millions!

And the things that are in the depths of the sea---in the darkest parts. Some are so ugly and scary looking. Lord are you saying something? The horrible things are in the deep darkness. Just like the Bible speaks. The things that come from hell are horrible and ugly. The natural world is a picture of the spiritual world. The fish and the coral in the shallow waters are pretty to look at and there is light that penetrates the waters.

*But what really has spoken to me is how You have designed the male species to court and to initiate by showing off. Humans are like that too. **You** did it! **You** created that!*

It made me think of You, the Bridegroom God. That it is Your job to do that---to draw us to You. You are the initiator. No one comes to Jesus, except the Father draws them as John 6:44 says.

You woo us and pursue us.

You designed it in such a way that nature is a reflection, a shadow of You. "But ask the animals, and they will teach you, or the birds in the sky, and they will tell you..."

What fascinates me, really wows me, is when a huge, huge flock of birds fly together at high speeds, quickly turning this way and that, and doing it without banging into each other. And then they land with precision, skill and accuracy onto tree branches, from high speed to no speed at all in a split second. The physics involved! Only God can do that! Only God can put those calculations in the brain of a bird.

The sign

Many years ago we lived on the high bluffs above the Nechako River. I found an old chair which someone had placed in an open area above the river, so at times I would sit, meditate, and pray there. One time, when I happened to glance down at the river, I saw red-orange streaks moving upstream in groups. I got up to look more closely. Sockeye salmon! They were swimming upstream to their spawning places. Wow! They kept coming and coming—seemingly no end to these travelling pilgrims.

For many years after, I watched for them along the Nechako and Fraser Rivers at around the same time of year, but I never saw them again in such abundance. Once I saw a smaller group but not as clearly as that one summer day when they were vivid against the rocky bottom.

I prayed at times asking the Lord to show me the salmon again.

Twenty years later, I was at Ness Lake Bible Camp fasting and praying for several days in September. Ministerial members had the privilege of going there, free of charge, for personal retreats. I was praying about some global things—some things being decided in the UN about Israel (things were tense in the Middle East), and praying for the church to awaken to *really know what time it is!* My burden was heavy. I had felt something was stirring on the global stage. I sensed a need for the church to be alert and awake as we are in the end times. (Not long after, the terrible ISIS sweep took place in the Middle East).

At one point I went for a walk around the camp acreage. There was a trail that meandered along the high shoreline, in and out of the trees. After exploring for a while, I sat on a fallen tree that had broken, maybe fallen in the wind. The inside of the tree and stump were a beautiful, red-brown—- cedar, I thought—and pieces broke off easily from the jagged crack. I broke off a piece and threw it into the lake from my high perch, the wood splashing and making ripples upon impact and then floating on the surface. The sun was bright and the water was clear.

I sat enjoying the warmth and quiet for some minutes. Suddenly I was alerted to motion in the water. A school of red-orange fish had showed up and were investigating the piece of wood. I realized it looked like one of them floating on the surface. It was the same color, length and size. It seemed they were checking out a "dead" brother.

I threw another piece into the water. Sure enough a school of these beautiful fish came again.

I threw in a few more pieces and it kept happening.

Then I realized there were 2 schools of fish. One had about 15 and the other about 25–30 red-orange sockeye salmon!

The previous week I had prayer-walked along the Nechako River several times and said to the Lord, "I have not seen the red sockeye salmon for about 20 years. Back then it was amazing sitting high up on the bank of the Nechako and seeing them swimming up river during my prayer time."

God heard my whisper and showed them to me a few days later!

I knew that if He answered this little prayer so quickly, He *also* heard my prayers regarding the burden I had in my spirit for the awakening of the church, and for the global things I was fasting about.

It was His sign for me!

Jesus enjoys humans and animals—and He has a horse

Animals are a big part of the world we live in—created for us to enjoy— because *He* enjoys them. It says in Proverbs 8 that Jesus enjoyed creating and He played in the middle of all this happening.

> *When He established the heavens,*
> *I WAS THERE*
> *When He inscribed a circle on the face of the deep.*
> *When He made firm the skies above.*
> *When the springs of the deep became fixed.*
> *When He set for the sea its boundary so that the water*
> *would not transgress*
> *His command. When He marked out the foundations*
> *of the earth…*
> *Then I was beside Him as a master workman (craftsman)*
> *And I was daily His delight rejoicing always before Him*

Rejoicing in the world, His earth and having My delight
in the sons of men! Proverbs 8:27-31 nasb

The Douay-Rheims Bible translation writes verses 30 and 31 this way:

I was with Him forming all things: and was delighted
*every day, **playing** before Him at all times; **playing***
in the world: and My delights were to be with the
children of men.

Jesus was *playing* in God's presence as the earth was being made. He was *playing* in the world and delighting in the sons of men! How He enjoyed creating all things! And He delights in us.

After reading the Bible many times, I noticed that Jesus has a horse. I had seen these verses, yes, but it finally sunk in. Jesus has a horse! Horseback riding is *His* idea and humans get to do on earth what He enjoys doing in heaven. Two scriptures in the Bible are about Him riding a horse:

Strap your sword on your thigh, Mighty One,
In your splendor and majesty!
And in your majesty ride on victoriously,
For the cause of truth, humility, and righteousness.
Psalm 45:3-4 amp

And I saw heaven opened, and behold, a white horse,
and He who sat on it is called Faithful and True,
and in righteousness He judges and wages war.
Revelation 19:11 nasb

Chapter Thirty-Three: Sweet Intimacy with Jesus

God Speaks Through the Skies and Wind

By the word of the Lord the heavens were made, their starry host by the breath of His mouth. Psalm 33:6 niv

The heavens declare the glory of God; the skies proclaim the work of His hands. Day after day they pour forth speech; night after night they reveal knowledge. Psalm 19:1-2 niv

I will take care of you

In a previous chapter I told the story of the dance team trip to Israel. On our way to Vancouver, a beautiful, double rainbow crossed the highway, giving us an inkling that it was for reason. A few weeks later, when terrorist activity escalated, and deaths took place, we understood that God had given us the double rainbow as a promise of His protection.

A circle rainbow

In May of 2001 I flew alone to Israel to meet up with the *Journey of Hope Watchmen for the Nations Gathering.* Five hundred and fifty Canadians had heard the call to travel there to ask forgiveness from the Knesset (Israeli government). In 1939, Canada turned away the SS St. Louis, an ocean liner carrying 937 Jews fleeing the Nazi holocaust. They were denied entry into Cuba, the United States, and Canada, which forced them to return to Europe; 254 later perished in concentration camps. This was an appalling sin our nation needed to repent from.

At the very beginning of this trip, when the airplane was rising into the skies above Vancouver, God spoke to me through the heavens. I saw something extraordinary: a circle rainbow. I was amazed. I had never seen one before though I had heard of it. It was a complete circle with the shadow of the airplane very distinctly flying in the middle of the circle. What a sight! I sensed God's assurance of His encircling hand of protection for this trip.

Sure enough, in London, we had a disturbing experience. We boarded the last plane of our trip—the flight from London to Ben Gurion airport in Tel Aviv, Israel. After settling into the cabin of the plane and waiting for some time, we were told to disembark because a security check had to be made. All our bags were to be taken with us. Finally, after some delay, we were told to board again.

We never did hear what that was all about.

This gathering was a traveling gathering. We stopped at a number of places and had worship and prayer times: Mt. Carmel, Bethesda, Tiberias, Jerusalem, the hills of Judah near Bethlehem, and the Knesset. About 13 of us had registered late. Because the tour buses were full, we latecomers followed the bus convoy in several rental vehicles.

Traveling from Tiberias to Jerusalem, our vehicle was in an accident. A large duffle bag, suddenly and unexpectedly, flew from the back of an oncoming jeep onto our lane, right in front of us. Our driver was not able to stop in time and drove over it. Praise God no one was injured, though our vehicle had to be towed due to undercarriage damage.

I understood then why God had given me a clear sign, the circle rainbow. He was with us, encircling us, and keeping us in His hand.

The angel of the Lord encamps around those who fear him,
and rescues them.
Psalm 34:7 nasb

This is not the end of the world

Discouraged, I drove to a lakeside park. I was disappointed with myself, with my reaction. It was not right what had been done, but my response to it should have been better. The situation hurt and frustrated me and my reaction to it hung heavy on me. It was a gray, rainy day adding to the sense of gloom I felt. I parked the car to face the lake, and prayed awhile. I dozed off. Suddenly I awoke with a start as if someone had wakened me, to see a brilliant, double rainbow right in front of me over the water. The vista had changed from gloom to glory. I felt God loving me and saying, *"This is not the end of the world"*. My spirit was picked up in God's marvelous way.

A skipping, cavorting whirlwind

> *Then the LORD answered Job out of the whirlwind.*
> Job 38:1 nasb

In 2011 Prince George House of Prayer hosted a conference called *After God's Heart*. We had spent weeks preparing and now it was the final afternoon before the conference was to begin in the evening. We had prayed much for a strong presence of the Holy Spirit and that people's hearts would be stirred, strengthened, and awakened. Our desire was for a fresh kindling of first love for the Lord and a resulting awakened prayer life in God's people, and that He would confirm with signs following.

I went to the church for the final tasks to be done, parking my car beside a tree that was in full bloom on that beautiful, sunny day in May. My car was the only one in the parking lot on that side of the church.

When I finished my tasks and walked to my car, a great gust of wind came and twirled in the blossoming tree. It was a whirlwind! White petals flew as the tree shook from the wind. Nothing else was shaking. No other trees. Then, after spinning in the tree and furiously shaking it around for a while, the wind skipped and cavorted through the parking lot, white petals twirling in the shape of the whirlwind. I marveled at the sight. I knew this was God's doing. I sensed a heavenly dance taking place, like a

kicking-up-of-heels. It was God speaking His delight about this conference and confirming His presence to be there. A sign.

As the leader I had felt a lot of pressure and warfare in preparation.
Now all that weight scattered with the wind and I felt joy and anticipation of what He would do. Everything was ready, and the Lord had come
and danced.

He makes the winds His messengers. Psalm 104:4 nasb

Flying in the skies, thinking from God's perspective

Flying from Prince George to Kansas City and on to Ottawa, in June
of 2010, God touched my heart as I looked at the earth from His perspective, from the skies. I wrote in my journal:

*Thank you, again, for this wonderful privilege of flying in the heights
with you! I love looking at what you have made below. I want to think
more from your perspective. What was it like to make it all, Lord? I
take it too much for granted and don't even know how to appreciate
it enough. Those snowy cliffs are spectacular!*

*Lord, life is so busy. I hope I am doing what you want me to.
Sometimes I think I want to slow down to really enjoy and think
about what you have made. To stop, think about, and thank You for
a flower, an animal, water, clouds, air, even bugs. It is stunning. You
are so amazing and creative (of course!). Creator God. The way You
made me — me to be able to have babies grow inside of me, come out,
grow up to adult people who are having children. Unbelievable! The
whole thing is so marvelous. We can think, feel, have different likes
and dislikes, interests. Lord, so amazing.*

And You desire to be known by us!

*Lord, I want to know You more. I want to, but also hesitate. Can I
really know You? You are God. I am human. A weak human. Yet*

You say we are "dark but lovely" to You (Song of Songs 1:5). I am drawn to You because you are drawing me. Draw me! (Song of Songs 1:4).

Chapter Thirty-Four: Sweet Intimacy with Jesus

Our Experiences Help Us Understand More of God's Heart

God lets us experience things like being a child. Jesus was a child at one time. We experience parenting. God is a Father. We begin to understand His heart more when we are parents. When we have a disobedient child, we begin to understand what God goes through in dealing with His disobedient children (us at times), and His breaking heart for prodigal Israel, as depicted much through the Old Testament. If you have a prodigal you are praying for, God says, "I have one too. I have been waiting for his return for over 2000 years. I know how you feel!"

He teaches us about Himself through many other ways too.

Jesus' house plans

One morning I was reflecting on our house building plans, thinking how this is a small reflection of Jesus: He is a builder of mansions and dwelling places, and of a temple in the coming kingdom. He lets us experience some of His heart through us building things.

As I read through chapters 40-42 of Ezekiel, I marveled. I really understood something for the first time. I had always skimmed through chapters like this, bored. I finally "got" it. These are Jesus' plans for God's house in Jerusalem in the 1000 year reign, the Millennium. We had pored over our house plans for several years while we built two houses. Plans have meticulous details: doors, windows, balconies, measurements of everything. Okay…*so that is why all those measurements are in these chapters.*

Precise. So many cubits this. So many cubits that. Very precise. Just like our plans. These plans in Ezekiel are dear to the Lord's heart, like house plans mean a lot to human home builders. One day His house will be built. And, even more, amazing, Jesus likes carvings of palm trees and cherubim.

> *...the galleries round about...were paneled with wood all around...**carved with cherubim (a certain kind of angel) and palm trees**; and a palm tree was between cherub and cherub, and every cherub had two faces, a man's face toward the palm tree on one side and a young lion's face toward the palm tree on the other side; they were carved on all the house all around. **From the ground to above the entrance cherubim and palm trees were carved...***
> Ezekiel 41:16, 18-20 nasb

Just like us, He has some very precise "likes". I get that now. Having being part of planning, designing and building two homes, I have a whole new perspective. Now I am quite interested in His plans. In the same way we humans like to show others our building plans and explain and describe the future house, Jesus also showed and described what His future house will look like. We are like Him, made in His image. He likes building and He likes specific things to be in His future house just like us.

Jesus builds with a budget, too

I was thinking about John 14 where Jesus talks about the mansions He is preparing for us, thinking about Him as a builder compared to us as builders. I thought, *but Jesus has unlimited resources to build with. We don't have the same privilege here on earth as He does up there.* So I said, "But Lord, we have a budget!" I heard him say, "So do I. I have to work with the amount of treasures you store up in heaven. I am trying to do my best with what each person stores up!"

Do not store for yourselves treasures on earth,
Where moth and rust destroy, and where thieves break in
and steal.
But store up for yourselves treasures in heaven, where
neither moth nor rust destroys, and where thieves do not
break in or steal.
Matthew 6:19-20 nasb

Chapter Thirty-Five: Sweet Intimacy with Jesus

He Loves Us That Much!

Being misunderstood is one of the most painful emotions

Being misunderstood is a disguised privilege because we will have experienced some of what Jesus walked through.

He was misunderstood by the leaders of Israel. The *spiritual* leaders. These were the ones who supposedly *knew* the scriptures and were waiting for the prophesied Messiah. Jesus came. They missed it. They not only missed the visitation, but they rejected and killed Him. The Son of God was misunderstood, rejected and killed!

Jesus humility is such that He does not need to be understood or recognized. He is mostly hidden. He knew when He walked the earth there would be those who believed. Others would not because they did not *want* to believe.

What grieves my heart is the rejection He endured: how little the Messiah was valued, and how He was constantly challenged and interrogated by the unbelieving Pharisees and Sadducees who were the spiritual leaders. Their aim was to prove him wrong. They challenged His authority (give the head a shake)! *The God of the Universe subjected Himself to that?* They asked, "By what authority are you doing these things, and who gave you this authority?" The God of the universe humbled Himself this way, permitting Himself to be questioned and challenged. He loved us *that* much!

Oh, God! The Lord of the universe! You put up with such humiliation. Lord I love you! He is *that* kind of ruler—how amazing He is!

If we are challenged, questioned, doubted, rejected, humiliated or misunderstood, we just need to look at Jesus. He, who created and gave breath to the very ones who interrogated Him, experienced far more rejection than we do. Jesus, *the Son of God,* who should have been received with reverence, fear, and love—was treated this way. And still is. God, who provides spring time and harvest, and keeps the universe going, is ignored, accused, and cursed. So if we go through these things to some degree, we are privileged, experiencing a little portion of the fellowship of His sufferings.

From my journal:

You are misunderstood so much! Railed at. Yet you do not defend Yourself. You just keep doing Your work. You wait for the right time. You know the right time. You make the right time.

*You were misunderstood. Your precious gift has been unwanted and rejected. You have not been wanted. You have been rejected. All these things that I have felt at times, God feels! I am realizing that some of the pain I experience, perhaps that is the very pain You experience. Lord, Your heart is to give extravagantly. You have given Your only beloved Son—-so extravagantly You gave. And millions upon millions refuse your gift. They don't get it. They **need** that gift.*

You have been revealing some of your heart to me. When I have been rejected you said to me "I am still not received by My people, Israel. I feel the same broken heart and pain."

When I have been misunderstood, you said to Me: "So often I have been misunderstood. People become angry with Me and turn away from Me. I cannot explain. They do not want to hear. I wait"

*When I have shown kindness and it was refused, it was painful. You said, "I know. Thousands upon thousands refuse My gift of forgiveness of sins and eternal life. I **died** for them, but they refuse* *it. It hurts. They refuse babies I send; beautifully-crafted treasures. They don't realize these become some of their greatest blessings down the road."*

When relationship with loved ones is broken, You say, "Satan continually works at kidnapping My children to get back at Me. He sows distrust about My love for them and works at fascinating them, vying for their attention and love, to take them from Me. "

When I am not heard, I think of You. You were not heard either. Jeremiah and the prophets spoke for You but the people did not listen.

Lord, You were not wanted. Even Your brothers did not want You at first. They made fun of You. No wonder You hide yourself, and reveal Yourself to those who diligently seek You. Thank you, Lord! I can understand a little bit of Your heart, even a little bit, because You have let me walk through a little bit of suffering. Help me to know You.

God, the One who carried them, was unappreciated and pushed away

Reading through the prophets in the Old Testament, I see the continual grief God had. He wanted relationship, but He was pushed away.

> *"...they have rejected Me...since the day that I brought them up from Egypt...they have forsaken Me."*
> *1 Samuel 8:7-8 nasb*

> *"...you have forgotten Me," declares the Lord God.*
> *Ezekiel 22:12 nasb*

> *"When your fathers tested Me, they tried Me though they had seen My work. For forty years..."*
> *Psalm 95:9-10 nasb*

They still came to the temple for the feasts but their worship was by rote, their hearts far from God. At the same time they were also worshiping idols and sacrificing their babies to them. God was disgusted with them. Yet He continually and patiently sent prophets to call them back. Jeremiah prophesied to them for 23 years, warning them of the coming calamity if they did not repent and turn back to the Lord. God kept sending him again and again. Even after He said it was enough, He still sent Jeremiah one more time saying that if they return to Him, He will not send these calamities on them. He was *longsuffering and merciful.*

So if you have gone through a long time praying for someone who seems to be going farther and farther from the Lord, and perhaps is rejecting you too, not wanting you in their life, let's remember how longsuffering God is. He is letting you experience some of what He has gone through and is still going through.

> *"I have spread out My hands all day long to a rebellious*
> *people, who walk in the way which is not good, following*
> *their own thoughts." Isaiah 65:2 nasb*

...and this is what they said to Him:

> *"Keep to yourself, do not come near me." Isaiah 65:5 nasb*

How lovingly He cared for them, carrying them, like a father carrying his little ones. But they pushed Him away, causing Him grief. As you read these following verses, some of you may identify with His heart, having experienced this with your child, or children.

> *In all their affliction He was afflicted, and the angel of His*
> *presence saved them. In His love and in His mercy He*
> *redeemed them, and He lifted them and carried them all*
> *the days of old.*
> **But they rebelled and grieved His Holy Spirit.**
> *Isaiah 63:9-10 nasb*

Don't be against God. He is your help

Eventually God brought judgments upon Israel to discipline them because they did not turn to Him. He said:

> *"It is your destruction, O Israel, that you are against Me,*
> *against your help." Hosea 13:8 nasb*

I will love them freely, for My anger has turned away

In spite of the fickleness of Israel, God did not end His relationship with them, but said in the books of Hosea, Isaiah and Jeremiah, "I will heal you." "I will heal your backslidings."

> *I will heal their backsliding, I will love them freely,*
> *for My anger has turned away. Hosea 14:4 kjv*

Many times He promised He would not hold back His love and comfort, and that Israel *will be* His bride. Isaiah 54 and 62 show the end of the story that His bridegroom love for them has not changed.

Oh, the patience of God, His love and longsuffering! He suffered long, so we at times are called to suffer long as well.

Israel is God's prodigal. Still. But she will return to Him because God will change their hearts:

> *"For I will take you from the nations,*
> *gather you from all the lands and bring you into*
> *your own land.*
> *Then I will sprinkle clean water on you,*
> *and you will be clean…*
> *I will give you a new heart and put a new spirit*
> *within you…*
> *I will put My Spirit in you and cause you to walk in*
> *My statutes,*
> *and you will be careful to observe My ordinances.*
> *You will live in the land I gave to your forefathers,*
> *so you will be My people and I will be your God."*
> *Ezek. 36:24-28 nasb*

You can pray this promise for Israel, and also ask God to give your loved one, who is a prodigal, a new heart as well, that He would put a new spirit in them, that they would love God's word and keep it, walking in His ways.

Pain eclipsed by glory—a young man's grief turned into a future

While waiting for the answer to our prayers, at times it feels like we are in a dark cloud. God hides Himself in dark clouds (Ps. 97), so the darker it gets, the closer He is to us. God meets and surprises us with something heavenly in our lowest moments if we turn to Him, crying out our pain to Him.

Here is a beautiful story of God's embrace in the dark cloud. This is a true story about a young Estonian man who lived most of his life in Finland. I read about him in a Finnish book my dad gave me, titled *Katso Mika Aamu*[9] *(Behold, What a Dawn)*. Finnish is my mother tongue.

Mika Piiparinen's father had been a strong support for him, his existence giving him a sense of security. Suddenly his dad was taken from him. His mother had died when he was a boy. He felt alone and grieved deeply.

Mika was an active participant in his church's young adult group. In 1937 they were excitedly planning a trip to Estonia, to the very area he grew up in. He desperately wanted to go with his friends to see his childhood vistas, but he had no money. He was sad and disappointed.

The day of departure arrived and the young people were elated, looking forward to this adventure with joyful anticipation. Mika was not able to go because no miracle had taken place. This raw fact hit him in the face like a winter storm. It was a big blow.

Discouraged and lonely, he walked the streets of Helsinki. He knew the only help for his sadness was by taking it to the Lord. He walked to his church and went downstairs to a windowless room in the basement. Shutting the door, the grey walls enclosed him from the world around him. *Why couldn't I go?* No answer came. He knelt and wept, lingering for a long time.

After some time, he began to feel peace and felt lighter. In that moment, music began to play inside him. He listened, amazed. *What is this?* He found a piece of paper in his pocket and began to scribble musical notes. He was hearing the accompanying music to a poem he knew that someone had written. The words of the poem depicted his innermost thoughts and feelings, and now God was giving him a melody to make the poem into a song. Surprised, he thought, *is this how these melodies come?*

At that time he had no inkling how and where the Lord would lead him, because the Lord's paths are mostly hidden from us. We need to surrender our own desires and plans and be open to His leading.

He was short on money for the trip. He didn't get to go to Estonia, but God gave him something else. This song was precious to him for the rest of his life. It was the beginning of his music-writing career. Throughout his lifetime he wrote music for many poems, turning them into songs which were sung in many churches for decades. For almost 20 years he conducted a church choir which also performed at many conferences.

This story moves me because I have seen God work this way in my life. I pray it gives you encouragement that whatever disappointment or sorrow you may be going through, God is planning to give you *something else in exchange* if you turn to Him in your pain, like Mika did. If tears are coming as you finish reading this story, let them come. They may have been bottled up for a long time. Vocalize your pain to God. Tell Him what it is. Our healing comes when we cry things out to the Lord and then wait quietly. He has something to give you in place of that deep disappointment.

It is Jesus' story. Out of death comes resurrection. Out of humiliation comes exaltation. Every knee will bow, every tongue confess that Jesus Christ is Lord.

Chapter Thirty-Six: Sweet Intimacy with Jesus

If What is Important to Jesus, is not Important To Me, am I Really Walking in Intimacy with Him?

God doesn't always explain everything to us immediately—He wants us to trust and obey. Those who follow Him are near and dear to His heart and as they are faithful in little, He gives more. We are defined by our obedience to His word, to His voice.

Intimacy grows as we say, "I want to be zealous for what You are zealous for, Lord. I might not understand it fully at the beginning but if it is important to You, I want it to be important to me. Teach me. Reveal more to me. Give me understanding and a willing heart."

In the Bible, I have seen that God is very zealous for some things. Zeal means to have passion, fire, enthusiasm, love, and fervor.

Zeal for His Father's house consumed Jesus.

Jesus was very angry when He found the temple court was turned into a marketplace: animals being sold and money changers doing their trade. He made a whip, overthrew the tables, and chased them out. The disciples remembered the words of Psalms (Psalm 69:9) that *"zeal for Your house will consume Me"*. Twice Jesus cleansed the temple: early in His ministry and then near the end of His ministry.

What exactly is the Father's House?

The second time Jesus overturned the tables He declared,

> It is written: 'My house will be called **a house of prayer;**
> but you are making it a den of robbers.'
> Matthew 21:13 nasb

He was quoting his Father's words from Isaiah 56:7:

> "For My house shall be called a house of prayer for all
> nations." nkjv

If Jesus was zealous for God's house, that it should be a house of prayer, we should carry that same zeal in our hearts. First, attending church should be a priority in our lives and in our families' lives. Second, we should have zeal for church to be a house of prayer for all nations: meaning, prayer meetings should be part of our life to participate in. If it is important to God, it should be important to us, His bride. If I lack zeal for it, the best way to adjust is to go to God in prayer and ask Him to give me a zeal for prayer and for attending prayer meetings at the church.

> ...if we ask anything according to His will He hears us.
> And if we know that He hears us in whatever we ask, we
> know that we have the requests that we have asked of Him.
> 1 John 5:14-15 nasb

I am exceedingly jealous for Zion

Another thing that Jesus has great zeal for is the city of Jerusalem and for Zion. Zion is another name for both Jerusalem or for Israel. It says in Zechariah 8:2-3 (nasb):

> 'I am exceedingly jealous for Zion, yes, with great wrath I am jealous
> for her.' Thus says the Lord, 'I will return to Zion and dwell in the
> midst of Jerusalem. Then Jerusalem will be call the City of Truth, and
> the mountain of the Lord of hosts will be called the Holy Mountain.'

God has His eye on Israel and on the city of Jerusalem. Jerusalem is God's city. Jesus called it the city of the Great King in Matthew 5:35. It is called by that name in Psalm 48:2 also:

> *Beautiful in elevation, the joy of the whole earth, Is*
> *Mount Zion in the far north, **the city of the Great King**.*
> *Psalm 48:2 nasb*

If Jesus has such zeal for Israel and Jerusalem, then I want to have it also.

I want the things that break His heart to break mine, the things that give Him joy to give me joy, and the things that He is zealous and jealous for, I also want to be zealous and jealous for.

Could you not keep watch with Me one hour?

I have fasted many fasts and prayed for many decades for a great prayer movement to arise. Having studied revivals in history, I found they were preceded by revivals of prayer; therefore, I have carried a prayer burden for the church to become a praying church. It has grieved me that only a small percentage of the church attend prayer meetings, including pastors, no matter how much I, along with many other intercessors, have prayed. (Thankfully there are some churches that are praying churches, with pastors who lead and carry the vision of intercessory prayer).

However, God has shown me that it was no different for Jesus, the greatest preacher who ever walked the earth. Huge crowds followed Him for 3 ½ years. They loved listening to Him teach and watch Him do miracles. Yet out of those thousands, only 120 obeyed Him to wait in the Upper Room for the promise of the Holy Spirit. Realizing that it was the same for Jesus, that few committed to wait in prayer, I have been comforted. He experienced it. Intimacy with Jesus deepens when we walk in His shoes.

Many want God's presence but few commit to doing their part of waiting and prayer, of drawing close to Him to get the deeper things of His heart.

I do believe, though, that this will change before the Lord returns, because it says in scripture that He will have a bride without spot or wrinkle (Eph. 5:27), and that she is a bride who has made herself ready (Rev. 19). Part of the bride's calling is to stand in worship and intercession.

God wants us to be a bride who feels His joys and pains and who cares about what is important to Him. Through the fellowship of suffering, our heart grows in compassion and understanding, and our intimacy with Him deepens. If we turn to Him in our painful darkness, He meets us, and gives us something divine in exchange for the pain, thus eclipsing the affliction with His glory. It is something we don't experience otherwise.

I will give you the treasures of darkness and hidden wealth
of secret places, so that you may know that it is I, the Lord,
the God of Israel,
who calls you by your name. Isaiah 45:3 nasb

Chapter Thirty-Seven: Sweet Intimacy with Jesus

How to Have a Revelation of God's Love

Ask

If you have never experienced His love for you personally, just ask.

Ask and it will be given to you. Matt. 7:7 nasb

If you have never received Christ into your life, take this first step.

Believe in the Lord Jesus, and you will be saved.
Acts 16:31 nasb

If you confess with your mouth Jesus as Lord and believe
in your heart that God raised Him from the dead, you will
be saved. Rom. 10:9 nasb

If you believe that Jesus Christ is the Son of God, and that He died on the cross for your sins, you will be saved. Just ask Him to forgive and cleanse you from your sins and ask Him to come into your life.

Some have done this but still may not have experienced that sense of His deep love and affection for them. Then, ask Him to do that for you.

Be childlike like David in the Old Testament was. That is the posture of spirit we need to receive from God. David talked to God this way:

O Lord, my heart is not proud; nor my eyes haughty.
Nor do I involve myself in great matters or in things too
difficult for me. Surely I have composed and quieted my
soul; like a weaned child rests against his mother. My soul
is like a weaned child within me. Psalm 131 nasb

When you are in heaviness or distress, do as David did: lean yourself against God. Pour out your heart to Him openly and honestly and experience Him ministering to you. To enter into the kingdom we must be like children (Matt. 18:34). To enter into knowing Him more deeply, we again must be childlike.

Just cry out continually for this revelation of God's love.

I love those who love Me, and those who seek Me diligently
will find Me. Proverbs 8:17 nkjv

Answered prayer reveals His love, so pray much, ask largely, and pray for many

Friends of ours came for dinner a few weeks before they moved to another province. We lived on a property on the edge of the town of Lake Cowichan, being the last house on the street with miles of forest starting from there. At one point, the wife was standing up talking to me as I sat near one of the picture windows. Suddenly her eyes grew big and a strange, bewildered expression crossed her face. At first I thought she was looking at me and I was puzzled. Then I realized she was looking over my shoulder. I turned and saw a huge bear face looking in the window right by my shoulder! It's one of those moments when your mind races—desperately trying to process because there isn't a grid for what you are seeing. I quickly got up, opened the door and clapped loudly to chase the bear away. We occasionally had bears from the forest wander across our yard, being the last house on the street. But this had never happened before that a bear came right up to the window and only a few feet from me!

My friend was very happy, saying she had prayed God would let her see a bear before they moved from Vancouver Island, because she had not seen one there yet.

Ha! Ha! So that was what was behind this! It was God's doing. My friend is a faithful intercessor who has prayed for many years for many things: Canada, revival, the outpouring of the Holy Spirit, the church, pastors, her family, and for many, many people. Now she had put in a little personal request and God went out of His way to grant it.

When He answers a little wish like this, it shows God's intimacy because no one else knows you have prayed that prayer, and no one else is praying it. It's just between you and God.

> *You understand my thought from afar…and are intimately acquainted with all my ways…even before there is a word on my tongue, behold, O Lord, You know it all. Psalm 139:2-4 nasb*

Okay, you might say, "Do I have to be praying for years before this kind of thing happens?" No. Remember my little girl asked the Lord for chocolates at Easter time, because we couldn't afford them. She got what she asked for. That box of groceries that arrived on our doorstep had a basket of chocolates included.

Hallelujah! He is the King of the Universe, and He hears and answers the smallest cry. Our love for Him grows when we talk to Him and He answers.

> *I love the Lord, because He hears my voice and my supplications. Because He has inclined His ear to me, therefore I shall call upon Him as long as I live. Psalm 116:1-2 nasb*

Fast

Some years ago, I wanted a deeper experience of God's love, so I went on a three-day fast for it. Soon I began to experience some of the things I wrote about in previous chapters. God loves a prayer like that. He is more than willing to show His love to those who seek it.

God reveals His love in His Word, the Bible

My parents gave me a Bible for my 10th birthday. It was a little King James Version, with thees, thous and haths. It didn't matter that it was in old English, I was determined to read it, begats and all. My goal was to read a chapter in the Old Testament and a chapter in the New each day. I didn't always keep the "each day" goal, but little by little I read through it. I loved the stories, though most of the prophets I did not understand. Would I ever understand those difficult passages? I remember praying and asking God specifically that I would understand the prophets one day. As I kept at reading through them over the years, what I saw was that God loved Israel, but they always rebelled and strayed. Then God brought judgments on them as a result of their evil ways. But what I noticed was that almost every prophet ended with God's promise to restore them to Him and to restore their land and fortunes. God said He was married to them—they were His wife—and He would draw them with chords of love back to Him. In the end they would turn to Him and be faithful to Him. Almost every prophet ended with that promise.

I saw a God of love in the Old Testament. It puzzled me when some said the Old Testament showed the wrath of God and the New Testament His love and mercy. I saw it differently. I saw His wrath, love and mercy in both the Old and New Testaments. God is the same, He does not change.

That was my revelation. By keeping reading and asking God to help me understand—even at a young age when I thought *would I ever understand* – God answered. I was thankful He later sent teachers to bring more understanding, and because I had a hungry heart for His word, I loved listening to their teaching.

Yes, God reveals His love in the Bible, in both the Old and New Testaments.

To have a revelation of His love, be real and honest with God

God wants us to be transparent and honest with Him. Like close friends, like husband and wife; if something bothers us, we say it. We don't pretend.

David had this kind of heart. He was transparent. He did not try to put on a façade of joy if he was anxious or fearful. He poured out his true heart thoughts to God. In this process of conversation, God brought him back to a right attitude if his heart was wrong.

> *The ropes of death entangled me; floods of destruction*
> *swept over me. The grave wrapped its ropes around me;*
> *death laid a trap in my path. But in my distress I cried out*
> *to the Lord; yes, I prayed to my God for help. He heard me*
> *from His sanctuary; my cry to Him reached His ears.*
> *Psalm 18:4-6 nlt*

The following psalm, below, has no author name. It shows this transparency—even doubting God, saying God has rejected him. But then he talks to himself, asking why he is disturbed and telling himself to hope in God, knowing he will praise Him again. These Psalms helped me because they show how real the writers were, and how to walk through hard times. We can pour our grief and questionings to God, even doubt. Wow! The whole point is: keep talking to God—in good times and bad. God will talk back to us if we keep talking to Him. Then encourage yourself in God, like this one did. Tell yourself to hope in Him and that you will praise God again no matter how hard it is now.

> *Why have you rejected me? Why do I go mourning*
> *because of the oppression of the enemy…why are you in*
> *despair, O my soul? And why are you disturbed within*
> *me? Hope in God, for I shall again praise Him.*
> *Psalm 43:2, 5 nasb*

Be real with God. He wants you to be that way. He longs for this kind of intimacy and trust. He created us to have real friendship: the friendship relationship you have dreamed of—the ideal relationship where someone knows your strengths and weaknesses and still loves you—is the kind you can have with Jesus. He is grieved when we don't enter into it. There is a longing in His heart for you.

> *"Jerusalem, Jerusalem, you who kill the prophets and stone*
> *those sent to you, how often **I have longed** to gather your*
> *children together, as a hen gathers her*
> *chicks under her wings, but you were not willing!"*
> Matthew 23:37 niv

It is not only *our* longing for friendship that is met, but also *His* desire for intimate fellowship with us.

If we lose our first love, God may allow us to fail to bring us back

Jesus disturbs us for our ultimate peace. We may have initially learned this walk of intimacy, but then have fallen away from it. God will deal with us: He will disturb our peace to create the need for it again.

Why does He disturb us?

Because relationship with Him is the most important thing.

In Luke 10:38-42 Jesus was at the home of Lazarus, Mary, and Martha, along with His disciples. Martha was busy preparing food, and impatient with Mary because she sat at Jesus' feet listening in rapt attention to everything He was saying, and therefore wasn't helping her. When Martha brought this to Jesus' attention, asking Him to tell her to help, He replied:

> *"Martha, Martha, you are worried and upset about many*
> *things. Only one thing is important. Mary has chosen the*
> *better thing,*
> *and it will never be taken away from her".*
> Luke 10:41-42 ncv

Martha missed the moment. It did not happen *every* day that *Jesus* came to *their* house. Mary was not going to miss a word He had to say! She was probably quite diligent in helping most of the time, but this was not the moment to lose.

The second reason Jesus disturbs our peace—if we have fallen away from pursuing Him—is because "one's effectiveness in the spirit realm is in direct proportion to one's relationship with Him, and this relationship is maintained only by time alone with God and His word."[10] (Billheimer).

Because of these two points, God will allow pain, failure, rejection, or whatever, to develop and maintain intimacy of relationship with Him.

Intimacy with the Lord is the key thing, and only out of it flows anything meaningful we accomplish in life.

God called David "a man after God's heart" even though he was far from perfect

David was formed and forged by God through trials: rejection, loneliness, the envy and rage of Saul, fearing for his life, and falling into sin. Through all this, he clung to God, and poured out his heart to Him continually. A lot of the Psalms, which are prayers he sang to God, were written by him. He loved God very much, very passionately. One of the songs he sang was called a *Shiggaion*, meaning "a wild, passionate song." He hung onto God's word, saying:

> *My soul is crushed with longing after your ordinances*
> *(laws, teaching, instructions) at all times.*
> *Psalm 119:20 nasb*

David was called "a man after God's heart" by God—even though he was far from perfect—because he loved the Lord and pursued him with *all his heart*. He understood God's desire for intimate relationship and he wanted to bring pleasure and joy to Him. He wanted to keep all God's commandments and words, desiring to live up to them. He knew the delight of meditating on God's truths and living them out in his life because they were God's love letter to him (and to us, also). He said:

How sweet are Your words to my taste! Yes, sweeter than honey to my mouth! Psalm 119:103 nasb

Open my eyes that I may behold wonderful things from Your law.
Psalm 119:18 nasb

The unfolding of Your words gives light; it gives understanding to the simple. I opened my mouth wide and panted, for I longed for Your commandments.
Psalm 119:130-131 nasb

Chapter Thirty-Eight

Intimacy Moves to Intercession: Partnering with God

When we experience intimacy with Jesus, it leads us into intercession:

> *As the bridegroom rejoices over the bride, so your God will rejoice over you. On your walls, O Jerusalem, I have appointed watchmen; all day and all night, they will never keep silent. You who remind the Lord, take no rest for yourselves; and give Him no rest until He establishes and makes Jerusalem a praise in the earth. Isaiah 62:5-7 nasb*

I am going to break these verses down:

First:

> *As the bridegroom rejoices over the bride, so your God will rejoice over you.*

We need to be lovers first, experiencing this intimate love relationship with Jesus. Out of intimacy, conception takes place: we receive revelation, we receive our assignments. Jesus only did what He "saw" the Father doing; it should be the same for us. We should wait on God until we hear His voice and not build golden calves. The children of Israel built a golden calf to worship because they got tired of waiting to hear what God had to say. They were waiting for Moses to return from the mountain where He was with God. Golden calves represent our ideas of what should be done. Even "Christian" things not born of the Spirit are golden calves. Abraham and Sarah, too, got tired of waiting for God's promise of a son to be fulfilled. Sarah contrived her own plan to make it happen. She gave her servant, Hagar to Abraham to have a son for them through her. Ishmael was born, and thousands of years later the ongoing struggle in the Middle East is a result of that man-made plan. God wants us to be doing things that are conceived by the Spirit, like with Mary, there was no intervention by man. In the same way as the Holy Spirit hovered over her, and she conceived, the Holy Spirit hovers over us causing His works, ideas, thoughts, and assignments to be conceived in our spirits.

Second:

Then, before these become fruitful actions, intercession takes place to birth them. Intercession will happen if we are practicing the first: spending time in intimate fellowship with God. We are both lovers and watchmen.

> *On your walls, O Jerusalem, I have appointed watchmen;*
> *all day and all night they will never keep silent. You who*
> *remind the Lord, take no rest for yourselves and give Him*
> *no rest until He establishes and makes Jerusalem a praise*
> *in the earth. Isaiah 62:6-7 nasb*

Those who spend time with God will become intercessors who stand in the gap in prayer for the things on His heart

We won't burn out if we follow this pattern:

Intimacy (lovers of God)…intercession (watchmen)…intimacy…intercession… intimacy… intercession. Like a wave. When we spend time with Jesus in intimacy, He reveals things to us on that mountain top. Then He leads us into the valley of intercession to battle through for the things He spoke to us in the times of intimacy. Then after battle, He calls us aside again, saying, "Come away with Me, My beloved!" He calls us to follow Him up the mountain of intimacy and revelation again.

If we follow His leadership, our strength will be renewed and we will bring God's kingdom purposes to birth all throughout our lifetime, in small and big ways.

Part Six

Jesus said, "Keep on the Alert... Praying"

Pray without ceasing.
1 Thess. 5:17 nasb

If you abide in Me, and My words abide in you,
Ask whatever you wish, and it will be done for you.
John 15:7 nasb

Now will not God bring about justice for His elect
Who cry to Him day and night?
Luke 18:7 nasb

Chapter Thirty-Nine

Golden Bowls are Filling Up with Prayers

Prayer pastoring

In January of 1997 I began on staff at Gateway Christian Ministries as prayer pastor. It was a very exciting time. I was given a large room in our chapel/youth/dance ministry building. I requested large bulletin boards for each wall: one wall for pictures and names of everyone in our church, one for our city, the third for our nation, and the fourth for the nations. Intercessory leaders chose 4-hour shifts to oversee, during which people came to pray. We had worship music playing quietly continually.

Tuesdays to Fridays at 7 am, groups came to pray for our church and missionaries. We had 8 missionary families in different parts of the world at that time.

Our prophetic intercessors met to pray on Mondays, focusing mainly on our city, praying for revival, the outpouring of the Holy Spirit, the pastors, the ministerial, and for the unity of the churches. God has promised the commanded blessing when the brethren dwell together in unity (Ps. 133), so unity was high priority in our prayers.

Another intercessory group met Tuesdays to pray through for the needs of the church family. On Wednesdays at noon, our church staff and anyone who wished to attend, joined to pray for our church.

A prodigal became a prayer missionary

On Monday evenings a small cluster met to pray for prodigals. They kept a book with the names of these prodigals and prayed faithfully for them, week after week. From those prayers, one young prodigal had a God encounter and his life changed so radically that he attended some of our prayer meetings. Later he moved to Kansas City to serve as a prayer missionary at the International House of Prayer for 13 years.

Praying for Canada and Israel

We had a monthly prayer meeting for Canada that was very well attended and another one for Israel for those who had a call to be God's set watchmen for Israel (Isaiah 62:6,7).

A 40 day fast

Early that year (1997), I became aware of a 40 day fast called by Bill Bright for revival to come to North America and the world. He was the director of Campus Crusade for Christ and had a burden to raise two million intercessors in North America to fast 40 days by the year 2000. This call kept coming to my attention through various sources. I knew this was on God's mind for us to participate in so I submitted this to our pastor and he agreed.

We brought this to the congregation. About 40 people signed up for a liquid fast, and 125—130 for partial fasting. Some joined from other congregations, as well as from other cities: one from distant Yellowknife in the Northwest Territories. People had heard about this fast and were eager to participate. During that time we had a lot of prayer meetings—three times a day—as well as waiting-on-God times. There was quite a prayer movement happening, with many people attending. Part way through, a pastor couple who led prayer in a church in Red Deer, Alberta came to help facilitate a 3 day round-the-clock prayer and worship time. Many people signed up to lead and attend 2 hour shifts. At the end of the 40 days, we had a final worship, prayer, and declaration event with other churches participating.

Signs in the heavens showing God's response

After this final evening, when I walked outside I was amazed to see three spectacular signs in the sky: a partial lunar eclipse, the Hale-Bop comet, and northern lights! This has happened often after fasts— signs to show us that God has heard, is pleased, and will answer in due time.

This fast was only one of many we did as a congregation, along with other churches. The following month, another church hosted a 24 hour worship/ prayer time which people from our church attended. God was building unity.

Prayed-for conferences

Our church had a yearly conference, a week with anointed worship and preaching by guest ministries along with powerful altar ministry times. We usually had 10 days of fasting and prayer leading up to the conference week. Also several people would pray in a side room during the preaching. These times were highlights because the presence of the Lord was very strong as a result of all the praying and fasting.

In 2000, we held another 40 day fast leading up to the annual conference. The Spirit of the Lord fell so powerfully during one of the conference sessions, that we warred loudly and prophetically with strong, anointed worship for about an hour or more, praying that strongholds in our region would come down—strongholds that had resisted a move of God. It was a memorable time—I don't remember such a meeting ever happening to that degree of intensity. God had revealed some of these strongholds to our prophetic intercessors with profound confirmations through dreams and other ways, and it culminated in that time of corporate warfare.

Fasting and praying for Canada and the nations

One of the 40 day fasts our church participated in was for the 10/40 Window, a section of Asia having the highest population but the least amount of Christians. Dr. Peter Wagner, the founding president of Global Harvest Ministries, called for this global fast. Many people from our congregation signed up.

For Canada we held a corporate fast one year, as well as having 24 hours of prayer one day a month, with people signed up taking one hour shifts in their homes.

Altar ministry, prayer shifts during preaching and a prayer chain
Regular prayer shifts took place in the prayer room during our Sunday services. Many people served in altar prayer ministry, faithfully praying for the needs of the people. A prayer chain was also in place, quickly mobilizing intercessors to pray when needs arose.

Praying for the churches of our city
Our church prayed every week for one of the churches in our city, praying for each of the many churches through the year. This lead to citywide prayer, fasting and worship events.

God has an appointed time
God is a God who hears and answers prayer. These multiplied prayers and fasts, along with the prayers and fasts of millions of others, are before God's throne in golden bowls. Angels are adding incense to them. They are stored up for the *right time*. God has an appointed time. These prayers have been filling up the bowls and are part of the outcome which will take place.

> *When He had taken the book, the four living creatures and*
> *the twenty-four elders fell down before the Lamb, each one*
> *holding a harp and **golden bowls full of incense, which***
> ***are the prayers of the saints.***
> *Revelation 5:8 nasb*

> *Another angel came and stood at the altar, holding a*
> *golden censer; and much incense was given to him, so*
> *that he might add it to **the prayers of all the saints on***
> ***the golden altar which was before the throne.** And*
> *the smoke of the incense, with **the prayers of the saints,***

went up before God out of the angel's hand. Then the angel took the censer and filled it with the fire of the altar, and threw it to the earth; and there followed peals of thunder and sounds and flashes of lightning and an earthquake. Revelation 8:3-5 nasb

You have...put my tears in Your bottle.
Are they not in Your book?
Psalm 56:8 nasb

Chapter Forty

How to Pray? Am I Doing it Right?

For we do not know how to pray as we should
Romans 8:26 nasb

The devil tries to keep us from praying

If we only spend 5 minutes a day in prayer thinking about God, this world will seem several hundred times more real to us than God.

"The one concern of the devil is to keep Christians from praying. He fears nothing from prayerless studies, prayerless work, and prayerless religion. He laughs at our toil, mocks at our wisdom, but trembles when we pray."(Samuel Chadwick)[11]

Am I doing it right?

Should I have a prayer list? Should I pray at a certain time of the day?

Is Bible reading a part of prayer? Can I pray sitting down, or should I kneel? Shouldn't we be praying without ceasing so a certain prayer time isn't necessary?

These and other questions might be going through your mind if you are beginning to step into a prayer life, or even if you have been praying faithfully for a long time. First, I commend you that you are desiring to do this. I am very excited that you have a desire to pray.

We only really learn to pray when we begin praying and keep doing it

Great men and women of God say that the best way to learn about prayer is to actually do it. That's how I learned. We are not to just seek teaching on how to pray without practicing it in our lives. Be not hearers of the word but doers also, the scriptures tell us. Do not stop when the trials or dry seasons come. Don't stop when you are emotionally down, or up. Just pray! Pray in every season—seasons of peace, confusion, faith, doubt, celebration, or grief.

I have found that once you step in, the Holy Spirit will guide you and teach you what to do as long as you persevere and don't give up. It took me several months of just "showing up" and stumbling through it the best way I could. My commitment was an hour a day. God honored that and met me with a "spirit of prayer"—the flow of prayer began and I began to see and get answers.

Do not quit! If you keep on, you will hit the oil well eventually.

Make it the most important thing you do every day

Sir Thomas Adney,[12] a historic mayor of London became restless when something interfered with his prayer time. Once, when attending a banquet, his prayer time approached and he tried to think of a way to excuse himself without being rude. He leaned over to a friend saying he had an appointment with a close friend that couldn't be postponed. Later he returned to his seat without anyone knowing he had stepped away for prayer.

This story encouraged me to be consistent in prayer, giving God undivided attention. I loved how he said he had an engagement with a close friend that couldn't be postponed. It helped me see more clearly that the Lord is a "Person" so I don't want to give Him a "no show".

Another saying that has stuck in my mind for decades is, "The most important appointment of your day is your appointment with God." The more I began to see Him as a Person, and that He wants me to keep an appointment with Him daily, the more real it became to keep it.

At first I tried doing it early in the morning. However, with three little ones, the youngest a one-year old, it didn't always work. Someone would wake up and need attention, so I allowed myself flexibility. If morning didn't work on a certain day, I spent an hour in the afternoon when the children were napping. When they grew out of naps, I taught them to have quiet time, each in their rooms with books or quiet toys. I left my door slightly ajar in case they needed to run and tell me something while I was praying.

Sometimes a whole day went by and I hadn't had my time with the Lord.

Then I would stay up to pray after everyone was in bed.

I believe each person can develop what works best for them. The key is to *keep your appointment with God.*

Priorities will be re-established

Don't let anything else take pre-eminence. At first it will be difficult: everything will come against you to stop the new habit—distractions, interruptions, conflict, failure, and discouragement to name a few. Just persevere. Don't quit. Even if you miss some days, get back on track. Let it truly become your most important appointment of the day.

You might ask, isn't that legalistic, too rigid? Answer: we brush our teeth every day, go to work, or go to school. Why would a regular prayer time be less than that?

Over the years it will become so natural you don't even think about it. You long for it because it is the very source of life. It's our place of conversation, our dialogue. God talking with me. Me talking with God.

God will get our attention if we drift away

If we drift away from it being a priority, or if we have drifted from our first love, God gently prods us back on the right track:

> *Your ears will hear a word behind you,*
> *"This is the way, walk in it,"*
> *whenever you turn to the right or to the left.*
> *Isaiah 30:21 nasb*

If we don't respond to His gentle prod, He has a way of creating disturbances to get our attention. If we have cried out to Him sometime in our past saying, "Lord, use me whatever the cost. Have your way in my life," well, God has His ways of answering that prayer. And I love Him for it.

The Holy Spirit helps us pray but we have to show up to pray

We don't know how to pray, but the Holy Spirit will help us. However, He can't help us if we don't start, if we don't show up. "For we do not know what prayers to offer nor in what way to offer them. But the Spirit Himself pleads for us in yearnings that can find no words." (wnt). I have found this verse keeps applying even if you have prayed for 40 years. Every time we pray we need to posture ourselves like a child, being aware that I am small and I need someone bigger to help me. We can say, "I don't know how to pray about this situation. Lord guide me to pray by your Spirit," and then wait.

Often He gives us words in English or in one's native tongue. Sometimes it is groans, or sighs—you don't have words, only an inexpressible yearning. Romans 8 makes it clear that this *is* prayer, even though there are no words, and that He is listening, paying attention, because it says He who searches the hearts knows what the mind of the Spirit is. (Rom. 8:27)

Other times He leads us to pray in tongues, a heavenly language. It is good because we know that the Holy Spirit is praying *the will of God* in the situation. If you have not been filled with the Holy Spirit, ask the Lord for it. He has promised to give it if we ask:

> So if you who are evil know how to give good gifts to your
> children, how much
> more will **your Father in heaven give the Holy Spirit
> to those who ask Him!** Luke 11:13 bsv

Praying without ceasing or a specific time to pray?

Some argue that they are continually talking to God so they do not feel a specific time is necessary. It does say in 1 Thessalonians 5:17 to pray without ceasing. This is keeping our spirit in tune with God even though our mind is focusing on what we are working on.

However, it is not possible to have a depth of communion and prayer in the middle of daily duties—when we have little children needing our attention, school, work, or when interacting with people.

In the same way that we want privacy and an atmosphere free of distractions when speaking heart to heart with a friend, so it is when speaking with the Lord. Not only do *we* need it, the *Lord* wants our undivided attention to speak to us the things of *His* heart. We need a time, or times daily, when we can employ our mind as well as our spirit in prayer. We need to truly engage, giving God undivided attention.

The Bible is full of great men and women of God who took time to be alone with Him regularly:

Enoch walked with God (Genesis 5:24).

Isaac went out in the field to meditate (Genesis 24:63).

Daniel prayed three times a day at a window (Daniel 6:10).

Jesus rose up early and went to a place of solitude to pray (Mark 1:35).

Everything Jesus did was an example for us to follow. He, who was the very Son of God, prayed. He spent much time alone with God in prayer, in enjoyable relationship with Him. And to know His assignments, to do the things the Father wanted Him to do. If Jesus prayed, how much more do we need to pray!

Hannah prayed and cried out to God in the temple (1 Samuel 1:9-11).

David spent much time alone with God, the Psalms being his journal. Sometimes he was lying in bed, meditating (Psalm 63:6), or singing loudly upon his bed (Psalm 145), or he was in the temple inquiring and gazing upon the beauty of the Lord (Psalm 27:4).

Habakkuk set himself upon his watch in a watchtower (Hab. 2:1).

From the example of these men and women, we see the need to separate a specific time to be alone with God and to have a place of prayer where you are alone with God.

What is my prayer closet?

> *But when you pray, go into your room and shut the door*
> *and pray to your Father who is in secret. And your Father*
> *who sees in secret will reward you. Matthew 6:6 esv*

What Jesus was emphasizing here was the need to be *alone* with God, separated from others. It was not about being in a room or a closet (kjv), because Jesus often prayed outdoors: in the Garden of Gethsemane, or on one of the Galilean hillsides. He went off alone to pray to his Father. *Selah! If Jesus needed to pray, and to pray alone, how much more do we?*

Ask the Lord to direct you to know the best place for you to pray. I often do prayer walks along nature trails, or I have taken my lawn chair out to a quiet lakeside park where I can be alone. I love to sit on my balcony in the early summer mornings as the sun is rising. However, when I was a very busy, young mother, I prayed in the living room when everyone was still sleeping, or in my bedroom during the kids' nap time. I remember getting up early each day during a week when we had a house full of company. There was no secret place of prayer in the house, so I drove to the riverside to pray. Tuomo, the kids, and our company all slept while I quietly slipped away. When the kids were a little older, I went for prayer walks along a country road. Twice I met bears on those walks, and a moose once. These encounters kept me home for two weeks or so, but the apprehension wore off and I was back on those trails again. During conferences, when there were meetings all day, if I missed a time of prayer in the morning because 4 women shared a hotel room, I slipped away to a prayer room at the church during an afternoon session. I felt it more important to have that time alone with God than take in every session.

David Wilkerson, the author of the best seller, *The Cross and the Switchblade*, had a recliner that was his "place of prayer". He liked to pray late at night. God will have a plan for you. Don't try to fit into someone else's way. Don't put on Saul's armor. Find out from God what is His time and secret place for you. It might be the bathtub, the park, your car, your bedroom, or a hillside.

Should I kneel, sit, or walk?

There is a time for each: a time for kneeling, a time for sitting and praying, and a time for prayer walking. I remember prayer meetings when I was a child and youth, us kneeling at old wooden pews. I remember pre-service prayer at my church in Prince George. We knelt in a basement room or the "fireside room", and cried out to God for His Holy Spirit to come. Kneeling doesn't seem to be done as much these days. Maybe it should. However, I think it is the posture of heart the Lord is looking for. What is the way that you can forget yourself and be in God's presence? Do that. I have knelt when there is something significant I have cried out to God for. I remember those times and places and I remember what I prayed. I remember my dad, too, kneeling by the living room couch, crying out to God.

When I enter warfare prayer, I shout, clap, pace and walk. I do that indoors in my family room, because I don't want to be shouting and clapping along a river trail.

Should I have a prayer list?

A prayer list is good, but God wants us to go deeper. We do not just pray through a "list" of things, rather God "burdens" our hearts to pray for the things on His heart at that particular time.

One preacher said it well, saying we need to wait on God in prayer until we experience this connection—this engaging with God when His Spirit begins to pray through us. He said it sometimes takes five minutes and sometimes several hours. He begins to pray through his prayer list until the connection takes place. Personally I have found God's creation brings me quickly into His presence, so as much as possible I like to go for prayer walks outside by a river, in parks, or just sitting outside with Him. Also, worship music helps me enter in. For some, music or being outdoors is distracting; they find a quiet room better. This speaker went on to say that when you enter the realm of praying in the Spirit (this doesn't necessarily mean praying in tongues, but it can be), that is where miracles happen. I can attest to that. You *know* you are before the throne of God, and you *know* with confidence that you are undeniably and totally welcome, and He is listening to you.

So a prayer list is a great help to get us into prayer because we don't always feel "anointed" to pray. The list will help us get going. However, don't let it become a legalistic bondage, though it will help you to be faithful to pray for the people God has given you a burden for.

A suggestion

During a season of my life I made a separate list for each day of the week, though keeping my immediate family in prayer daily. (Later, when I was a prayer pastor at our church, and when I led the House of Prayer, there were separate, focused meetings for each specific area)

If you do this, you will not be overwhelmed by one long, enormous list which you can't maintain. By having daily focuses, many people, missionaries, areas of ministry, nations, etc., will be covered weekly by you.

Sometimes I dropped the list or made mention of the items on the list briefly at the end of my prayer time because I had spent most of the time on what God put on my heart that day. This is the same for Bible reading. God wants us to be faithful to pray and read the Bible, but to also be sensitive to what His Spirit is highlighting. Be ready to drop the structure—the prayer list or Bible reading plan—if He is showing up in a special way. If a verse from the chapter you are reading is highlighted by the Holy Spirit stay with it.

God's Love Letter, the Bible

Is Bible reading part of prayer time? What is prayer? Is it just us talking? No, it is us in a dialogue with God. We need to listen for God to speak to us, too. The Bible is God's Word and He speaks to us through it. He also speaks to us directly by His Spirit—a thought comes to us during prayer time: direction for the day, a text to write someone, a call to make—those assignments that are from Him for us to do. Or even a revelation. Mostly He speaks through His word, kindling something in our spirit when we read.

Reading my Bible is very important to me. I wrote earlier that I started when I was 10 years old with a goal of doing one chapter in the Old and one in the New Testament each day, though I didn't keep my goal perfectly. However, over the years I have read the Bible through many times. It is God's love letter to us, revealing how much He loves us, and teaching us to love Him with all our heart, and to love our neighbor as our self. In it He shows in many ways how He responds to our whole-hearted love, by loving us back, showing up, answering our prayers, blessing us, and correcting and disciplining us. He tells us that we are His ambassadors, speaking for Him, declaring who He is by preaching the gospel of the Kingdom in words and actions. He tells us how to do that by knowing our gifts and callings, and serving others through these. He reveals the plans of His heart to us, how everything will unfold in the end times, leading into the age to come. We don't have to be in the dark.

We should read the Bible asking Him to speak to us through it and with expectation that He will. If we read without a life of prayer and listening, we will be reading with our intellect only, rather than with our spirit. Reliance on intellect alone produces lifeless, mental gymnastics.

Timothy, guard what has been entrusted to you, avoiding worldly and empty chatter and the opposing arguments of what is falsely called knowledge.
1 Timothy 6:20 nasb

As we pray, asking Him to reveal His word to us, understanding will come. I don't mean we just pray, "God help me to understand, speak to me now, please." That is good, but what I mean is that we have a consistent prayer life aside from Bible reading. Abide in Jesus, and then when you pick up the Bible it is a living word.

We have received…the Spirit who is from God, so that we may know the things freely given to us by God.
1 Corinthians 2:12 nasb

Something from the passage we read will become a "living" word to us. As we spend time with God and study His word, He speaks life to us, and we can in turn share this life to others. I have often found that the scripture I read in the morning is the very one He wants shared with a person He directs me to, or who calls later that day asking for prayer. That is what our abiding in Christ does—it releases the scripture to become a life giving word through the Holy Spirit to others.

The Lord God has given me the tongue of disciples that I may know how to sustain the weary one with a word. He awakens me morning by morning. He awakens my ear to listen as a disciple. Isaiah 50:4 nasb

This passage above is actually a prophecy about Jesus. It is about His prayer life: how God would awaken Him morning by morning to listen to the Father, to get His instructions for the day, so He could "sustain the weary one with a word".

Jesus continually modeled for us how to live. If He needed to awaken to listen to the Father in the mornings, how much more do we? *Help us to harken to the promptings of Your Holy Spirit to get up to listen, so we can sustain others with the word You give us.*

Answers to prayer are exciting, but they only come if we spend quality time in prayer

Each answered prayer excites us and builds our faith for the next prayer assignment God gives us. We need to persevere and develop prayer in our lives to become a good habit that we will not easily slip back from into a prayerless state, because things happen when we pray.

Pat Robertson said on his TV program that God wants "stretched out prayer" like the church prayed when Peter was in prison. A miracle took place. God wants this kind of praying, not just little, light, blessing prayers, though these are important, too. At the end of the day, if someone asked, "What did you really pray about today?" would you remember?

When I discovered prayer, which is abiding in Jesus, and when I learned to bear His burden and to persevere in it, I tapped into an incredible source of power. I realized that something happens when I pray that does not happen when I do not pray, and saw that knowing God in my weakness was a great source of power and strength.

God wants us to discipline ourselves into a habit of prayer.

Let it become a life-giving habit that is hard to break.

Let it become such that if you miss your daily prayer time

You feel it deeply.

Chapter Forty-One: Asking

Ask: My Teenaged Friends got Saved Though my Prayers Weren't That Great

You do not have because you do not ask. James 4:2 nasb

He gives to those who simply ask

> *Ask, and it will be given to you...If you then, being evil, know how to give good gifts to your children, **how much more will your heavenly Father give the Holy Spirit to those who ask him?"** Luke 11:9–13 nasb*

Imagine! God gives <u>much more</u> than earthly parents do!

God's lavish generosity

> *He who did not spare His own Son, but delivered Him over for us all, how will He not also with Him **freely give us all things?** Romans 8:32 nasb*

> *Now to Him who is **able to do far more abundantly beyond all that we ask or think**...be the glory. Ephesians 3:20, 21 nasb*

Keep on asking, and you will receive what you ask for.
Matt. 7:7 nlt

My teenaged friends got saved though my prayers weren't that great

We were moving. It was time to downsize drastically while we were waiting for our house to sell. As I was going through my library of books, clearing out those which I had not looked at for years, I picked one from my "discard" pile to look at more closely. It opened to the first blank page and there was a personal note from someone. My eyes quickly scanned to the bottom of the page. It was from my grade five teacher, Mrs. Kydd! But she had dated it 1974? I was nineteen years old at the time. My curiosity was peaked—why did I receive a book from my grade five teacher when I was nineteen? I read the note:

Marja,

May you derive as much pleasure from the reading of this book as I have. The piece of reading you wanted is on pages 170–177. This book is a gift to you in appreciation for your two notebooks – Soc. Studies which I still use to show pupils from time to time as an incentive for them.

Sincerely,
Mabel Kydd 1974

It started to come back. I had remembered a story Mrs. Kydd had read to our class years before. I wanted to track it down so I could read it to children we were ministering to in Prince George. I had written her and she sent me this book. What a treasure!

Her note brought back more memories—a wonderful story of answered prayer.

My family moved from Canberra, Australia to Port Arthur, Ontario, Canada in 1965. I was ten and placed in grade five, Mrs. Kydd's class.

I quickly acquired a friend named Barbara*. She and I loved school, loved the challenge of learning, and were both artistic. We competed for marks and artwork in a friendly way, inspiring each other. We not only wanted top marks, but colored our maps artistically, added colorful art to all our work, and tried to be as neat as possible in our penmanship.

In high school we took a volunteer job working in the cafeteria kitchen during lunch hour, loading and unloading the dishwasher. This way we enjoyed a free hot lunch and were able spend time together.

In the depths of my heart I wanted Barbara to come to know Jesus personally. She attended a church that didn't present a clear salvation message, and I knew she was not born again. I wasn't a great evangelist—not quite sure how to talk to her about the Lord. But I prayed for her.

We lost contact when I married, and Tuomo and I moved to Prince George, BC, several thousand kilometers away. I continued to lift her up in prayers from time to time, asking God for her salvation.

Many years later I had a strange experience. My husband and I attended a Christian banquet at a hotel in our city. Throughout the evening I kept thinking about Barbara. When it was time to leave, I pushed my chair into place, pondering why Barbara was coming to my thoughts in such an overwhelming way. When I turned to leave, a woman greeted me. It was Barbara! I was stunned.

She had been sitting further back in the conference room and had recognized me. At the close of the event she bee-lined to my table. She told me she was married, had a child and was living in Prince George now, having moved recently…and *she had received Jesus into her life* in her later teen years! We set up a time to visit to do a lot of catching up.

I was awed and blessed that God went out of His way to let me find out He had heard my prayers and answered them. He is a God like that—letting us in on what is happening. I love Him for it!

Interestingly, I had another friend also named Barbara**. She started attending C. D. Howe Elementary during my grade seven year. She was

---

* *name changed*

** *name changed*

a Dutch girl and I loved her immediately. We became fast friends and visited at each other's homes. She was also a church-going girl, but I sensed she did not know Jesus as her personal savior so I attempted to share the gospel with her. It wasn't received too well, so I decided I would not use words any more. I resorted to prayer. We continued our friendship. I was maid-of-honor at her wedding, and then our lives parted when Tuomo and I married and we moved to Prince George. We kept up through letters.

One day I received a letter from her. She wrote how she had gotten saved, along with her husband, mom and brothers—it was household salvation! I was ecstatic. Again, God went out of His way to let me know that my weak prayers were answered.

These salvations of both my friends named Barbara increased my faith in the power of persistent prayer, weak as they had been. I had just lifted them up in simple prayers from time to time, asking for their salvation. He is a God who hears and answers.

> This is the confidence which we have before Him, that, if
> **we ask anything according to His will, He hears
> us.** And if we know that He hears us in whatever we ask,
> **we know that we have the requests which we have
> asked from Him.** 1 John 5:14-15 nasb

I asked the Lord to encourage me

I was very discouraged. I could not seem to pick myself up, so I prayed and asked the Lord to please encourage me. Later that day there was a knock at the door. A friend stood there holding a vase with a long-stem rose. She had driven 15 km out-of-town to my house in the country to bless me this way. I knew it was God! He was behind this because she had no idea what I was going through or about my prayer. I felt "heard" by God. He is amazing!

I have sought first Your kingdom—please provide some new clothes

I read to my girls from one of Arthur Maxwell's *The Bible Story* books. That day's story was about the lilies of the field, radiantly dressed even though they don't work or spin, and much more beautiful than Solomon in all his glorious clothing. What caught my eye in a new way were these words:

> *If God so clothes the grass of the field (with these lilies),*
> *which is alive today and tomorrow is thrown into the*
> *furnace, **will He not much more clothe you?**...**seek***
> ***first His kingdom and His righteousness,***
> ***and all these things will be added to you**.*
> Matthew 6:30, 33 nasb

I could not afford new clothes—that was a luxury. But faith rose in me as I read these verses, so I prayed, "I have sought first Your kingdom, Lord. I would like some new clothes. Would you please provide?"

A few days later a friend from another city, visited. She gave me $50, saying this was for new clothes. Thank you, Lord!

I mentioned to the Lord I would like a specific dress I saw in a shop

I told the Lord I would really like it, but it was around $60, much too expensive for me to afford. A few months later I received $20 as a gift in the mail for my birthday, and when I went shopping, that exact dress was on sale for $16!

God's amazing answers regarding houses all throughout our lives

It started when my husband and I were very young; we had only been married for 4 months. A pastor wanted to sell his duplex to us, one which was new, only 6 months old, and very attractive. At that point in our marriage, we had not even begun dreaming of owning a home. However, we went to look at it because this pastor seemed keen on selling to us, for some reason. I remember thinking, *I love this place! But to own it? How can we?* We went home and Tuomo said, "Let's pray and ask the Lord". So we knelt down by our bed and asked if it was His will, and would He provide the down payment money if it was. Within a day or so, a money order arrived in the mail from Tuomo's uncle. He had decided to send money gifts to all his nephews and nieces. This money, together with Tuomo's half month's wage, and a small, short-term loan from his brother along with his co-signature (because we didn't have credit yet), was sufficient for the down payment.

We were not the only ones who received money from our uncle, but for us it was a direct answer to prayer. How exciting it was, and it greatly built our faith.

We were so green regarding house buying that we didn't know how to make the monthly mortgage payments. We thought a bill would come in the mail. After three months, there was a knock at the door. An official looking man wearing a suit and carrying a briefcase stood there; he was from the mortgage company and wanted to talk to us. We sat at the kitchen table and within a few minutes things were cleared up. He was sent to see if we were really going to be able to keep this house. We had the money—that was not the problem—we just needed to know how to pay!

Be specific

Some years later we sold the duplex because we had invested in business.

I had searched in the newspaper for rental houses, but for what we needed, little was available. We had 3 little boys at the time, plus we ran a business out of our home, so we needed a house to accommodate all of this. I was getting anxious because we were just days away from having to move and we had no place to go...

I had read in a book, *Adventures in Prayer* by Catherine Marshall, that when you ask God for something, you need to be specific. So I thought about our family and business situation and described a house to the Lord that would meet our needs. I asked for a playroom in the basement that wasn't too fancy as the boys could be rambunctious at times. I asked for three bedrooms upstairs, an office room in the basement with shelves for products we carried in our business, and a park nearby. I asked for drapes, for green carpets, and for brick-red linoleum. Lastly, I told the Lord the rent amount we could pay monthly.

Finally, at the eleventh hour, a house showed up. At that point I didn't have time to view it because I had a paperwork deadline to meet, and I was busy packing, so Tuomo went. He came back saying he had taken it. I asked him what it was like. He was vague, saying it was fine, though it had a few holes in the walls. *Oh, no! What has he rented?*

I stayed at our old place until the very last moment to clean after everything had been moved out. Finally I was able to go to the new house. I was apprehensive. *What am I going to see?* When we drove into the yard, I was impressed with the outside appearance and tidy yard, and it was right beside a pretty little park. *Wow! So far so good.* I went in and was awed: green carpet throughout, red brick-looking linoleum in the kitchen and dining area, drapes at all the windows, three bedrooms upstairs, an office room downstairs *with shelves*, a big playroom with chip board walls—perfect for the boys. There was even a guest bedroom.

A little puzzled, I asked Tuomo about the holes in the walls as I hadn't seen any. He grinned and said, "Two fireplaces!"

God answered my prayer *specifically* and above what I had asked.

Should I call?

Many years later we were in the process of moving to Vancouver Island to build a house. We sold most of our furniture. I had learned the "drill": ask the Lord specifically. I asked for a furnished rental home for the duration of the building project, one suitable for hosting our large family.

I didn't have to search much when one came up on Kijiji: a fully furnished home with a large deck on 1/3 of an acre near Lake Cowichan. And the price was right, It sounded ideal. *I could take the grandkids swimming!* There was one problem. Our house had not sold. But somehow I knew we would be moving by the end of summer. I thought, *should I call? It's only May and I don't know when our house will sell. And we can't move until it does.*

I picked up the phone and called anyway. Within minutes the landlady tearfully poured out her life to me. Her oldest son had died about a year earlier, and she was undecided about renting the house. I switched into ministry mode and talked to her about the Lord and offered to pray with her. She said she'd had a salvation experience many years ago, but had not been attending church for a long time. It was a divine appointment—the Lord showed up in our time of talking and prayer.

A few months later our house sold. I called this lady again, just to check if her house still happened to be available to rent. Yes it was!

I really enjoyed the house—it was tastefully and creatively decorated with eclectic furniture and pictures on the walls. It was where I began writing this book—in idyllic surroundings, both inside and outdoors. That was where those 17 elk surrounded our house. We had many elk visits, and some bear visits, too. I took grandkids swimming, hiking on trails overlooking the lake, cross-country skiing at the nearby park, and for drives to find elk. God answered my prayer above and beyond what I had asked. Not only did I have these blessings, but also the landlady and I became good friends and met for Bible study and prayer times during the two years we lived there.

Praying for our neighbors resulted in salvations

We have moved many times in our 50 years of marriage. With each move, we began praying for our neighbors and asking God for their salvation. As we prayed regularly, in almost all those neighborhoods we led people to the Lord. In two of the places, deaths in families opened the door for us to share Christ.

On Gagne Street, three children, ten years and under, lived next door and they often played with our girls. The oldest boy accepted Christ at our Vacation Bible School event. Later, Keziah, our daughter who was around 8 or 9 at the time, brought his sister, Jane*, into our home. Kez asked to borrow my big Thompson-Chain Bible, and the two girls headed downstairs to the family room. When they came upstairs, she informed us that Jane had accepted Jesus as her savior. Keziah had memorized the "Roman road" scriptures and showed them to her from the Bible, leading her to the Lord.

---

* *name changed*

Early one morning we saw an ambulance in their driveway. Their mother, who was quite young, had suddenly and unexpectedly died. When we offered to help in anyway, her husband asked if her celebration of life could be held at our church. The pastor presented the gospel message in a beautiful, simple way. Their youngest daughter listened carefully and responded, receiving Jesus into her life. Praise the Lord!

Some years earlier we lived in a home on 5 acres in an area with only a few other families further up the road, who we prayed for. I regularly went for prayer walks in the opposite direction of the houses. Because no one was around, I would freely pray out loud. One day as I was walking and praying aloud, I glanced up and saw a young man walking toward me. He was one of the sons from a family of ten. I was a little embarrassed, knowing he had heard me. I decided to face it head on, and said, "Hi! Just so you know, I wasn't talking to myself. I was talking to God." He was a bit startled, but responded in a friendly way, so I told him about Jesus and encouraged him to talk to God, too. A week or so later he died in a car accident! What a shock. We reached out to the family, and the celebration of life was held in our church. Later I led his 14 year old sister to the Lord. A few years later she called me in tears saying another of her brothers had been in a serious motorcycle accident. That time I was able to share Christ with her father.

God determines our appointed times and our boundaries

We moved often and with each move lives were touched by the Lord. It seems it was God's plan to move us from place to place so that we would be praying for these neighbors and sharing Christ with them.

We need to ask, "Why am I here?" God places us strategically and supernaturally for a *purpose*. He determines our appointed times and establishes the boundaries of our habitation, as Acts 17:26 says.

When we simply start praying for the people around us, regularly asking, God answers, opens doors, and leads in wonderful ways.

An accident that resulted in a house

Back during those difficult years, we rented for almost 15 years because our financial situation had gone south. We had lost our house, and the houses Tuomo had invested in.

In 2002 I was in a car accident that caused a deep cut to my forehead. It was sutured in emergency at our hospital. Some weeks later, when I had an appointment with my own doctor, he took a look at the scar and said it wasn't done very well, offering to redo it. In the meantime, the insurance company had been waiting for a report about the healing process. I thought and prayed about whether I should get it redone and came to the conclusion not to do it. When I called the insurance company, they offered a settlement. I didn't realize this was even an option. Some weeks later I was called by them to pick up a check. It was $10,000. I was shocked.

There was a house for sale on our street, just two houses down from us—an older home needing renovation. We were able to purchase it, using the settlement money as a down payment. My husband, along with friends did a beautiful job renovating. It had a yard with mature trees, shrubs and flowers and after some TLC, the yard looked lovely.

We lived there for 10 years.

Then we bought a lot and Tuomo built a home, which we sold after living there for less than two years. We moved to Vancouver Island, supposedly to retire near two of our kids' families. Again Tuomo built a home. After five years of investing into the lives of our nine grandchildren there, we felt the Lord speaking to move to Alberta to be near the two kids' families we seldom saw because of distance. The grandkids on Vancouver Island had grown up during those five years and were now busy into part time jobs, school, cadets, and youth group. The eight grandkids in Alberta were younger, at a stage when grand-parenting is impactful.

We sold our house and were greatly surprised by the amount we were able to sell it for. There had been a sudden jump in the house market on the west coast just months before. We had no idea—just felt the Lord directing us to move. As a result, we were able to pay off our mortgage and buy five acres with a lovely home overlooking a river valley in Southern Alberta, mortgage-free.

This domino effect started from a car accident! "God causes all things work together for good to those who love God, to those who are called according to His purpose" (Romans 8:28)

Truly God answered my prayer from thirty some years earlier, that I would see the goodness of the Lord in the land of the living. I had declared the words of Psalm 27:13, many times over, "I would have despaired unless I had believed that I would see the goodness of the Lord in the land of the living."

God answered our teenaged son's prayers

Our son, Steve, was in air cadets and really enjoyed it. After a year I wasn't sure if he was to carry on because our schedule was hectic, and having 5 kids in many activities involved a lot of driving from our out-of-town location. Steve prayed. It became clear God wanted him to keep on, so he did, and he later received top cadet award at survival camp. Years later, Steve has served as President of the Squadron 744 Administration Society for many years, volunteering in many ways. Also, all his children have been cadets through their teen years and are now civilian instructors as adults, one an officer.

As a young teen he prayed for a job and God answered—he was hired by a farmer for haying season. Several times he prayed for a way to make money so he could go to youth conferences and retreats. One time, when he was 13, God did a miracle for him through prayer. He wanted to go to a youth ski retreat. We were financially super-tight, so we could not pay, for sure. It was two days before the retreat and there was no money for it. He had wanted to use family allowance money, something I gave to each of my kids when they turned 13, to buy their clothes and personal items. I said, "No, but pray for a job opportunity." I prayed also, with earnest, heart-felt prayers, that it would work out for him to go, especially because I saw he was not complaining but had resigned himself to pray.

He realized he could deliver catalogues, something our church school had a contract for. I helped him with this, driving while he ran from house to house, dropping off the catalogues. God did a miracle: several hours before departing to the retreat he was still delivering catalogues, but he made it!

God at times, gave him a word of knowledge. He "just knew" that one of his friends was going to be there at the retreat. He spoke it out and then earnestly prayed it would happen, and sure enough, a way was provided for his friend, also.

Our daughter wanted to hear from God about her calling

Our youngest daughter, Keziah, had been frustrated as a teenager for some time because she didn't know what God's calling was for her life. A couple of her siblings seemed to her to effortlessly hear from God and it bothered her that she didn't. I encouraged her to start asking, just simple short prayers every day. Two years later a visiting pastor/prophet ministered at our church. He saw her standing in the hallway with a few people, walked up to her and prophesied, saying, "You have intellect. I see you with your bags packed and a ticket in your hand. You're going to travel. Don't think Prince George is the only place on the horizon." It was a clear word from the Lord, and it witnessed in her spirit and in ours. She began to look at going into college and university, taking hospitality administration for 4 years. She did an internship in the United States at a Hyatt Hotel, and a year of university in Melbourne, Australia. Upon completing her degree with honors, she was hired and served as the operations manager of the church for ten years, truly being fulfilled in her calling, and having traveled and used her intellect as the prophetic word stated.

Just ask!

Bible people who asked and received

In the Bible there are many stories of simple asking prayers and God's answers:

Jabez asked to be blessed and kept from causing pain
(1 Chron. 4:9-10).

David asked for direction in warfare (2 Sam. 5:19, 22-25).

Bartimaeus asked for sight (Luke 18:35).

Joshua asked for the sun to stand still (Josh. 10:12-14).

Hannah asked for a son (1 Sam. 1:10, 20).

Jesus (and us) were told to ask for the nations (Psalm 2:8)

Conditions for receiving

We need to be abiding in the vine, Jesus, and abiding in His word, having a close walk with the Lord:

> *If you abide in me and my words abide in you,*
> *ask whatever you desire,*
> *and it shall be done to you. John 15:7 nasb*

We need to walk with integrity:

> *No good thing does He withhold from those who*
> *walk uprightly.*
> *Ps. 84:11 nasb*

> *If I regard wickedness in my heart, the Lord will not hear.*
> *Psalm 66:18 nasb*

We need to ask with pure motives, not for selfish ambition.

> *You ask and do not receive, because you ask with wrong*
> *motives, so that you may spend it on your pleasures.*
> *James 4:3 nasb*

Keep asking

Answered prayer moves us to love and worship Him, and launches us to keep on praying.

> *I love the Lord, because **He hears my voice and my supplications**, because **He has inclined His ear to me**, therefore **I shall call upon Him as long as I live.*** Psalm 116:1-2 nasb

In the above verses, love erupted in the heart of the psalmist because God heard him. God paid attention to his request.

And because God heard him, he said he will call on God all his life. Answered prayer can initiate a lifetime of seeking the Lord. For me it has been this way. When I experience answers to prayer, I know I will get more answers, so I just keep asking!

Chapter Forty-Two: Intercession

Intercession

The airplane crash

I drove to Fort George Park in Prince George to pray (one of my favorite prayer places), but because it was raining hard, I sat in the car. I began to pray for each of my five children beginning with the oldest. When I prayed for Steve—our second oldest who was 21, and had recently graduated from college in Calgary—intense weeping hit me; I *wailed* out loud! Fortunately, because it was pouring rain, people were not walking about, otherwise they would have heard my loud wailing prayer and wondered about that crazy woman in the car. I was weeping like someone who had lost a loved one through death. It was very intense.

Two hours later Steve called from Calgary and told a very tragic story. He had just witnessed his boss crash his plane during a test flight. Steve had been in the air-control tower watching with binoculars. Although I was 800 kilometers away, God had moved on my spirit with intercession and travail, completely bypassing my mind. Steve ran 2 kilometers to the crash site, hoping for the slightest possibility of his boss's survival. He was the second person on the scene, preceded only by a person driving by. The police came shortly after. Tragically, his boss had died. As Steve processed this horrific tragedy, he realized he should call the boss's son, otherwise he would hear of his father's death through the news.

All this the Holy Spirit knew, so He moved me to pray with deep travail. Steve was alone processing these things, so the Holy Spirit knew an intercessor was needed for him to have grace to walk it out and do what was needed in such a tragic situation.

God looks for an intercessor who will pray His purpose through

Intercession is not necessarily as intense as it was in the above story.

To intercede means to stand between God and the person, or people group you are praying for. It can be normal talking prayer—it is still intercession if you are praying for others.

We can form a list and pray for those things. It is good and things do happen at that level. But at times, the Holy Spirit moves us to engage with Him in a depth of prayer where we begin to experience a flow of the Spirit. It is the Spirit praying through us: it can be in our own language or in a heavenly language, or even in groaning and sighing wordlessly. At this level we *feel* things happening even though we cannot see the outward manifestation yet.

Many people give up before they experience it. I wrote earlier in the book, that for me it took two months of waiting on God daily before I entered into this level of intercession. I read my Bible, prayed through my lists, and read a Christian teaching book if I ran out of things to pray.

Then one day the spirit of prayer hit me. It was different praying. I felt something happening in the spirit realm and I felt satisfied when I finished. Something *had* happened! People I prayed for were touched by God, though they did not know I was praying for them. It strengthened my faith greatly

Daniel prayed and fasted in mourning for 3 weeks (Dan. 10). After 3 weeks, a heavenly being appeared to him saying his prayers had been heard on the first day, but the Prince of Persia (a ruling demonic principality) had resisted and hindered him from bringing the answer. But because Daniel prevailed in prayer, the answer came. Therefore we need to *keep praying*. We don't know what is going on in the spirit realm but somehow our prayers make a difference in the battle that demons and angels are waging. Daniel was not consciously coming against demons, or even aware of this battle. He was just mourning, praying, and fasting. He knew from Jeremiah's prophecies that 70 years of exile in Babylon were now completed and it was ***now time*** for the Jews to return to their own land.

The definition of intercession in Greek is "to entreat". In Hebrew it is "to come between".

God wants us to stand between man and God, entreating Him, praying for salvations, for the needs of others, or for maturing of believers so they become fruitful and effective in their ministry calling. Everyone has some kind of ministry calling, whether to serve with their hands, or to speak (1 Peter 4:10, 11, Romans 12:6-9, 1 Cor. 12). This intercessory praying can be for an individual, church, city, nation, or nations, or for the lost neighbors next door, colleagues at work, your relatives, or those globally.

Jesus intercedes for us

He always lives to make intercession. Hebrews 7:25 nasb

It is good to know that even if no one else is praying for us, Jesus is.

God looks for an intercessor to pray His purposes through

I searched for a man among them who would…stand in the gap before Me for the land. Ezekiel 22:30 nasb

He wants to fill us with His Holy Spirit to pray His heart, mind and will through us

…But the Spirit himself intercedes for us… according to the will of God. Rom. 8:26-27 nasb

A depth of sacrifice is involved in intercession

The effective, fervent prayer of a righteous man avails much. James 5:16 nkjv

Fervent in Greek means to be "hot, as boiling liquid" or a "glowing solid." That speaks of great intensity.

Intercession is a type of prayer that involves the intercessor being in a spiritual battle and *actually feeling* what the person or group (church, city, or nation) is going through: heaviness, despair, hopelessness, oppression, tormenting fear, great irritation, anger, anxiety, or strife for example. At first you may think it is something you are personally going through, but as you think it out, you realize there is no reason for it. You may try to pray through for a release for yourself, thinking it is you feeling this way, but nothing happens, no breakthrough takes place. You might even ask others to pray for you and still it doesn't lift. God is allowing you to feel these things so you can identify to pray effectively for those who are going through them. These kinds of feelings may direct and stir us to pray for the persecuted church, for a bereaved person sorrowing the loss of a loved one, for abused children, those caught in human trafficking, or someone contemplating suicide, etc. You may have suicidal thoughts yourself, and wonder why because you are not prone to this. That heaviness is actually someone else's so you can intercede effectively for them. Later you may cross paths with this person and the Lord opens a door for you to minister to them.

We don't always know who it is for or what it is about. We don't need to. The Spirit will pray effectively through us if we give ourselves to it.

God wants us to learn to let that heaviness be the birthing pain on behalf of others. The pain is God's crucible to release anointed prayer that breaks the oppression and brings heaven's help into the situation. As we pray through, the heaviness lifts and we sense a breakthrough in the spirit realm.

Interceding, prevailing and travailing for a Holy Spirit breakthrough

We had an intercessory prayer group that met each week at the church for several hours. One year it seemed our intercession level rose higher and higher, and a sense prevailed that God was going to break through in our church, and in our city in a heightened way. We had been praying continually for a move of the Holy Spirit, for revival—for all the churches to experience this. In the summer our church did a 3-week fast on top of all the prayer. That fall the prayer meetings were very fiery. Some of the men joined us and we were like warriors pressing through in the spirit realm for a victory. I remember one of the men would whale around with a stick and roar, like a warrior in battle. None of us had a problem with it because we were all roaring or praying loudly in tongues. We knew we were pressing through for something significant in the spirit realm. Even at home I would wail and pray; the Holy Spirit praying strongly through me. We knew something was going to be birthed soon.

Sure enough! Later that fall we had special speakers come and our church filled up to around 800 people one evening during the conference. Our seating capacity was 450, but people kept coming and coming. We seated them on the floor in the aisles and some sat on the edges of the platform. The Holy Spirit was poured out powerfully during those days. People fell on the floor and shook uncontrollably under the power. We took some of the people downstairs to pray for them as there wasn't enough room for prayer ministry upstairs.

The presence of the Lord was sweet and strong, doing powerful and deep things in people's lives. One woman was on the floor lying on her back, vibrating—her whole body bouncing—praying loudly in tongues. It was a God encounter moment for her which empowered her to later become the intercessory prayer leader of the church, lead a women's recovery ministry center, and lead and facilitate Bible studies. Another person who had gone through years of grief was filled with so much laughter she could not stop for a long time. God washed away the grief. She was a woman who would not normally be caught doing something like that in public, but the Holy Spirit took over and anointed her with the "oil of joy for mourning". For another it was the first time he was filled with the Holy Spirit and he lay on the floor receiving God's love poured all over him. These are just a few of the things that happened during those days. Pastors of other churches, along with their congregations, joined us for these times because there was such an ocean of refreshing that had broken out in our city. For several years we had a number of these "Fan the Flame" gatherings, and this refreshing continued being poured out.

Our intercessory group had prayed regularly for all the churches of the city for about six years. The prayers crescendoed that fall after the 3-week fast, and it culminated in this wonderful time of outpouring where many churches "drank from this well" and were refreshed.

This refreshing led to these churches working together for an evangelistic thrust, a story found under the title, *Prevailing Prayer*.

Often God gives you a word for the people you pray for regularly

Many times God will use the intercessor to also bring a word from Him to the person, church, etc. As we intercede, travail, and pray the burden through, the heavens open and we hear what God is saying and He uses us to speak a word of faith, a word of knowledge, encouragement, prophecy, or wisdom to that person or situation.

Intercession is laying down one's life for another

In this process, intercession, prevailing prayer, travail, and supplication may all take place. The intercessor lays down their life for the other(s), standing in the gap. It is not just a matter of praying mere words, rather it becomes a matter of fighting a battle for someone, so we become the target of spiritual warfare. Often the person who has prayed regularly for that other person will be the one who feels the travail when it is time for that prayed-for-person to be birthed into the kingdom, or if that person is already in God's family, to be birthed to a higher realm of knowing God.

Tuomo's high school buddy

Tuomo and some friends had begun to pray for an unsaved fellow student at trade school. His name was Mark. One evening Tuomo felt a deep burden to pray for him, the Holy Spirit stirring him to do intense battle in prayer for quite a long time. He fell asleep on his knees. The next day at school, Mark called Tuomo aside and told him that something strange had happened to him the previous night. Tuomo said, "I know." "How can you know?" Mark asked with surprise. Tuomo said, "We'll talk at lunch," because classes were starting. At lunchtime, Mark recounted a startling dream or vision he'd had in the night in which he was a fish in an open sewer. He saw Tuomo fishing on the shore, and Mark swallowed the baited hook. The fishing rod became a Bible and Tuomo reeled him in. As Mark came out of the filth, he turned into a beautiful swan and flew away. He was greatly moved by this dream/vision. Tuomo said, "We need to talk. Can you come to my place tonight? The reason I knew something had happened was I got a deep burden to pray for you last night, praying until I fell asleep on my knees. I received peace that something had happened."

That evening, Tuomo shared the plan of salvation with him starting from Genesis to Revelation, a two hour Bible study, which he chuckles about now (it doesn't have to be a 2-hour thing). They both knelt down and Tuomo led Mark in the sinner's prayer. He invited him to study the Bible with him, which they did weekly, inviting a few other Christians to join as well.

The principal heard about this Bible study. He asked Tuomo to lead the school's weekly 20-minute devotional for the entire school of several hundred students, which he did for two and a half years.

Pray. You may be the only one praying

There are some situations that God will bring to your attention and you are the only intercessor.

Other times you may be a co-intercessor, or support intercessor, standing with someone else like Aaron and Hur held up Moses' arms while the battle took place in the valley (Ex. 17:8-16). The three of them were the intercessors for the battle to be won, Moses carrying the primary burden and Aaron and Hur supporting him.

Other times there may be many lifting up prayers for a specific person or situation for a season.

Steve's plane crash

On May 1, 2014 we received horrific news that Steve's plane crashed just west of Calgary. He was in a coma for a week and we didn't know if he would survive, or if he did, would he have brain injury as most of the broken bones were in his head and neck. He had a badly broken ankle, fractured ribs, several fractured vertebrae, broken skull, broken jaw, and crushed facial bones—a total of 35 broken bones in his body, including 13 teeth. Thirty-one of those breaks were in his neck and head alone. He came out of the coma and within a day or so he wrote on his white board— writing because he couldn't talk (his jaw was wired shut and he had a tracheostomy)—asking for his lap top. Tuomo watched him enter all his logins and pins to check his banking information. His brain was fully functioning. NO brain damage, praise God! However, pneumonia hit him full force and a life-and-death battle ensued. He pulled through, eventually making a full recovery, though with numerous surgeries over the years to remove metal and screws that caused infections.

Over 750 people joined a Facebook group which Moses, his older brother set up. These people prayed him through. I feel Steve's life was preserved because of the prayers of these brothers and sisters in Christ. He was severely injured, but God wanted him alive, so He raised up a wall of prayer. All our family felt carried by those prayers, as well. Many continued to pray as he underwent further surgeries in the following years.

By God's grace, he was able to complete his work contract from hospital, directing his work crew from there. He completed it on time, and in budget. He recovered from this tragic accident so well that he was back to work within a few months.

The amazing thing is, he had no broken bones in his hands or arms. Our boys did not have middle names, so when they were young, we told them they could choose a middle name for themselves. We read the Bible daily with the family, starting from Genesis. When Tuomo read Exodus 31, Steve, who was around 8 at the time, declared, "That's me! Aholiab!" Bezalel and Aholiab had been appointed by God to make the tent of meeting, the ark of covenant, the mercy seat, the furniture and utensils, the priestly garments, and the fragrant anointing oils. It says that God had put skill into their hearts to do these things.

We saw that Steve had skill with his hands from a very young age, and knowledge to do things many didn't. Even at around 8 or 9, he was ready to build. He walked down the road to a property where a house was being built, and offered to work. He was hired to collect and pick up construction debris that had fallen on the ground. That was the beginning of his construction resume.

God had anointed his mind, his arms and hands to build and fashion all kinds of things. Before he left for Africa for five years of mission work, when he was 21, he was prayed for by the leaders of the church. Our pastor prophesied Exodus 31 over him—the same scripture Steve had claimed for himself as a child!

In this plane crash, God spared his brain, his hands, and arms. These had been anointed for God's work.

Delays and disruptions may be God's opportunities

Wherever you go, always be perceptive and ask, "Why am I being sent here? Do you want me to be praying for someone?"

These delays may be God's opportunities. He may want you in a certain place at a certain time to make a difference through prayer as the following story recounts:

Another suicide intercepted: Heaven and earth worked together

One Sunday morning, in the fall of 2006, I went to my favorite river trail for a prayer-walk before Sunday service. The sun warmed me pleasantly as I walked and prayed. At a certain point there was a makeshift bench, so I sat down for a while. The sun was behind me, so it cast my shadow onto the glistening river surface. The shadows of three big trees beside and over me were like three big angels reflected on the water. They were stationed around me. *BIG angels*. It was as if they actually *were* there. I felt a strong heaven and earth connection. Little did I realize why they were there!

After a while, I got up and carried on toward the bridge, my usual turn around point. I was all alone on the trail, which was fine by me. I loved early Sunday mornings—so peaceful and quiet.

Suddenly the silence was broken! A car raced helter-skelter into the parking area by the bridge and a young woman burst out the door and headed straight for the water, crying loudly as she went. She threw her purse and kept running headlong into the river. Her boyfriend ran after her and grabbed her as she lunged into the water. Without thinking I ran too, to help. She was desperate to get away from him; determined to drown herself, crying and yelling at him to let go. He held her while she fought him, soaking wet. I went and held on to her as well and told her that God wanted her to LIVE! I kept speaking words of life to her, praying. She was strong and fought us both, but the two of us were able to keep her from breaking away. She didn't want the young man to help her, but gradually calmed down as I held her. I talked about Jesus, about how God had a purpose for her life. She was very cold, so I took off my sweater and put it on her. Finally she walked back to the car with her boyfriend and I stayed close by until they drove off. I had given them my phone number.

The sweater I gave her was my favorite—one which I had bought brand new, a very rare occurrence. Most of my sweaters were from thrift stores.

One day, maybe a year later, I browsed through the racks at the Value Village thrift store. Suddenly my eyes grew big, because THERE was my favorite sweater—the very one! With great joy I bought it back.

I never did find out the outcome of this young woman, but I kept her in my prayers for a time. My hope is that she also has been "bought back", redeemed by the blood of the Lamb.

What I know is that God had angels posted on that river trail that morning; heaven was poised and ready to work with earth to rescue a despairing girl. We walk in works foreordained as Ephesians 2:10 says.

Instead of being judgmental, God wants us to be "prayermental"

It's not hard to see imperfections in the church. The natural tendency is to criticize and tear down. However, the true bride of Christ will stand in the gap and lay down her life in intercession rather than gossiping, criticizing, or tearing down, thus being aligned with Jesus rather than being aligned with the accuser of the brethren, Satan. We are all weak and broken people who are being restored by God, and we need one another to build each other up.

We need to have the heart of Jesus, who is for us, always interceding on our behalf. Likewise, when we see failure and brokenness in the body, we need to be like Him and stand in the gap in intercession.

Therefore He is able also to save forever those who draw
near to God through
Him, since He always lives to make intercession for them.
Hebrews 7:25 nasb

Prophetic Intercession

We are all called to intercede. However, some have a prophetic gift coupled with intercession, so they seem to pray in a different way because this gift helps them sense the heart of God in a matter by the Spirit. However, if you don't have that gift, never be intimidated by it to hold back from praying. Your prayers are just as valuable. Short, heartfelt prayers spoken out are powerful and make a difference. Whatever 2 or 3 agree is done in heaven, and one chases a thousand and two ten thousand.

Chapter Forty-Three: Prevailing Prayer

Feeling Dumb but Doing it Anyway

That was real dumb! Maybe he thinks I have a gun in my purse. I felt awkward in my bumbling attempt to share the gospel…

I am not a bold, brave evangelist. Far from it. A big chicken, in fact. But I know God has called us to be witnesses, so I often pray that He would use me this way even though I am weak in it. I worry often that I might say the wrong thing, and therefore I miss many opportunities.

Our pastor preached a message on evangelism, a good message to preach from time to time, and challenged us to share Christ with someone. I try to be a doer of the word, not just a hearer, so I couldn't shake the challenge even though I was out of my comfort zone again.

I began to pray for God to open a door for me to share Christ with someone.

Not long after, I had an errand to pick up some health products from people we knew as acquaintances, products which they sold from their home. As Larry* was writing the invoice, I struggled within myself. *Should tell him about Jesus?* Finally I blurted, "Are you ready to die?"

Startled, he looked up. *That was real dumb! Maybe he thinks I have a gun in my purse.* I quickly went on to say that we all die one day. It could be any day. Are you ready to meet God? Do you know if you will go to heaven? He was cavalier and said he's not worried, saying he almost died once because of a health situation, and it was very peaceful. And besides,

---

* *name changed*

who can know if they will go to heaven or not? We won't find out until we die. He said he is a part of a certain church (that doesn't preach a clear salvation message, neither did I think he was active, and I sensed he was not born again) and went on to say he believes what he believes. I told him that you *can know* if you are going to heaven or not and your church and ours read the same Bible which tells us how to be saved and how to *know*.

He quickly ushered me out, not being comfortable with the direction of the conversation.

I began to pray for Larry on a regular basis, asking God for the salvation of his soul.

About six months later, on a day that I felt quite down and couldn't seem to pick myself up, my phone rang. It was a lady from our church calling in a prayer request for the prayer chain which I facilitated. Dutifully, but with a heavy heart, I picked up my prayer chain notebook and pen to write out her request. "This request is for Larry Adams, a man my husband knows through work. He is dying of cancer."

My heart leapt. The heaviness vanished in a second. "Larry Adams?! Praise God!" I exclaimed. She was surprised at my reaction. I quickly explained that I had witnessed to this man six months earlier, and the first thing that had come out of my mouth was, "Are you ready to die?" I had thought those words were real dumb, but *God* had put those *exact words* in my mouth!

Suddenly I had much faith to pray for this man's salvation. I saw that God had me on a pre-planned path. We walk in works that God has prepared. After praying for some time I sensed I should visit him. I carefully prepared by taking some *Power for Living* leaflets that were included in our church's bulletins each month. I often read those and saved them because the stories from people's lives were very encouraging and inspiring. I found a couple of stories of people with cancer. I also took some booklets that explained how to receive Jesus as savior.

When I arrived at his home I was invited in, but to my dismay he had out-of-town visitors. Two brothers and a sister were in the living room with him and they all had strong drinks in their glasses. Larry's wife,

Shelley*, was not there, perhaps at work. I chatted with them for a while, but at the same time shot up prayers asking God to direct me. *How do I share Christ with Larry in front of these people?* Finally I thought I better dive in as I may not have another chance and this is about life-and-death—about eternal life and eternal death. I lunged forward, not knowing what the reaction was going to be in the room. I don't remember exactly my words and sentences, but shared about Jesus and the pathway to salvation. I gave Larry the material I had brought with me, explaining what was in them. I think I prayed—not the sinner's prayer because he was not at that point yet—but a prayer for him in his difficult state.

I had no idea how the siblings were reacting as I did not look at them while I was talking, keeping my focus on Larry. Finally I got up to say good-bye and all the siblings stood up and thanked me profusely, shaking my hand. I was surprised at how glad they seemed about my visit and the things I talked about. As I drove away, I realized these people had no idea what to say to their dying brother, and they were relieved someone had come with words of truth and life.

I kept praying much for him and his wife and siblings. A few weeks passed. Because our family was going on a holiday, I thought I need to call and see if I can visit him one more time because it might be too late if I wait until we get back. When I called, his wife answered and was immediately open for me to come. She said he had gone downhill very quickly and was given a few weeks to live. When I arrived, she said she had made sure no one else was there so we could talk freely. It seemed like a very wide-open door. Larry was sitting up weakly on the edge of a hospital bed set up in the living room. I sat beside him. He could only speak quietly and slowly because his strength was gone. He told me he had accepted Christ into his life! Oh, my heart jumped for joy. He said a friend of theirs had flown up from Texas (I believe) to visit, and she had shared the same things I had spoken a few weeks earlier. He had received Jesus into his life! I hugged him and said, "You are going to heaven! I will see you in heaven one day!"

---

* *name changed*

His wife began to weep and said, "Of course he is going to heaven because he has been a good man!" I went and held her and said, "Yes, he is going to heaven, but not because he is a good man. He is going to heaven because he has received Jesus Christ into his life."

She said she has read the material I had left with them and had liked them.

After our holiday trip, I phoned them again. Shelley answered and said he had passed away two days after my visit.

Prevailing prayer is praying through to victory, not stopping until the job is done. It is not letting go of God until He answers. It is not giving up.

Praying for 300 to attend prayer training

In the 1980's I started leading a prayer group in our home with the blessing of our pastor. About 8–12 people attended regularly and the main thing we prayed for was for a prayer movement to be birthed in our church. After we had prayed for a long season, I told the group about the *Change the World School of Prayer* training I had attended which had greatly encouraged and inspired me to keep praying an hour a day. I shared how I felt the Holy Spirit was saying we are to have a CWSOP training event in our church, and they agreed.

I had learned God's way, which is to *pray it in!* So we began to do that—to pray for this event and for all the people God wanted to attend—with faith and fervency. After praying for a season, I presented it to my pastor. He was favorable to us organizing this event at our church, giving us the go-ahead. We continued to pray week after week. I contacted the CWSOP ministry organization in Ontario, and they said they would come if there were 125 people minimum attending, and suggested we advertise it to other churches to make sure we had enough people. We took this to God in prayer, and sensed we were to ask God for 300 to attend. For 8 months we prayed persistently, persevering with our request. When all was said and done, we had just over 300 attendees and most of them were from our church.

God answers prevailing prayer when we have heard from Him, and are specific, staying focused with what He told us to pray for

Heaven's Gates, Hell's Flames

In the last chapter I wrote about a great outpouring that came on many churches in our city after a season of much intercession. The pastors continued to meet together regularly to fellowship, pray, and enjoy this refreshing.

This led to these churches working together to do an evangelistic outreach where 100 or so people responded to the gospel.

There is a back story I need to tell:

I had heard about a drama production that my nephew's church had performed in Winnipeg as an evangelistic outreach, called *Heaven's Gates, Hell's Flames*. His stories about it fascinated and grabbed my heart, and I felt stirred that this *needs to be done* in Prince George.

I began to pray earnestly that it would be done in our city.

Not long after, my husband and I made a trip to Wichita, Kansas, where our son's family lived. They had just welcomed their third child into their home and we were thrilled to go and meet her. While there, I noticed an ad in the Christian newspaper, that a church in Wichita was hosting *Heaven's Gates, Hell's Flames*. I was excited—I had to go and see it! We were able to do that, a leading of the Lord.

I sat back and watched this drama unfold. It consisted of a number of scenes of families, co-workers, and friends going about normal life events. One scene was about a family of four who were driving after church. The kids argued in the back seat about which fast food restaurant they would go to. Then they talked about the service, and the son thanked his dad for leading him to the Lord that morning. They all celebrated it. The mom talked about how she missed their youngest daughter who had died in an accident the year before. The son asked if this sister had accepted the Lord, and she said, yes, she had, and now they would all be together in heaven one day. Suddenly a car crash! They all died, finding themselves at heaven's gates. Angels were everywhere and there was a great book, the book of life, where the names of born again believers are recorded. Asking if their names were in it, the angel looked into the book and nodded, affirming they all were recorded. They ran up golden stairs into the arms of Jesus who was waiting for them. He embraced them with joy. Then He stepped aside and a little girl came running, calling out, "Mom! Dad!" The family was ecstatic as they were reunited. It was very moving.

Many scenes like this were portrayed, but some about dying without Jesus. Demons came to take those ones to hell. Very sobering.

I was deeply moved and convinced that we had to do this in our city. Information for hosting this drama production, and a video for $20 were at a table. I bought it, even though the $20 was a sacrifice at that time.

I watched the video at home. From it I learned this production had already been performed in many churches over several decades and God was using it greatly to bring people to salvation. A church in Modesto, California extended their drama production for 28 days because people kept coming and coming and getting saved. A total of 81,000 people attended and 33,000 accepted Christ during that time. These people were directed to attend the 250 churches of that area. Modesto and sur-rounding cities, in a small radius, had a population of about 1.5 million or more, and had many churches.

I *knew* this was meant for our city, but how do I take the next step? *With much prayer.* I knew God would lead me.

I felt the pastors who continued to meet together were the group to take this on. But how to present it to them was the question? I gave the video to our pastor and he presented it to them. They took it on! I was excited.

The intercessors prayed. One of the men took it on as a serious prayer assignment, crying out to the Lord, on his hands and knees in his kitchen, that God would use this to bring people to salvation.

My task was to organize a 40 day fast preceding the production. Each of the participating churches chose a week to 10 day segment of the 40 day fast.

The Civic Center was rented, altar ministry people were trained, and congregation members were encouraged to invite unsaved people.

About a week before the drama, several people from the *Heaven's Gates, Hell's Flames* organization, arrived with all the props and to train local people from the churches to be the actors.

Finally the day arrived when everything was ready! I don't remember how many times we presented it, but all in all, over 100 people went forward for prayer. Many salvations took place and others came forward to rededicate their lives to Christ. I was thankful to God for the harvest of souls that came through this harvesting net that was cast out.

When God gives a vision and his people persistently pray it through to fulfillment, adding fasting to the mix, His kingdom purposes advance in a wonderful way.

God has set it up in such a way that when we work with Him—partnering with Him, and together with God's people in unity—He brings in a harvest.

Hearing an answer to my prayers on a boat on the Sea of Galilee

In the 1990's I prayed often for Thailand that God would send apostles and prophets there, naming specific ones to the Lord. I was burdened that the spiritual atmosphere of Thailand needed an apostolic/prophetic thrust to break it open to another level.

In 2013 I led a team from Prince George House of Prayer to Israel. One day our group sailed on a "worship boat" on the Sea of Galilee along with many other Christians visiting the land. As the boat glided across the sparkling waters, a worship team led us in worship and praise to God out on the open deck. It was wonderful to worship together with people we didn't know, except by the Spirit, on the Sea of Galilee. The majority of the people were from Thailand. At one point, the pastor of the Thai group came to talk to me (if I recall, our groups had been introduced according to the country we were from, so he knew we were from Canada). He asked if I knew Wesley Campbell, who is a Canadian apostle. I told him, "Yes, his wife, Stacey is speaking in my city at this present time." He went on to say they'd had Wesley, Patricia King, Chuck Pierce, and Cindy Jacobs at their church.

I journaled later, "Lord, I prayed *a lot* for Thailand to get these speakers, and now You showed me the answer to these prayers! Bring a great harvest in Thailand, and bring the church to maturity."

God let me hear answers to my prayers *on the Sea of Galilee*. Who would have guessed?!

He hears the prayer of the righteous. Proverbs 15:29 nasb

How strong is our desire to get an answer?

Daniel didn't stop; he fasted and prayed for 3 weeks until he got an answer from God (Dan. 10).

Jacob wrestled with God to gain a blessing. He didn't let go. There is a time for this and it pleases God. God blessed Jacob and called him a prince because he prevailed with God and man. (Gen. 32:24-29).

Elisha, the prophet, was angry with Joash, King of Israel, because the king only struck the ground 3 times with his arrows. He said he should have struck 5 or 6 times, then he would have destroyed Syria completely. Now he only got a partial victory (2 Kings 13:14-19).

God is pleased with faith that keeps knocking.

Jesus told a parable to show that we should pray at all times, and not become discouraged. It was about a widow who kept coming to a judge asking for justice. The judge was unwilling at first but finally conceded because of her persistence. Jesus went on to say:

> *Now, will not God bring about justice for His elect who*
> *cry to Him day and night, and will He delay long for*
> *them? I tell you that He will bring about justice for them*
> *quickly. Luke 18:1-8 nasb*

We need to determine the will of God in a situation and then boldly keep asking for that outcome.

Ed Silvoso spoke at a conference, saying that sometimes it takes persistent prayer to bring a stronghold down. A concrete wall does not come down with one hit of a sledgehammer, but with many, many hits. Cracks begin to form and finally the wall comes crashing down. Likewise some spiritual strongholds need persistent prayer that may take months or even years.

When we get the word from God, after asking for it, we then need to pray for its fulfillment.

There had been a 3 ½ year drought in Israel, which Elijah had prayed in, but now Elijah got a word from God that it was going to rain. *Then* he set to work, praying the rain in. He kneeled down seven times with his face between his knees. He sent his servant out seven times to see if a cloud was forming. Finally after the seventh time the cloud appeared. He *knew* the rain was coming, and it did. (1 Kings 18).

Why doesn't God answer our prayer immediately?

If we look at the story of Daniel praying and fasting for 21 days in Daniel chapter 10, I think we get our answer. An angel appeared to him on the 21st day, saying that on the very first day of his fast, his words were heard and he was sent to Daniel. However a demonic prince, the prince of Persia, resisted him for 21 days. Then Michael, an archangel, one of the chief princes, came to help this heavenly messenger so he could get through to Daniel with his message from heaven.

There are 3 heavens: 1. The natural sky (Psalm 104:12 esv), 2. The second heaven which is the realm of the prince of the power of the air (Eph. 2:2, 6:12), and 3. The third heaven where God dwells (2 Cor. 12:2, Rev. 12:19). When we pray, our prayer is heard immediately and the answer is sent on its way, but there is resistance. Somehow as we prevail in prayer, this resistance is overcome. Angelic forces are sent to overthrow this demonic resistance.

Interestingly, Daniel was not aware of this spiritual battle in the heavenly realm. He just kept fasting and praying. We don't have to know all that is happening in the invisible realm, just be obedient to do our part.

The book of Daniel encourages me because in another prayer assignment it says he experienced extreme weariness (Dan. 9:21) before he got the message from Gabriel. Another time he was exhausted and sick for days *after* receiving a vision (Dan. 8:27). Why does that encourage me?

Because I go through those same things when I am fasting and praying. Sometimes I have felt so weak I thought I can't go on, feeling tempted to quit. Seeing it in the Bible settles my heart that it's okay. It is part of the warfare. Just keep going!

If you have received a word from the Lord about something, pray it in. Don't stop. Persevere. Add fasting to fortify your prayers.

Don't quit until it's finished!

Chapter Forty-Four: Travailing or Birthing Prayer

What You Weep and Pray for, God Sends You Into

I have seen this happen often. The people I have prayed for with travail and tears, I have been sent to, to encourage or lead them to Him. Nations I have prayed for with deep travail, I have been sent to, sometimes to pray there on site, or to preach and teach there as well as pray. I observed this in the lives of others too, how God has sent them to see the fruit of their prayers and tears. He lets us see the results, though often it may be years later. I am going to tell some stories, but first I want to talk about travail.

Travail is deep prayer. It is about birthing. Bringing forth new life. A new level. It is about yearning groans too deep for words, often with tears. It can be for a day, weeks, or even some years on and off, depending on what God is birthing.

Hannah birthed a prophet after years of painful unanswered prayer

Hannah, who was barren, prayed year after year to have a child. Each year her family went to Shiloh to the house of the Lord, and there she would not eat but only weep. One year she went into the house of the Lord, and "she, greatly distressed, prayed to the Lord and wept bitterly" (1 Sam. 1:10). She prayed with such intensity that the priest thought she was drunk and rebuked her. She was in travail, basically praying, "Give me children or I die!" She made a vow to the Lord, saying that if You give me a son, I will give him back to You for all the days of his life. She birthed a prophet, Samuel.

Paul travailed

*My dear children, for who I am again in **the***
***pains of childbirth** until Christ is formed in you.*
Galations 4:19 niv

After people had come to Jesus through new birth, now Paul travailed, praying fervently that they mature in Christ to become like Him.

Our prayers at times are groans

... groanings too deep for words. Romans 8:26 nasb

That is powerful praying. This groaning can mean just that, groaning without words. It can also include praying with tongues, heavenly languages that we can receive when we are baptized in the Holy Spirit. God knows exactly what we mean without using earthly words.

Jesus travailed

In the days of His flesh, He offered up both prayers
and supplications with loud crying and tears.
Hebrews 5:7 nasb

Travail is birthing prayer. When a woman is in labor, and when it gets closer to the baby being born, it turns into transition labor. She often cries out and writhes because the pain is very great. Jesus was birthing sons and daughters into the kingdom through His travail.

Childbirth is a picture of birthing things in the spirit

God has always created something in the natural to be a picture of the spiritual. Childbirth is a picture of birthing things in the spirit: revival, salvation of souls, maturing in Christ, healing and miracles, birthing God's kingdom purposes in our nation and nations. When we are in "transition labor" spiritually, our prayers get desperate and intense, often feeling deep pain and anguish in our spirit. Like Hannah did. Like Jesus did. Think of Jesus travailing in the Garden of Gethsemane where He sweat as if it were drops of blood.

Travailing prayer does not come on us all the time, just like a woman is not in travail (labor) all the time—only when she is birthing a baby. If we pray for something specific on a regular basis, when it is time to be birthed, our spirit picks that up and travail kicks in. We don't always realize why we are feeling this way—weepy, distressed, in anguish—but as we go into prayer and stay with it, God starts to put the pieces of the puzzle together. Our mind catches up to what our spirit has already picked up long before.

Don't think you are "losing it" if you pray this way, or that someone is "losing it" when you see them pray like this. They may even wail and move about as if in pain. It is the travail of the Spirit birthing something. Remember, even the priest misunderstood and thought Hannah was drunk.

This kind of prayer is mostly done in secret. Sometimes God brings it into the congregation.

Travail for Africa—the horrors of genocide

Many years ago, when our five children were very young, the African Children's Choir from Uganda visited our church for the first time. I listened to the stories of many of them being orphaned in tribal fighting. I could hardly bear knowing what these precious children had endured.

When we arrived home that evening, I asked my husband to put the kids to bed as I was so deeply burdened I had to pray. I ran out to the forest, fell on my face and wailed loudly, agonizing over the plight of these children and many like them. My heart was ripped apart in grief for those suffering this way.

Some years later I watched a documentary about the genocide that took place in Rwanda in 1994. Members of the Hutu ethnic majority murdered as many as 800,000 people, mostly of the Tutsi minority. Christians meeting in churches were attacked and killed.

This led me into deep travail for Africa for some years—about the injustices, the killing, the poverty, the child soldiers, human trafficking, and the abuse and oppression of widows and orphans. I could hardly bear knowing of so much grief in the world.

I have discovered that what you weep and pray for, God sends you into. In 1998 I went to Africa and preached in several churches in Malawi. Then in 2001, I went and taught the *Power Perfected in Weakness* course in three Bible Schools in Zimbabwe, Malawi, and Zambia. These doors opened because God had moved me in travailing prayer for Africa for many years.

I believe God's promise, *"If my people...humble themselves and pray and seek my face and turn from their wicked ways...I will heal their land."* (2 Chron. 7:14). God has promised healing of the land if we repent and pray. That is why I speak and write about prayer so much. I am grateful God opened this opportunity to sow seeds into Africa about the power of prayer.

Further unfolding—God brought this to my attention

In the spring of 2020, I preached a message about travail at Lake Cowichan Christian Fellowship in the town of Lake Cowichan, British Columbia. I told of the terrible Rwandan genocide, and how God moved on me in travailing prayer for a prolonged season, and then sent me to Africa.

When I checked the news later that day, I was shocked to see an article posted *that very day* about the genocide that took place in 1994, stating that businessman Felicien Kabuga, known to be the financier of the Rwandan genocide, had been arrested after 26 years of hiding. May God have mercy on him! Thank you, Lord, that the hidden things of darkness are being exposed. Jesus promised that God will bring justice if we cry to him night and day. This man being arrested does not bring justice to the terrible suffering that took place, but it is a beginning. Somehow God will make all the wrong things right one day as He says: "He will make sure that justice is done. He won't quit or give up until He brings justice everywhere on earth." (Is.42: cev). As intercessors we are partnering with Him for that outcome.

What amazed me was how God moved me to check the news that day to see this report about his arrest, on the exact day I preached about it. I could have missed the news. God goes out of His way to let us see what our prayers are helping to bring about. Though He has so much to do, at times He reports back, which shows how much He values us partnering with Him.

After 5 years of fervent prayer for the West Coast, God moved us there

I never imagined when I started leading a zoom prayer meeting for the West coast of Canada, that one day I would live there, even though it had been a pattern in my life. I should have known since God had sent me several times to the countries we had prayed for at out church's early morning missionary prayer meetings. My heart had been deeply burdened for China, Japan, Thailand, Malawi, Zimbabwe, Zambia, and Israel. Amazingly, the Lord sent me to all these countries several times to pray and minister on site after years of praying for them from a distance.

Now it happened again. This time He sent us to actually live there in the West Coast, the place I had prayed for, for 5 years.

Before our move, I had prayed for Canada regularly on my own, as well as with others at our church, at PGHOP, and on a national conference call. However, I was specifically carrying the West Coast on my heart even though I didn't live there, nor did we have a plan to live there. Most of those who were part of the Coast Guard call, as it was named, didn't live there either, but had a God-given burden to pray for this region. Obviously God has something in mind since He had raised up intercessors to pray.

There have been prophetic words about the west winds touching down and blowing across the nation from the west, as well as serious words about a major earthquake. Therefore God has raised intercessors to pray that what can be averted will be, and that people will turn to Jesus.

I remembered something one of my intercessor friends told me that gave some direction for our zoom prayer call. She. with her family had made a holiday trip to California. One day her husband and kids went out, but she remained in the hotel room alone. She gazed out the window and asked the Lord what He had in mind for this city. He said, "Earthquake." She began to pray the earthquake would come at a time of day when there was the least amount of traffic so lives would be spared. They returned to Canada and within a short time the earthquake hit. God had heard her prayers: there were few casualties even though there was significant damage to infrastructure, because it came at a low traffic time. So this became one of the things we prayed for on the Coast Guard call.

After we moved to Vancouver Island, our Coast Guard group continued praying, and I also joined local intercessors to pray with them.

An 8.0 Earthquake Shook Up Vancouver Island

Upon checking the news the morning of January 23, 2018, I found there had been an 8.0 earthquake at around 2:30 in the morning, off the coast of Alaska. Due to a tsunami warning, thousands of people along the south and west coasts of Vancouver Island had been awakened and evacuated to higher ground in the middle of the night. There had been a possibility of up to 20 meter waves. I watched a video clip of bumper to bumper cars moving up the hill in Port Alberni. Loud warning sirens had been activated and repeated every 10 minutes. In Greater Victoria, local emergency officials knocked on doors and told people to head to higher ground. Alerts had been sent via cell phone and email. Residents near water were advised to either move two blocks inland to higher ground or to an upper floor of a multi-story building. There was a picture in the news of Tolmie Park in Victoria, crowded with cars, it being one of the highest points. In Tofino, many people made their way to the emergency center until the warning was lifted 2 hours later. Praise God that this time disaster was averted. God answered. We lived inland on the island, so it didn't affect us; we didn't even know about it until later.

Intercession can change things

In the scriptures there are examples of judgments that were averted or alleviated due to the intercession of God's people (Ex. 32, Amos 7). Other times they were not. God said that even if Moses or Samuel pleaded for the people He would not change His mind about the judgment He was about to bring (Jer. 15:1). Our prayer on this call had been that earthquakes would not be severe and would not take lives. God answered and averted disaster. After this 8.0 earthquake, we prayed fervently for those who had been evacuated in the night, to be awakened to the frailty of life because in a moment one can be swept away. We prayed they would think, "Am I ready to meet my Maker?" and that they would hear and respond to God's call to repentance and salvation in Him.

Our prayers are not in vain, though sometimes it may be many years before we see the answers. Ecclesiastes 11:1 ncb and 11:5-6 nasb, states:

Cast your bread upon the waters, and eventually you
will get it back.

Just as you do not know the path of the wind and how
bones are formed in the womb of the pregnant woman, so
you do not know the activity of God who makes all things.
Sow your seed in the morning and do not be idle in the
evening, for you do not know whether morning or evening
sowing will succeed, or whether both of them
alike will be good.

I hear God say: "Keep working! Keep praying! I will show up! I am going to show up!"

Chapter Forty-Five: Travail or Birthing Prayer

Instantly his Muffler Fell Off!

Here we were, a company of several hundred, marching up a hill on Queensway on our way to Fort George Park. A car pulled up alongside and the driver's angry face glared at us. He opened his window and cursed loudly. Instantly his muffler fell off and its terrible roar reverberated in the street! It was rather comical, actually. All I could think was that God was for us saying, "Shut up!" His hand silenced this man who thought he could curse what God was doing. We were marching in the Lifeline Parade, standing up for babies in the womb—these little ones who cannot defend themselves.

How can I live in a world where this atrocity was happening?

For years I had wept for these babies who were slated to die. I could not stop. I could hardly bear it that we lived in such a world where this kind of atrocity was happening every day, every hour, and every minute—where innocent, helpless babies were murdered because of immorality and inconvenience.

In Chapter 12, as I was writing about how God was teaching me to pray, I touched on this area of the murder of these little ones. In this chapter, I write to show where this weeping travail led to.

You may recall I wrote that my husband had attended a Pro-life meeting in the fall of 1983 and came home with a handful of material. He plunked these on the living room coffee table and there they sat. He is not much of a reader, but I am. I was the one who picked up the book, *The Silent Holocaust* and as a result, my life went into tailspin of more than three years of weeping about this horrific murder of innocent children in the womb. I could not stop. I was pregnant with my fifth child when I read the book along with other literature. I cried in my prayer times, even in the shower. I cried when I bathed my newborn baby, thinking about the saline solution abortions that babies go through where their skin burns in the amniotic fluid. They kick and fight through this slow, agonizing process of death and yet some are born alive. I cried in my living room, praying loud, agonizing prayers when the boys were in school and my daughters were having their naps at the far end of the house. I could hardly bear living anymore. How could I live in a world where this kind of atrocity was happening every minute?

They sacrificed their sons and daughters to demons

I read in the Bible that one of the reasons God's judgment fell on Israel was for the shedding of innocent blood. Babies were sacrificed to Molech and Baal. In Israel! *God's chosen people* were doing this?!

> **They even sacrificed their sons and their daughters
> to the demons, and shed innocent blood...** *whom
> they sacrificed to the idols of Canaan; and **the land was
> polluted with the blood...** Therefore the anger of the
> Lord was kindled against His people
> ...Then He gave them into the hand of the nations, and
> those who hated them ruled over them.*
> *Psalm 106:37, 38, 40-41 nasb*

> *For behold, the Lord is about to come out from His place to
> punish the inhabitants of the earth for their iniquity; and
> the earth will reveal her bloodshed and will no longer cover
> her slain. Isaiah 26:21 nasb*

On account of these verses, I knew God was not looking kindly on Canada, either. There is a lot of innocent blood crying out to Him. I was deeply burdened by this, thinking of the future of our children and their children. Will they be the ones to bear the judgment of God on our nation for our generation's horrific sins? Therefore I became very earnest to do everything I could to avert this if possible. Perhaps our children and children's children would have a future and a hope.

Together our intercessors cried out to God

After months of agonizing on my own, I began to share this burden with the intercessory prayer group that met at our house. I laid out the material on the coffee table; pictures of aborted babies, some born alive after the horrors of saline abortion, were spread out. My intercessory friends perused these and listened as I shared the burden. They were stricken and picked up the burden. Together we cried out to the Lord for many months.

Pamphlets in mailboxes

God began to show us what to do. I ordered thousands of pamphlets called, *Children, Things We Throw Away*, from Last Days Ministries (Melody Green). We organized a blitz of the city, delivering these to mailboxes. Many participated by taking sections of the city. At the same time we prayed earnestly that God would speak to people through these pamphlets.

The hospital board changed their format because so many Christians signed up as members

The Catholic Church faithfully and relentlessly spearheaded the Pro-life group in our city. Together with them we were able to vote in directors onto our city's hospital board because a large number of believers signed up as voting members. Others were willing to run for a position on the board to make a difference. Tuomo worked tirelessly, calling people to sign up, as well as encouraging some to run for the board. At one Hospital Board AGM he put forward a motion that abortion be stopped in our hospital. Many people spoke to it. One pro-choice director stated that only 20% want abortion to be stopped. However, putting this to a vote, a show of hands was done at the meeting. 99 voted against abortion. 51 for. So much for 20%! The membership grew so profusely that the hospital board had to move the AGM to a large concert venue to accommodate all the voting members. Soon the hospital board pro-life directors outnumbered pro-choice directors. One Christian prolife woman served as both director and later as chairman of the hospital board for a season. This growing pro-life influence became such a concern that policy was changed. Directors would no longer be voted in but rather appointed by the government.

Families marched across Canada covering the miles on foot

In the 1980's a Lifeline March was organized across Canada—a relay where pro-lifers took segments of the highway connecting their home city or town with the next one. Our family, along with others, took the last 26 km from Prince George to Quesnel, BC (117 km between these two cities). It was a long march on a hot summer day. We took turns to rest our tired feet in a van that travelled with our group of a dozen or so walkers. Arriving in Quesnel, we marched to a rally at a park and passed the baton to the next group who headed towards Williams Lake. This way all of Canada was prayer-walked.

The white hearse, white casket, and children in white gowns

The Pro-life March I began this chapter with, took place in September of 1988. I was on day six of a water fast praying for this atrocity to end in Canada. A funeral home graciously lent us a white hearse and a small, white baby casket to use in the march. Two men in suits carried it, walking somberly behind the hearse. Following them came groups of children in white gowns, each group representing a year that abortions had taken place in our hospital. We had acquired the numbers of babies aborted each year and made a sign for each year. The children carried these signs in groups, each group representing the number of children aborted that year. It was sobering to realize how many children were missing from our city because they had been murdered in the womb. Others followed behind. It was when we were marching south on Queensway, that the enraged person drove up beside us, cursing vehemently. God would not allow it, instantly slamming his muffler to the ground. He shut up right quick and rumbled away in humiliation. I pray he remembers that moment. May it be etched in his memory and bring him to repentance. To truth. To Jesus. To forgiveness.

CHP gained over 100,000 votes in only one year of existence

We realized that to effect change, we somehow needed to affect our government. That same year we signed up as Christian Heritage Party members and Tuomo became campaign manager for our riding. We worked hard to get more Christian politicians into our government. It was an excruciating several months of commitment. I remember our washing machine broke down in the middle of it all, which added more work to our already overloaded schedule. I drove to the closest laundromat once a week to fill up many machines with the dirty laundry of a family of seven. Often one of my sons came along to help.

CHP came in as the 4th federal party after all was said and done, having gained over 100,000 votes in their first year of existence. Even media acknowledged it as quite an accomplishment.

To truly affect change, we needed to pray for Canada corporately

After these exhausting two months my husband and I understood that to truly affect change, we needed to pray for Canada corporately. In January of 1989, we began a monthly Prayer for Canada group with 15—25 people attending for many years.

The hidden cries of many began to come together

When we pray, God moves us onward and upward progressively. As we met faithfully, we saw something rising in Canada—a prayer and repentance movement called *Watchmen for the Nation*. What we were doing in our small corner began to rise into a national movement. I know there were many crying out to God across Canada in their hidden places as well, and God was hearing all our collective cries.

Watchmen took this to a whole new level. Together we repented for national sins over a period of many years in gatherings across Canada. The first was the sin of turning away Jews who fled the holocaust on a ship called the St. Louis in 1939. As I wrote earlier, our country refused to admit these refugees who were desperately fleeing for their lives from the Nazi regime which was bent on annihilating them. It took a number of years to deal with this particular sin, in the form of many diverse gatherings. One was a "train of tears"—a literal train that carried intercessors who wept and prayed as they travelled from Vancouver to Winnipeg. Then survivors of the St. Louis ship were located and invited to Ottawa. We asked forgiveness from them for this terrible treatment that Canada had handed them in their hour of despair. They were treated royally as honored guests. One final step was asking forgiveness from the Knesset, the Israeli parliament. Five hundred and fifty intercessors traveled to Israel for this assignment in 2001.

This journey of repentance, the *Journey of Hope*, took many years.

As a result, this happened…

What was done in the spiritual realm through this repentance and intercession, affected our nation in such a positive way, that in 2006 a God-fearing man, who did not bow to political correctness, was elected as Prime Minister. PM Stephen Harper led our country for 10 years. He made a trip to Israel in January of 2014 and delivered a bold speech, the first speech to the Knesset by a Canadian prime minister. He acknowledged our Canadian government's terrible sin of refusing the Jewish refugees in the 1930's. He made it clear that Canada was standing with Israel, declaring them to have the right to exist as a state and defend their borders. Most of the rest of the world up until that time, had been outspoken against Israel, or silent. One by one other nations have since stood up and now a number of them, beginning with the United States under President Trump's leadership, have moved their embassies to Jerusalem from Tel Aviv, fearlessly acknowledging Jerusalem as the capital of Israel (Canada has yet to do this as of this writing). Also many Arab nations have normalized their relationship with Israel, something unheard of for decades.

Further Watchmen gatherings focused on other sins of Canada. One highlight was the One Heart Gathering in Quebec City where we prayed Jesus' John 17 prayer to be fulfilled, for us to be one so that the world would believe. There was repenting for disunity in the body of Christ and disunity in Canada, particularly between the French and English.

Another voice crying in the wilderness for the unborn

In the meantime, the burden for the unborn has been taken up by thousands. Faytene Grassechi, leader and director of *4MyCanada*, has led large prayer gatherings, called *The Cry*, in Ottawa and other parts of the nation, with thousands joining to fast and pray for Canada to have righteous laws enacted to protect babies in the womb. She has also led a virtual prayer wall for life for many years, working tirelessly for it to be 24/7. This feat was accomplished in the summer of 2022, with praying groups now covering each hour on line across our nation. Faytene has influenced many young adults to carry a burden for babies to be protected, as well as a burden for the government of Canada. She has led multiple teams of young people into the halls of our parliament where they have met and prayed with and for MP's. Many young adults have been encouraged and mobilized by her to put their names forward to campaign for a parliamentary seat, as well as campaigning herself for a seat in New Brunswick. She also influences through her television program, FayteneTV. All this with an unrelenting back drop of intercessory prayer and fasting.

Estimated 10,000 participated in March for Life

There has been an annual March for Life in Ottawa where thousands have come together on Parliament Hill to demand protection for babies in the womb. In researching for numbers attending, I found a police estimate stating over 10,000 participated in 2019. Abby Johnson, who was a former Planned Parenthood worker was a guest speaker. Her story has rocked the abortion world and has been made into a movie called *Unplanned*, a movie which exposes the deception and corruption of the abortion industry.

Many faithful voices are fighting valiantly

Many other groups and ministries have fought valiantly in this battle for the unborn, including (and especially) the Catholics who have been steadfast and faithful before others caught on: Pro-life, Pregnancy Crisis

Centers, National House of Prayer, Campaign Life Coalition, Battle for Canada and the Canadian Firewall (a 24/7 prayer ministry on line) to name some.

The most prolife president in the history of the U.S. Roe vs. Wade overturned June 2022

The United States has had a growing movement against abortion over the years, so overwhelming that in June of 2022, the Supreme Court voted to overthrow Roe vs. Wade. It was a monumental victory! It was after the most prolife president in the history of the United States appointed pro-life judges. This man, President Donald Trump, has been the most vilified president in the United States, but not surprisingly because he has fought for righteousness in many ways that even a lot of Christians are not aware of.

The golden bowls of prayer are filling up

God is a God who hears and answers prayers. We have not seen a complete victory yet, but from these reports we see things are progressing and growing. The golden bowls of prayer before God's throne are filling and He says to His people, "Your prayers are not in vain."

Answers to corporate and individual travail for a prayer movement

In February of 2023, a revival spontaneously began at Asbury University in Wilmore, Kentucky, which became a 24/7 worship and prayer movement where hundreds of people, young and old, gave their lives to Jesus, or rededicated themselves to the Lord at the altar. This went on for several weeks. "It was attended by approximately 15,000 people each day. By its end, the revival brought 50,000–70,000 visitors to Wilmore, representing more than 200 academic institutions and multiple countries…the revival was additionally significant because of its spread on social media, particularly among Generation Z, the most irreligious generation in US history. "[13] This revival spread to many universities and Bible colleges in USA, in fact, when I checked the CBN news after writing this, even this very day (May 1, 2023), they reported a massive worship, prayer, and evangelism gathering of young people at the Oklahoma University Stadium with 60,000 in attendance. And they were encouraging students to do this in the stadiums of their university campuses.

The prayer movement has snowballed around the world with many online prayer calls and initiatives. Dutch Sheets has close to 1 million praying along with him daily on his *Give Him 15* online talk and prayer. International Prayer Connect (IPC) is a group that connects regularly with over 5,000 prayer networks that together include **130 million intercessors**. These 100 million+ prayed for China on January 22, 2023, for the Middle East on April 17, for Israel on May 28, and for India on October 31—in a global mission initiative called 110cities.com. That is amazing—millions of intercessors praying together with a focused target on the same day! When we are one, the world will believe (John 17:21).

A goal of one million intercessors were called to an *Isaiah 62 Global Fast* for Jerusalem and Israel for May 7-28, 2023. It far exceeded that goal. Additionally, the 100 million plus from the 110cities.com joined to pray for Israel and for global revival on the final day of this 3 week fast (May 28). It was a day of powerful worship and prayer, with many countries allotted an hour segment each.

One of the most moving segments was by a worship team of children from Chennai, India. These young girls worshiped the Lord with abandonment and interceded with amazing knowledge of God's heart plans from the scriptures. It was evident they knew the scriptures because their deep, spirit-led intercession was scripture praying. These ones, who were lost in God in abandoned travail and intercession, prayed with greater maturity, depth and knowledge than most adult believers. What is truly remarkable about them is they are children from the Royal Kids ministry: children who are orphans, or abandoned, human-trafficked, used and abused. They have been rescued, restored and healed by the loving touch of God's heart through this ministry. They are loved, valued, provided for, educated, and taught about the love of Jesus.

What this global fast and prayer showed was the unprecedented escalation of prayer and worship all over the world!

From the ends of the earth we hear songs,
"Glory to the Righteous One."
Isaiah 24:10 nasb

But have we seen the final breakthroughs yet?

I love Antero Laukkanen's words. He was a member of the Finnish Parliament for two terms from 2015-2023. Though he did exemplary work in serving the nation, he clearly states his two main callings were personal intercessory prayer and also calling the body of Christ in Finland to intercessory prayer for their nation. When questioned if all this prayer was accomplishing anything, he states in his book, *Kansanedustajan Salainen Elama (The Secret Life of a Member of Parliament), "I only do my work and God does His... the responsibility to pray is ours, but the responsibility to answer prayer is God's. How freeing!"*[14] God spoke to him in a time of discouragement, saying, *"If I didn't force humans to think the way I wanted them to in paradise* (Garden of Eden), *I won't do that in the Finnish Parliament either. Finland carries the responsibility themselves for their decisions. The important thing is, that you have told them what options Finland has: either the way of blessing or of curse. The choice is always with the human himself... God does not force us into anything. He invites."*[15]

Chapter Forty-Six: Fasting

Calls to Fasting—
Surprising Adventures with
Unexpected Bonuses

I started adding fasting to prayer early in my life, in my teens. My pastor fasted often and it inspired and challenged me. One fall, he called the congregation to a one-week fast for salvation of souls. We were a small Finnish-speaking church in Thunder Bay, Ontario, and since there were thousands of Finns in our city, he felt a burden to reach them for the Lord. So I launched into it. It was difficult! After a few days I had toast and tea after school. We knocked on doors and delivered a Finnish Christmas magazine to Finns during that fasting week, having found their addresses in the phone book. We were seeking an opportunity to share the gospel and minister to them. I don't remember if I actually finished the fast.

Some years went by. I married, and my husband and I moved to Prince George, BC. The Lord led us to a church where the pastor fasted faithfully on Wednesdays. Again, it inspired and challenged me and I began to do that on a regular basis. Later I added Fridays as well. I found these fasts helped me to stay alert for God's voice and alert in my Christian life.

You haven't even fasted about this yet!

I knew of people who had done longer fasts, but I had never done one until during a time of earnest prayer, I heard God say, "You haven't even fasted about this yet!" In Chapter 13 I wrote how He called me to a 3-week fast, which had long-term, unfolding repercussions and writing this book is one of them. Though I wondered if I could do it, He gave me grace, and amazing answers continued to unfold over the years.

Saddam Hussein's scud missiles

In 1991, Saddam Hussein threatened to launch scud missiles into Israel from Iraq. It was a time of great anxiety and fear. My husband's two sisters and their families live in Israel, so because of this ominous threat, we feared for their lives and for Israel as a whole. We had carried Israel in our hearts and prayers for many years. We kept in touch with our family through this life-threatening time. Everyone in Israel was ordered to seal off one room in their homes and to pick up gas masks. They knew Saddam was good for chemical warfare.

Tuomo and I both fasted for five days. The day came when 35 of these big, long-range scuds were launched into the cities and towns of this small nation. That was before the Iron Dome.

When all was said and done, not one person perished from the missiles. A few senior people died, most likely from stress. There was some damage to buildings but no people perished from actual missile hits. Once more God covered His chosen people under the shadow of His wings.

We were not the only ones fasting and praying, but we played a part in it. Five years later I traveled to Israel. My sister-in-law showed me the place where a scud had landed in a park, about 200 meters from their home. It missed all the numerous apartment buildings in that heavily populated area. How carefully God directed the missile, making it all the more evident that He was taking care of them! The danger was close, but did not touch them.

> He will cover you with his pinions, and under His wings
> you may seek refuge; His faithfulness is a shield and
> bulwark. **You will not be afraid** of the terror by night, or
> **of the arrow that flies by day (missiles)**…for He will
> give His angels charge concerning you, to guard you in all
> your ways. Ps. 91:4-5, 11

Dream about 9/11, Manhattan, NY

In the summer of 2001, I felt God call me to a fast. There was a sense of urgency about it. I had read in emails about a 40 day global fast for Israel, and so I joined in, eating only one meal a day in the evenings.

On September 1 of that year, I woke up to a strange dream that I was on the bridge in Manhattan, New York, and the skyline of tall buildings was in my sights. I was walking with a friend who was pushing a large hotel vacuum cleaner across the bridge. Then she pushed it up the side of a tall building (you know how dreams can be so strange at times). Suddenly the grey vacuum cleaner dust broke out of the vacuum and floated horizontally across the sky like a cloud. End of dream.

I was puzzled. I knew the dream meant something, but what? I shared it with my friend, who was the executive secretary of our church, because she was the one in the dream.

The following week, on September 11, 2001, the pastors of our city were at Ness Lake Bible Camp gathered for our annual ministerial prayer retreat. As we began our time, one of the pastors arrived from town and told us the shocking news of two planes crashing into the Twin Towers in New York! We got on our knees to pray.

Our church called an emergency prayer meeting for that evening. Before the meeting, I had a chance to watch some of the news clips and was shocked when I saw smoke pour out of the Twin Towers—shocked because it was just like the gray vacuum dust floating away from the side of the building in my dream. *This* was what God had shown me!

I don't know the results of the corporate global fast for Israel but I know that radical Muslims hate both Israel and the United States, at times burning flags of both nations. I have learned to trust that when we respond to a call to fast, God's Kingdom purposes are advanced.

In Revelation 5:8 it speaks of 24 elders falling down before the Lamb, each holding a harp and golden bowls full of incense, which are the prayers of the saints. Revelation 8:3–5 talks about an angel who was given much incense to add to the prayers on the golden altar. The smoke of the incense along with the prayers went up before God out of the angel's hand. Then the angel took the censer and filled it with fire from the altar, and threw it to the earth, resulting in peals of thunder, sounds, flashes of lightning, and an earthquake—and the trumpet judgments began. God keeps our prayers in a bowl *and adds incense to them* and then releases His purposes. Our prayers are required. Heaven adds the greater part. Heaven and earth work together—the bridegroom and the bride, side-by-side.

I believe the fast positioned me to receive this dream. God let me know what was going to take place, though I only understood it when it was happening. He doesn't always tell us to do something about it, but lets us know ahead of time, so we know that He is in control even in these shaking events. We are His friends, and He discloses His secrets to His friends (John 16:13-15, Amos 3:7)

Not long before 9/11, Habakkuk 1:5 had come up 4 times at our intercessory prayer meeting. Several in the group had gotten that scripture and it came up in a video we watched that day:

> *Look among the nations! Observe! Be astonished! Wonder!*
> *Because I am doing something in your days – you would*
> *not believe if you were told. Hab.1:5 nasb*

I have learned to pay attention when the same word comes out of the mouths of 2, 3, and 4. The scriptures say that by 2 or 3 witness a matter is established. It becomes something to press in and pray about seriously.

Out of context, Habakkuk 1:5 sounds exciting. But if you read the context, it is warning Judah that God was sending a "fierce and impetuous people", a dreadful army of Chaldeans, to march through the earth and seize captives, houses and lands. What especially caught my attention after 9/11 happened, were these verses from chapter one:

> *They **fly** like an eagle **swooping down to devour**...All*
> *of them **come for violence**...They mock at kings, and*
> *rulers are a laughing matter to them. **They laugh at***
> ***every fortress and heap up rubble** to capture it. Then*

*they will **sweep through** like the wind and pass on.*
Hab.1:8-11 nasb

The words in the verses matched precisely with what happened: the planes "flew", "sweeping" in to destroy. They were all coming for "violence", to turn these "fortresses" into "rubble". They "swept" through the buildings and "passed on". Many passed away: innocent hostages on those planes, close to three thousand in the buildings, and the terrorist attackers. It was a tragedy of horrific proportions.

This scripture and the dream, where I was walking in Manhattan on the bridge and saw what later I realized was the smoke pouring out of the Twin Towers, were highlighted to us *before* 9/11. When it all unfolded, we realized God prepared us so that we knew this was not a surprise to Him. Somehow God was in the middle of it and was going to work out His purposes through it. He said He will shake everything that can be shaken before He returns. (Hebrews 12:26-27).

Chapter Forty-Seven

Other Types of Prayer–Peace in a Tragedy

Supplication

Supplication is urgent praying where we flee to God in desperation, needing a breakthrough and inner peace. Supplication is *earnest* praying, more than just praying. If we battle with anxiety over any situation, God has given us the perfect verses:

> *Be anxious about nothing, but in everything with **prayer** and **supplication** with **thanksgiving**, let your requests be made known to God. And the **peace of God which surpasses all comprehension**, will guard your hearts and minds in Christ Jesus. Philippians 4:6 & 7 nasb*

Peace in a tragedy

When we received a call from our son, at 5:30 one morning, that our grandson had taken his life, a flood of emotions walloped us like a tsunami and rolled us around mercilessly in its force. I jumped up to dress but my husband pulled me back to bed and said we are going to pray first. We raised desperate, disorderly, jumbled prayers to God—cries for help. Then we raced out the door to make the 45 minute drive to their home. Tuomo drove while I called our pastor, our family, and intercessors, waking them up to pray. It felt like I was surfacing and gulping for air while being tossed around in this tsunami. We needed God's peace to be able to stand alongside our son's family through this horrific tragedy.

Our grandkids met us at the door. We embraced and clung to each other. The police were talking with our son and daughter-in-law, coroners were doing their work, and a family services counselor stood by unobtrusively, ready to offer support as needed. After some time, they all left and it was just our family together.

As we sat, an incredible peace flooded me. I marveled. It was tangible. It was incomprehensible. It was not logical. It was supernatural. It was from heaven.

God was there! He came to help us in this tragic, horrific moment, faithfully keeping His promise to never leave us nor forsake us, and to give us peace. I think of the verse in Isaiah 60:2 where it says when there is darkness, God's glory comes. That is what it felt like.

> For behold, **darkness will cover** the earth and **deep**
> **darkness the peoples**; but the Lord will rise upon you
> and **His glory will appear upon you**. nasb

There were still many tearful, difficult days, but that initial miraculous peace gave confidence of His ongoing nearness as we walked through this grief. And He did carry us through. God has promised that:

> Light arises in the darkness for the upright.
> Psalm 112:4 nasb

Whenever a circumstance starts getting too "dark", I try to remember these verses and ask God for His glory and light to appear in that situation.

I can join David in my praise and thanksgiving to God for hearing our desperate supplication:

> Blessed be the Lord, because He has heard the voice of
> my supplication.
> The Lord is my strength and my shield; and **I am helped**.
> Therefore my heart exults and with my song I shall thank
> Him. Psalm 28:6&7 nasb

I love the Lord, because He hears my voice and my supplications.
Because He has inclined His ear to me,
Therefore I shall call upon Him as long as I live.
Psalm 116:1&2 nasb

Fire!

Something was not right! My eyes hadn't opened yet, but I could sense too much light in my bedroom. I snapped them open. I could hear a crackling noise that shouldn't be happening, and the room had an eerie, pink glow. *Fire!!* I leapt out of bed to look through the window shades. Our outside sauna was in full flame, just feet away from our patio roof overhang. The flames were already starting on the detached garage behind the sauna and leaping up the weeping birch tree that stood beside these outbuildings. *If that tree falls on the house, the house will be on fire!* Tuomo was out-of-town on a business trip on that fiercely cold winter night. As I raced to the phone, I yelled upstairs to wake Keziah, who was the only kid still living at home. I called 9-1-1. We rushed to move our cars out of the way to facilitate the fire crews. In the ten minutes we waited for them to arrive, the flames advanced, leaping 12 feet above the roof. It was spectacular, but fearful. I feared the neighbors shed might catch fire, and then their house. Fire trucks from two fire halls rolled in with lights blazing, turning the neighborhood into an eerie, flashing-red scene, like something from the movies. They arrived at 4:30 am, and worked until 7 am to make sure the fire was out. A few crew members continued to monitor it until the fire inspector came later in the morning.

As dawn was breaking, I looked at the smoldering, black ruins of the sauna, the partly burned garage, and weeping birch. It looked like a war zone. Adding the bitter cold to this mixture, and the initial conclusion of the deputy fire chief—that a spark from the sauna had most likely started it—caused a heavy gloom to settle on me. *It can't be a spark!* It had been several days since we had last used the sauna and there had been a good dose of minus 20 weather in the nights since then.

Later that morning the fire chief and another firefighter did a proper investigation to determine the cause. I looked out the kitchen window and was surprised at what I saw! Instead of the bleak, black mess, tiny ice particles were falling from the sky. The sun was shining at such an angle that the ice particles looked like a veil of gold dust covering the blackened wasteland. I could only make out the shadows of the men through this glittering veil. It was beautiful. Not only that, I felt God's voice speak that His glory was going to cover this darkness. It did, in more ways than one.

This was an attack from the enemy, as we were involved in much prayer for breakthrough and revival for our city and nation at Prince George House of Prayer. The glory? Unity in our ministerial grew during those years and we had many city wide worship and prayer events together as churches. Also, our insurance covered everything very well and we actually came ahead through this set back. And…it was determined it was not a spark that caused the fire, but arson. It had been lit. Glory did appear!

Look for the glory. It will appear.

I have often done what David did in Psalm 18, which is one of my favorite Psalms. In it he cries out to God in desperation because his enemies were too big for him. *David's enemies too big for him?? David*, who single-handedly and fearlessly downed Goliath (with God's help)! *That David* cried out saying his enemies were too big for him?! Find out the rest of the story in the chapter on Spiritual Warfare and one of my best stories about supplication is in that chapter as well.

Compassionate praying

This is when we are moved in our hearts about a certain situation, often accompanied by tears. I believe we are very effective when God moves our hearts. It says about Jesus, that He was moved with compassion for the multitudes, and healed the sick.

However, we need to know the difference between the compassion of the Holy Spirit working through us, and human compassion. Some are naturally compassionate in their personalities, easily in tears—even unbelievers. That is different from God's compassion. Human compassion is from the soul and can lead us to make ungodly judgments about matters, even protecting someone from God's dealings without us realizing it. Knowing God's word helps us to pierce and divide between the soul and the spirit (Heb. 4:12).

Talking with Jesus

Having a conversation or dialogue with Jesus is a form of prayer. I remember hearing a story about a woman who was having a hard time praying. Finally she pictured Jesus coming for a visit, sitting down in a chair across from her. She even poured a cup of coffee for Him and one for her. Her prayer life unlocked into a freedom she hadn't experienced before.

This story helped me as there have been times I have tried to figure out how to pray about something. Then I thought I will talk it out with Jesus as a friend, like this woman did. One time poised this way, before barely finishing a sentence, God's presence came so tangibly it brought me to tears.

Thanksgiving

From time to time I journal my thanks to the Lord. I look back at all the answers to prayer and blessings He has given over the last while. Instead of asking and interceding, I give Him thanks. As a result, His Spirit lifts me up because He inhabits the praises of His people (Ps. 22:3).

Jesus healed ten lepers and told them to go show themselves to the priests to be declared cleansed, according to the instructions of God's law. Only one leper returned to give thanks to Jesus. He fell at His feet, loudly glorifying God.

> *And as they were going they were cleansed. Now one of them, when he saw that he had been healed, turned back, glorifying God with a loud voice, and **he fell on his face at his feet, giving thanks to Him.** Luke 17:14-16 nasb*

Do I remember to say "thank you" enough? He is always at work, though we don't see Him working. One pastor said, "God takes our garbage out when we don't even realize it." Wow! Children do not appreciate all that parents do in raising them, but when they mature and become parents, and have these responsibilities (like taking the garbage out), they begin to appreciate more and more what their parents went through to raise them. Likewise, as we mature spiritually, we become more aware of all that Jesus is doing behind the scenes. We become more thankful rather than always seeking to have *our* needs met, like babies who are self-focused.

It moves my heart in sorrow when I read about how God feels when the people He lovingly raised and cared for, reject Him and go their own way.

When Israel was a youth I loved him, and out of Egypt I
called my son.
The more they (the prophets) called them, The more they
went from them;
They kept sacrificing to the Baals and burning
incense to idols.
Yet it is I who taught Ephraim to walk, I took them
in my arms;
But they did not know that I healed them.
I led them with the cords of a man, with bonds of love, And
I became to them as one who lifts the yoke from their jaws;
And I bent down and fed them. Hosea 11:1-4 nasb

...doesn't that sound like parents who have done the same for their children, and in spite of this, the children are unappreciative, ungrateful and reject them? God feels the pain, just like human parents do. (Praise God that many children are not like this, but it does happen often).

It is good to say 'thank you' often because we live and move and have our very being because God has granted it. Behind the scenes, it is by His power that we exist. Our very breath is a gift from him.

Praying in tongues

Jude 20 says praying in tongues builds our faith, so it is good to do this on a regular basis. Also, when I don't know how to pray about something in English, I pray in tongues because I know I am praying the will of God when I pray in my heavenly language (Rom. 8:26-27)

Sometimes in our prayer group we switch into tongues together. As intercessors we know that God is doing something powerful as we corporately pray this way. Then after a while, we begin to pray in English—boldly declaring words of faith from the Lord regarding the situation we are praying for. I believe those English prayers are often the interpretation of what we prayed in tongues.

The power of sighs and groans when we don't have words

Don't think you are not praying when you don't have eloquent words. True prayer is not beautiful words but a spirit connection where our spirit engages with God. (Rom. 8:26 nasb)

God sent execution angels to destroy the wicked people of Jerusalem. These people had been given a lot of time to repent from their wickedness, but they refused, so now time was up. However, God first ordered an angel with a writing case to mark all the people on the forehead who had '**sighed and groaned**' about the 'abominations' (atrocities) being committed, to be spared. Then the execution angels were to deal with the wicked with no pity. This is a moving story. God hears our wordless groans and sighs and records them. The names of these ones were recorded, so we know ours are too, if we have done the same. (Ez. 9)

Waiting on the Lord

Earlier I wrote about the pastor's wife who came to our prayer group for the first time. It was the day I felt we were to wait on God in silence for an hour. I worried through that time, thinking she would not want to come back. However, the very opposite happened. God *met* her during that hour—it was her moment with God. She became a powerful intercessor.

Often we do not wait. God is forming a bride who waits on Him until she hears *His* heart to do *His* will. We often, individually and corporately, get tired of waiting, and build golden calves instead, creating our own 'good' plans of ministry and action rather than 'doing what the Father is doing'. Jesus did not rush about doing a lot of 'good' things. He only did

His Father's will which He heard from Him during times of prayer, often rising up early in the morning and at times praying through the night

Truly, truly, I say to you, the Son can do nothing of
Himself, unless it is something He sees the Father doing;
for whatever the Father does, these things the Son also
does in like manner. John 5:19 nasb

The children of Israel got tired of waiting for Moses, and for God, who were up on Mount Sinai. They built a golden calf instead, and worshiped it with dreadful results. (Exodus 32)

Lord, help us to keep waiting for You—to be led by You, to hear Your voice and do Your will. It says of Jesus in Isaiah:

The Lord God has given Me the tongue of disciples, that I
may know how to sustain the weary one with a word. He
awakens Me morning by morning, He awakens My ear to
listen as a disciple. Isaiah 50:4 nasb

Jesus modeled for us what we also need to do. As we take time to wait on God and listen as a disciple, He will also give us the tongue of disciples to be able to encourage and refresh weary ones with a word from God.

God is forming a bride who knows how to sit expectantly before Him. Worship music is very helpful for waiting on God. Also being surrounded by God's creation is conducive to hearing from Him. Reading the Bible is another way if we stop to wait for the Holy Spirit to speak, and then write down those revelations so we don't forget. I've been encouraged years later by reading through my journals about the things God has spoken to me.

You may have other ways to wait. Whatever works for you, keep doing.

Some feel waiting is wasting time. It is actually the opposite. All the things we accomplish, the good ideas that come without intimate connection with God, are for nothing and will burn. Only the things that are born from that place of encounter with Him will last and be rewarded. (1 Cor. 3:12-15)

There are other promises and benefits of waiting on God:

1. God is good to them.
   The Lord is good to those who wait for him, to the person who seeks him. Lamentations 3:25 nasb

2. He saves them from difficult situations.
   It is good that he waits silently for the salvation of the Lord. Lamentations 3:26 nasb

3. He favors them.
   The Lord favors those who fear him, those who wait for His lovingkindness. Psalm 147:11 nasb

4. He acts on behalf of them.
   Nor has the eye seen a God besides you, who acts on behalf of the one who waits for him. Isaiah 64:4 nasb

5. Our strength is renewed.
   *Yet those who wait for the Lord will **gain new strength**; they will mount up with wings like eagles. They will run and not get tired, they will walk and not become weary. Isaiah 40:31 nasb*

6. He blesses and gives direction
   Blessed are those who wait for him…your ears shall hear a word behind you, saying, "This is the way, walk in it." Isaiah 30:18, 21 esv

7. He listens to our cry and answers
   Blessed are those who wait for him…He will surely be gracious to you at the sound of your cry. As soon as He hears it, He answers you. Isaiah 30:18, 19 esv

8. He is gracious to us, will have compassion on us, and give us justice.
   Therefore the Lord waits to be gracious to you...to show
   mercy to you. For the Lord is a God is justice; blessed are
   all those who wait for Him. Isaiah 30:18 esv

Last but not least, we have seen this fulfilled in our lives:

9. We inherit the land.
   Rest in the Lord and wait patiently (longingly) for Him...
   those who wait for the Lord, they will inherit the land.
   Psalm 37:7-9 nasb

I waited three days for the Lord to speak to me, being tempted to renege on the call to ministry because I felt disqualified. At the end of day three a phone call came from a prophet living in another country who'd had a dream about me. It confirmed my call. God acts on behalf of those who wait for Him.

One preacher talked about how much we *WAIT* in life—at the doctor's office, the dentist office, the bus, for our parents to come and get us. It is the same with God. Take time to wait for God. It is simple. He went on to say, that if you do, in an hour or less you will be in the spirit. When Jesus told the disciples to wait—that was simple—they just waited and the Holy Spirit came. They didn't shout, stress, or press. They waited!

Praying with faith to sell my granddaughter's and my books

An idea began to take shape while I was driving. I often pray for creative things to do with my grandkids, things that "click" with their personalities and motivational gifting. God's ideas are the best! I was on the road when this idea came.

Savannah was coming to spend a weekend with us soon. As I drove, I remembered an announcement about a craft fair being hosted at our church. *Maybe we could sell our books there. Writing is our craft.* I had written three books, and Savannah, who was 13 years old, had written two. I had missed the deadline for registering for a table, being out-of-town.

The idea persisted so I called and we were able to get a table, late as we were. God was helping.

A visiting preacher made a statement in his message, saying *God will work for us when we move forward in faith.* He was speaking about Jonathan and his armor bearer when they climbed up a steep incline to confront their enemies above them, Jonathan said "God will work for us". He had gotten a sense from God to do this risky thing, and they moved forward in faith and were successful.

God had given this idea, so I asked Him to work for us as we were stepping forward in faith, asking Him to give us favor and make this time successful, that we would do well in sales. I told Savannah what God had spoken to me. She was all in and we prayed together with Grandpa joining in.

When we tallied our sales at the end of the day, we had sold over $400 of books. Praise the Lord!

When the three of us were driving to church the next morning, I recounted how God had unfolded this plan, moving it forward with blessing as we stepped into it in faith. It was time to give thanks to God, which we did, and not be like the nine lepers who didn't.

When you have taken time to wait on God, having an ear of a disciple to listen for His instructions, then you can pray in faith because you know what He spoke will come to pass. Sometimes immediately, other times with persevering prayer over time.

> *Therefore I say to you, all things for which you pray and ask, believe that you have received them, and they will be granted you. Mark 11:24 nasb*

> *This is the confidence which we have before Him, that, if we ask anything according to His will, He hears us. And if we know that He hears us in whatever we ask, we know that we have the requests which we have asked from Him.*
> *1 John 5:14, 15 nasb*

If God *didn't* speak it to you, it will *not* happen:

> *Who is there who speaks and it comes to pass, __unless__ the*
> **Lord has commanded it?** *Lamentations 3:37 nasb*

...but *if* He has spoken it to you, when you pray it, it will happen:

> *If you abide in Me, and My words abide in you, **ask***
> ***whatever you wish**, and it will be done for you.*
> *John 15:7 nasb*

Praying in agreement

> *If two of you agree on earth about anything that they*
> *may ask, it shall be done for them by my Father in heaven.*
> *Matthew 18:19 nasb*

God meant for husbands and wives to pray together. They are a prayer cluster of two as Matthew 18:19 describes. The enemy seriously fights marriages to prevent us from moving into this calling of prayer. If you are married, pray that you not only have a good marriage, but that you become a prayer cluster of two, praying the purposes on God's heart into being.

If you are not married, ask God to give you a prayer partner to pray with.

Remember the two ailing, elderly sisters in Hebrides, Scotland, who prayed together non-stop and a great revival broke out. I know two senior ladies who recently did the same. They began to pray faithfully for the mobile home court one of them lived in, praying for each family every week. Within a year, after resisting the gospel, the manager of the trailer court accepted Jesus as his savior and was burdened that his adult children also come to know the Lord.

My friend was deeply troubled because of a family member who was suicidal, so we prayed in agreement. She was set free.

Fasting added to prayer

If you are wondering if fasting is necessary, Jesus said, "Whenever you fast…" (Matt. 6:16 nasb). He didn't say, "If you fast", but rather, "when you fast." It is a part of our walk with the Lord. Some breakthroughs do not happen without fasting added to our prayers:

> And when He had come into the house, His disciples asked
> Him privately, "Why could we not cast it out? So He said
> to them, "This kind can come out by nothing but prayer
> and fasting." Mark 9:28, 29 nkjv

Praying the scriptures to overcome my many fears

When I was in my early 20's, I struggled a lot with fear: fear of speaking to people, fear of answering the phone, even. I struggled with belonging, fearing I would be rejected, where do I fit? I recall a preacher saying that whatever you are going through, there is a scripture in the Bible to match it. Find that scripture and pray it. War with it. I found some scriptures which I memorized and began to declare:

> For God has not given us a spirit of fear,
> but of power and of love and of a sound mind.
> 2 Tim. 1:7 nkjv

> The LORD is for me; I will not fear; what can man do to
> me? Ps. 118:6 nasb

> The Lord is my light and my salvation; whom shall I fear?
> The Lord is the defense of my life; whom shall I dread?
> Psalm 27:1 nasb

I often prayed this throughout our dark night of the soul years:

> I would have despaired unless I had believed that I would
> see the goodness of the Lord in the land of the living. Wait

for the Lord; be strong and let your heart take courage; yes,
wait for the Lord. Psalm 27:13-14

Truly, we have seen the goodness of the Lord in the land of the living, though it took many years of trusting Him and holding onto this promise.

The Scriptures tell how things will unfold at the end of the age—we can pray in agreement with His word

In the Bible God reveals to us what is going to happen to Israel, the nations, for believers, and unbelievers. As we read His prophecies, we can pray for those things to happen. He wants His bride to pray in agreement with His plans.

For example, even though the Middle East seems to be endlessly unresolvable and volatile, the Bible tells us in Isaiah 19:24-25, that one day Israel, Egypt, and Assyria (modern Syria, Iraq, Jordan, and Iran) will together be a blessing on the earth. No matter how impossible that seems, that will happen because God said so. I often pray that scripture, thanking God for His promise to fulfill it.

He is a covenant-keeping God and remembers His promises. He hears and answers our prayers for their fulfillment. In Isaiah 62, He tells us to *remind Him* and *give Him no rest* until He makes Jerusalem a praise in the earth. Mind boggling. Just do it!

God cares about the individual in the middle of national shakings

God gave a prophetic word to a person who most might not pay attention to. In the middle of all the judgment prophecies that God spoke to Israel and the surrounding nations, He inserted a personal word for Baruch, the scribe who was writing out all the prophecies. In Jeremiah chapter 45, it appears Baruch was overwhelmed with the coming judgments. He cared about and believed God's prophetic words, while most didn't. Most mocked Jeremiah and his words, believing the false prophets instead. God went out of His way to speak to Baruch, promising that He will keep him alive through all these shakings.

He cares about the individual in the middle of national and international upheavals. If He bent down to encourage Baruch, He will do the same for you and me, no matter what shakings and judgments hit the earth—if we are ones who care about God's purposes. We can pray this scripture back to Him, asking for a personal word also, to strengthen us that no matter what shakings come, we can walk confidently. He has promised to *strongly* support the one whose heart is completely His (2 Chron. 16:9).

We find hidden treasures tucked away when we faithfully read the Bible through and through. Words that bring us hope. Words that we can turn into prayer for ourselves and for others.

Prayers Jesus prayed

There are many prayers in the Bible that Jesus and the apostles prayed, which we also can pray.

Most everyone knows the Lord's Prayer from Matthew 6, a prayer that Jesus taught His disciples and which is prayed all over the world. The entire chapter of John 17 is also a prayer Jesus prayed, and one we can pray. Also, He told us to pray for workers for the harvest fields (Matt. 9:38)

Regarding global shakings just before He returns, He said to pray this way:

> *But keep on the alert at all times,*
> ***praying that you may have***
> ***strength to escape all these things*** *that are*
> *about to take place,*
> *and to stand before the Son of Man. Luke 21:36 nasb*

Praying the Word back to God, rather than praying the problem

We can be confident that we are praying the will of God when we pray the Bible. It also helps remember God's word more, and helps us understand more clearly His plans for us and the nations. When we pray the word back to God, revelation increases.

We can thank Him for what He is saying in that particular chapter or verse, and ask Him to reveal more of the meaning. As more revelation comes, we can turn it into a prayer, praying for ourselves and for others to walk in whatever God is saying in that passage. So often we pray the problem rather than the word of God for the situation. However, if we meditate on the word and pray it, we become like a tree firmly planted by streams of water, yielding fruit, and having green leaves that don't wither, and whatever we do, prospers (Psalm 1). This will not happen overnight, but if we stick with it, when we look back we will see how much God has blessed us.

Chapter Forty-Eight:

Spiritual Warfare: Six Police Cars and an Ambulance Rescued my Stolen Purse

How many times has something very intense happened before a breakthrough? It is normal. There is a birth, death, and fulfillment of a vision that takes place. God gives a vision for something and we begin to pray for it. Then warfare hits and it becomes a great challenge to keep pressing through against all odds. There is a point of actual death because the battle is too great and we can't go on. In faith we lay it out before God: *If You called me this, then You, Lord, can make this happen. It is only by Your doing it will be accomplished.* As we do this, and having done all we keep standing, God does His part. Something finally breaks open, sometimes softly at first, but the gentle winds begin to blow again, the music begins to play, and we move into the fulfillment of what He showed us and called us to do.

Help! My enemies are too big for me!

There have been times when I felt my enemies were too big for me. I knew I was done. I thought all the Bible heroes never wavered. They were men and women of great faith that I could not measure up to...until I read the Bible more. *David said* his enemies were too big for him?! Yes, I saw it in Psalm 18. *David* who slew Goliath as a young teenaged boy? At this later date, he was at the end of his rope, about to perish. *He* was terrified and distressed and cried out to God? Yes, David.

I LOVE God's response. Ha haa! He shook the foundations of the earth because He was angry. Smoke came out of His nostrils! Fire from His mouth. He hurled hailstones and coals of fire. Riding on a cherubim and clothed in dark clouds, He thundered in the heavens with His voice and released lightning flashes in abundance, routing the enemies of David. Yaaaah!!! One of the names of God is *Yah*, meaning the most vehement one (Strong's Exhaustive Concordance 3050). It is the warrior name of God. I love that Psalm. When I was cornered like this, or someone I had been praying for was cornered like David, I dove into praying Psalm 18 back to God. He responded.

I don't know what else to do!

Something I had fasted and prayed for many years, covering it from every angle I could think of, only grew worse. Finally, in desperation I said to God, "I don't know what else to do. My enemies are too big for me. You need to come and fight for me like you did for David in Psalm 18!" A week later a prophet visited our church. He walked to Tuomo and me, and described the situation we had been fervently praying about— in precise detail. He declared the purpose of God over that situation and warred against the spirits that were involved. He said this year we would see breakthrough. I went home and transcribed these words that were audio recorded into my journal. Tuomo and I prayed these words over and over, and I did some more targeted fasting. Within 4 months this situation began to shatter. Through this prophet we received new ammunition. By writing out the prophetic word and decreeing the things the Lord had said, we stood in agreement with Him. Within a few months this stronghold crumbled, and breakthrough came. It was a miracle. Paul told Timothy to war with the words spoken over him. We need to do the same.

Timothy, my son, in accordance with the prophecies
previously made concerning you, that by them you fight
the good fight. I Timothy 1:18 nasb

The battle before the breakthrough

When God calls into long-term ministry, there are usually long-term trials and heavy warfare to try to get us off track from fulfilling God's plan. The enemy always tries to abort the purpose of God.

There are short term assignments too, and the same takes place in one form or another. At times I find myself drained, unable to properly think to get normal daily tasks done. It feels like I am trudging through sludge. I can't seem to focus and it is difficult to press through. I feel anxiety and irritation. Prayer doesn't flow easily. Then suddenly there is a divine reversal.

One time I felt like every normal enjoyment of life was sucked from me.

It was a Sunday afternoon and I had lunch to prepare and serve, followed by a family bike ride. I felt like a robot, functioning mechanically. Later, though I had no desire to go to church that evening, I got everyone ready and we went because that was what we always did. I *loved* going to church so this was not normal. Every step seemed like a ponderous effort. Suddenly during preaching, the power of God hit me and a strong prophetic anointing fell on me. When the preaching ended, I shouted out a confirming prophetic word. Our church moved into establishing a Christian School, which was the topic of the message, and it was a sustained ministry for 25 years.

We walk in works that God has foreordained, and to walk out these assignments, there is a battle to press through. The enemy always tries to hinder what God desires to release on earth.

When breakthrough takes place, there is a divine reversal and I feel normal again, in fact, energized. The tasks that took three days to accomplish during the spiritual battle, I can now accomplish in a day. *I get it now: the last three days I was in warfare. That's why I felt like I was plodding in sludge!*

Death in us works life for others and when life comes forth, we have joy. We give birth to something through the battle. It may not be a prophetic word. It is whatever assignment God has for you to fulfill. If you press through and don't draw back, God will use you to bring life.

My stolen purse got half a dozen police and an ambulance involved

It seems the devil sends the same demon(s) to harass on similar assignments. My purse was stolen both times before I went on trips to Israel to the All Nations Convocations. *At church!!*

The first time I was at a table in the church foyer signing up people for something after the service. There was a raised plant shelf immediately behind me where I placed my purse. After everyone left and I put everything away, I went to retrieve my purse. It was *gone*. When I told my family, Ben, my son said, "Now I get it! I saw a man pick up a coat from behind you. I think he dropped his coat onto your purse and picked up his coat with the purse." This took place a foot or so behind my back, unbeknownst to me.

We had one clue. Ben knew what the man looked like.

We called the police but they were reluctant to act because purse snatchings are common and rarely recovered. Thus my husband and son became a vigilante team. I called the credit card company to freeze my card. They informed me it had already been used at a convenience store to purchase a case of cigarettes. Upon getting the address of the store, my vigilantes rushed to that location to question the cashier about this person. As they were talking, the very man Ben had seen taking my purse came in to get a refund for empty bottles. My husband walked up to him, saying, "Hi, how are you? Did you enjoy church this morning?" He was a little puzzled and said, "Yes". Then Tuomo said, "I'm sure you did, since you stole my wife's purse. I want it back." He rudely protested and tried to walk away, but Tuomo grabbed his arm saying, "You are under citizen's arrest!" The thief retorted, "Get your hand off me or I'll break your arm!" "Okay, let's see about that," was my husband's response. The cornered thief sized up my husband and realized he was dealing with a bigger man than himself. He complied, saying the purse was at his place.

They walked some blocks to his house and then Ben went back to get the car and call the police (this was before cell phones, so he had to go to a phone). After completing the call, Ben drove to the house. He saw several police cars had arrived. Suddenly more police cars roared in as well as an ambulance, with siren blaring. Ben was alarmed because he could not see his dad. *What had happened?! Where was he? Was he okay?* To his relief, he saw Tuomo appear from behind a corner with a water hose.

Before the police arrived, the thief had gone into the house and locked the door, refusing to co-operate with Tuomo. Two police arrived and demanded to be let in. No response, so one of them began to kick the door in. A woman opened the door. At that moment, the officer accidentally dropped his pepper spray and shouted to the other officer to grab it quickly before the thief does. The thief immediately leapt forward, grabbed it and sprayed him. In agony, the officer backed out of the house. The other officer called for help and numerous police cars raced to the scene. Tuomo managed to find a water hose to help ease the officer's pain before the ambulance arrived.

Everything was recovered and the credit card company reversed what had been charged by the thief. Although the police had been unwilling to help, my purse theft ended up having six police cars and an ambulance involved. God was thorough in taking care it.

Resistance and breakthrough

Three times when I attended Ears2Hear Summits of Canadian prophetic intercessors, I had much warfare. Twice I had to drive in heavy snow; once behind semi-trucks that sprayed muddy snow on my windshield. I had no window washer fluid left to wash it away. The highway was terribly rutted with compacted snow and slush, so I could not pull to the side because the shoulders were snowed over. There was no choice but to keep going. I called on God to help guide me as I could barely see through the windshield. Another time an unbearable tooth ache assaulted me the day before I was to fly out. I had the tooth removed the next day just hours before my flight to Ottawa. Then my glasses broke in one of the airports along the way.

At these gatherings we did prophetically-led, targeted corporate warfare prayer, which the enemy hates because it greatly advances God's kingdom and hinders his. *Prophetically-led* means we prayed what God was saying to pray. We had heard from Him. It is often during these times, when there is an open heaven and God pours out prophetic vision with great clarity, that there is preceding tremendous resistance from the enemy.

Corporate worship, warfare and prayer

I love to participate in conferences and prayer gatherings where we worship and war in the spirit, targeting specific focuses God has highlighted, led by those who understand wisely the sphere of authority we have. When a company of apostolic and prophetic leaders, together with prophetic intercessors, war this way, the enemy's power is broken, and God's kingdom advances. I believe in the power of united prayer. One chases a thousand and two, ten thousand. It is exponentially multiplied.

I have attended many of these kinds of conferences and gatherings in Canada, Israel, and the United States, ranging in size from 20 to 3,000 people. These are not just times where there has been anointed preaching and teaching, but also where we have joined together in strong, united, warfare worship and prayer. I love teaching and preaching. However, it goes to another level when a company of people, after being strengthened in faith through preaching and teaching, rises to war and pray together in faith.

At one conference we prayed with unrelenting focus for North Korea. At another, we prayed for the nations of our world. Each nation was presented and prayed for, one after the other during a 10 day conference. We have prayed for Israel at critical junctures in their modern history. Also in numerous gatherings we have prayed for Canada (my nation) in many major cities across our land.

My cry, along with countless others, is for a global, great awakening to come, for the Joel 2, Acts 2 outpouring of the spirit on *all flesh*, for a mighty harvest of souls, for hearts to turn to the Lord, for prodigals to return, and for the promised great awakening in Israel, as well. Where two or three are gathered, the Lord has promised to be in their midst, and whatever two agree, touching anything on earth, will be done by the Father. When we pray according to His will, He answers.

God's appointed time

Though some nations of the world are experiencing a great harvest, some prayers have not been answered yet. Neither have all the prophetic words regarding Jesus, Israel, and the nations been fulfilled yet, though most have. God has an appointed time. He calls for his bride to work alongside Him in the ministry of intercession to bring it about. The Spirit intercedes through us with groans too deep for words. The golden bowls of prayer are filling up. Every prayer we pray in solitude, or in gatherings of a few or thousands, adds up to filling these bowls. When they are full, God acts.

Confirming signs

God often gives signs after these kinds of gatherings. One time after a gathering in Edmonton, as two of us were travelling home, we stopped to watch a phenomena at a lake. A strange cloud hovered low over part of it. It was not a morning mist because it was later in the day and the sun was shining. It was not smoke. What was it? It was a picture of the glory of God.

Another time crowds had stopped at another lake along the highway. People were walking in the water, many of them almost across the lake, and still only ankle deep. It was strange—it looked like they were walking *on* water. The lake bottom was only a few inches below the water level, giving this illusion. Though there was a scientific explanation, there was a sense of God's presence declaring, "I will do unusual things". It was a wonder. Something that made you wonder.

There have been signs in the sky, like the eclipse of the moon, a comet, and northern lights, all three together, after a 40 day fast.

God gives these signs to confirm our prayers have been heard in heaven and He is faithful to watch over His word to perform it—even though it might not happen in the time frame we are expecting. Just like with Abraham and Sarah, it took 25 years for God's promise of a son to be fulfilled. God takes His time. His promises to Abraham and His promises spoken through all the prophets about the nation of Israel are not completely fulfilled yet. But they will be.

We can pray for His end time plan of a great outpouring of the Holy Spirit, and of glory in the midst of darkness

It is good to know the word of God, to read it a lot because then we can know what He is planning to do. The world is shaking and people who do not know Jesus are fearful of the future. Those who trust in the Lord, can read the book He provided *to know what will happen*. There are many prophecies for the nations in the scriptures, some by name and some for the world in general. We can pray these specific prophecies back to the Lord. Overall, before His second coming, there is a plan to pour out His Spirit in the midst of darkness. When darkness covers the earth, His glory will be revealed (Is. 60:1-2). Many people will turn to the Lord and signs and wonders will follow the preaching of the word in unprecedented ways (Joel 2:28-32, Acts 2:17-21). We can be confident that God has a plan in all the upheaval of nations. He is working to usher in a new era, the millennial kingdom. In the middle of the shakings He will take care of those who love and trust Him.

The Lord is good. A stronghold in the day of trouble.
***He knows those** who take refuge in Him.*
Nahum 1:7 nasb

Because he has loved Me, therefore I will deliver him;
I will set him securely on high, because he has known My
*name. He will call upon me, and I will answer him. **I will***
***be with him in trouble; I will rescue him and** honor*
***him.** Psalm 91:14, 15 nasb*

***Do not be afraid of sudden fear,** nor of the onslaught*
*of the wicked when it comes; for **the Lord will be your***
***confidence** and will keep your foot from being caught.*
Proverbs 3:25, 26 nasb

Jesus is a Man of War

The Lord (Yah) is a man of war: the Lord is His name.
Exodus 15:3 nasb

The Lord will go forth like a warrior. **He will arouse his**
zeal like the man of war. *He will utter a shout, yes, He*
will raise a war cry. He will prevail against His enemies.
Isaiah 42:13 nasb

I indeed come now as the **Captain of the host of the**
Lord. *Joshua 5:14 nasb*

Jesus is a Bridegroom, but He is also a Warrior King and Judge

Psalm 45 is a wedding Psalm about the marriage of the Lamb. In verses
2 and 8, He is described as fairer than the sons of men and clothed in fragrant garments. Verses 9–17 beautifully describe the wedding. However,
He is also described as a mighty warrior:

Gird your sword on Your thigh, O Mighty One,
In Your splendor and Your majesty! And in Your majesty
ride on victoriously, for the cause of truth and meekness
and righteousness;
Let Your right hand teach You awesome things. Your
arrows are sharp;
the peoples fall under You; Your arrows are in the heart of
the King's enemies. Psalm 45:3-5 nasb

At the end of the age, He will return as a warring king to remove wickedness and to rule and reign on the earth with His saints.

And I saw the heavens opened, and behold, a white horse,
and He who sat on it is called Faithful and True, and **in**
righteousness He judges and wages war.

His eyes are a flame of fire…
His clothes are dipped in blood, and His name is called
The Word of God. And the armies which are in heaven,
clothed in fine linen, white and clean, were following Him
on white horses. From His mouth comes a sharp sword, so
that with it He may strike down the nations…
Revelation 19:11–15 nasb

We were born into a war and for war

Think not that I am come to send peace on earth.
I came not to send peace, but a sword. Matt. 10:34 kjv

There are times we are to let God fight on our behalf, but there are times when we are to enter into battle with Him.

There is a battle going on—whether we are aware of it or not—the battle between God's kingdom and Satan's kingdom. It is not a battle between flesh and blood, but against principalities, powers, and rulers of the darkness of this world, against spiritual wickedness in high places (Ephesians 6:12).

We are the ones who wrestle against these invisible forces. There are times of earnest, spiritual battle, and God has drafted us into His army. If we are sluggish and lazy, He has ways of disturbing our peace to get us moving.

The Old Testament is a picture

Have you ever wondered about the Old Testament? So many wars and so much bloodshed. That warfare is a picture of the spiritual warfare we encounter and are called to fight. Only our warfare is mostly done in prayer, by obedience to God's word and His will. There is a time for physical war also. Romans 13 states that the military is part of God's ministering army. However, if we are doing our homework of loving Him and our neighbors through prayer and actions that come from a place of prayer, the police and army don't have as much to do (ie. The Hebrides Revival).

The Old Testament also pictures the literal war that will be waged at the end of the age when Jesus comes a second time. Joshua and David are pictures of Christ when He comes as a warrior to war against the antichrist and the wicked kings and rulers of the earth (Rev. 19).

What exactly is doing spiritual warfare?

It is taking authority over the powers of darkness and taking for God what is rightfully His.

How do we do it?

There are two keys causing the enemy to flee:

> *Submit yourselves therefore **to God,**
> resist the devil, and **he will flee** from you. James 4:7 kjv*

The first key is submission to God

To the degree we submit to God, His word, and His will, to that same degree we have authority over powers of darkness. 2 Chronicles 16:9 says that God *strongly* supports those whose heart is *completely* His. Psalm 23 says He prepares a table for us in the presence of our enemies if we follow Him as our Shepherd.

Abraham was willing to sacrifice Isaac, his promised son, when God asked him to, testing him. Because he was obedient, even to this degree, trusting in God's goodness, God promised him:

> *...your seed shall possess the gate of their enemies. In your
> seed all the nations of the earth shall be blessed, **because
> you have obeyed My voice.** Genesis 22: 17–18 nasb*

Even we are blessed in this generation on account of Abraham's obedience because Jesus, our Savior, came through his lineage. How many generations will be blessed by your obedience and my obedience?

We have authority when we are under authority

Jesus submitted Himself to God the Father, even submitting to death on the cross. It brought victory over Satan and ongoing victory even to this day and through the ages (Phil. 2:5-11). Because He submitted He was exalted and now every knee will bow to Him. If Jesus who was God, submitted to the Father, how much more should we submit to Him and His word.

Just as Jesus did, we also gain authority over our enemies by submitting to God.

> *Oh, that My people would listen to Me, that Israel would*
> *walk in My ways!*
> *I would quickly subdue their enemies and turn My hand*
> *against their adversaries. Psalm 31:13-14 nasb*

The second key is resisting the devil

There are times we need to do active spiritual warfare with supernatural weapons. Not everything that happens to us is a trial from God to test us. Some things are attacks from the enemy that need to be resisted. You can know the difference between a trial from God and an attack from the devil. The trial comes with an accompanying grace to endure. Whereas there is no grace to endure an attack from Satan. It is to be resisted.

When we have prayed much about a certain focus, there comes a time when God calls us to not just pray about it, but to war. Our voice even rises as we move into an offensive position spiritually. We, in essence, say, "This far and no more!" I often switch to walking and pacing aggressively, and clapping to "hiss" the enemy out (Job 27:23) when that spirit of warfare prayer comes on me. When this happens corporately in a prayer gathering, there is shouting, clapping, loud praying, and declaring. Some do prophetic actions like karate moves, or banging with sticks. It's not something you manufacture. It is divinely led.

David's mighty men

I think of David's mighty men. He had three top warriors: Adino, Eleazar, and Shammah. Adino slew 800 at one time. Eleazar slew his enemies until he was exhausted and his hand stuck to the sword. The rest of the army had fled, but he fought them himself and the Lord gave him a great victory. The others came back later only to take the plunder. Shammah defended a field of lentils alone. The enemies were gathered as a troop on this field and everyone had fled except Shammah. He held the ground, killing the enemies and winning a great victory by the hand of the Lord. David had 30 others who were valiant, recognized warriors. I believe God's people are called to be warriors like this in the spirit realm, not backing down an inch but fighting through to victory in prayer.

God wants us to have tenacity to prevail like these mighty men did. It may feel like God is ruthless and severe sometimes. Well, army boot camp is no bed of roses. Soldiers are put through rigorous training to withstand the stress, hardship, and pressure of the battlefield. Likewise, God knows the stress, hardship and pressure of the *spiritual* battlefield, so He trains us rigorously through the circumstances of life. He doesn't want us to be soft. Diamonds are formed under great pressure, olive oil through crushing, and seeds grow in dark soil.

The weapons of our warfare

There are many weapons; God has given us an arsenal. The weapons of our warfare are mighty to the pulling down of strongholds (2 Corinth. 10:4).

Some of our spiritual weapons:

- Fasting and prayer: in Daniel 9 and 10, because Daniel fasted and prayed, Michael the archangel was able to push back the Prince of Persia, a demonic principality, to help a messenger angel get through to Daniel. Also Esther 4, and Ezra 8 are stories of fasts.

- <u>Worship</u>: in 2 Chronicles 20:21-22, worshippers were sent out to battle in front of the army. Confusion came on the enemies and they killed each other and fled in panic.
- <u>High praises</u>: Psalm 149 says high praises executes vengeance on nations and punishment on peoples, binding kings and nobles.
- <u>Declaring the scriptures</u>: Jesus spoke the scriptures to Satan, and he left (Luke 4).
- <u>Clapping</u>: Psalm 47 (nasb) shows how through clapping and shouting God ascends and subdues nations under Him. Also Ezekiel *21:14-17 (nasb) says: "You therefore, son of man, prophesy and clap your hands together; and let the sword be doubled the third time."*

  Job 27:23 (nkjv) *"Men shall clap their hands at him, and shall hiss him out of his place."*
- <u>Musical instruments</u>: Isaiah 30:30-32 describes how God beats upon the enemy with every beat of tambourines and the music of lyres.
- <u>Shouting</u>: the walls of Jericho came crashing down when the trumpets blasted and the people shouted. (Also 2 Chron. 13:15.)
- <u>Warring with prophetic words</u> (1 Tim. 1:18, 2 Chron. 20:20).
- <u>Speaking to the mountain, binding evil forces and casting them down</u> (Mark 11:23, 2 Corinth. 10:3-5)

There are other weapons not normally thought of as weapons:

- <u>Truth</u>: it sets free (John 8:32)
- <u>Humility</u>: God gives grace to the humble, which is divine enablement to overcome the tactics of the evil one (1 Peter 5:5-8)
- <u>Tithing</u>: God rebukes the devourer (Malachi 4:10-11)
- <u>Taking care of the poor and afflicted</u>: our recovery will speedily spring forth, darkness will break off, God will answer our prayers (Isaiah 58, Ps. 41)
- <u>Unity</u>: resistance breaks when we walk in unity. Something shifts in the spirit realm. The "world will believe" when we are one and

we love one another (John 17:21), and the commanded blessing comes when we dwell in unity (Ps. 133).

- <u>Prayer of helplessness</u>: David cried out to God that my enemies are too big for me, come and help! God thundered from heaven with coals of fire, smoke, hailstones, and an earthquake. (Ps. 18, 2 Sam. 22:7)
- <u>Having done all, standing your ground and trusting God</u> (Eph. 6:13)
- <u>Prayer of relinquishment</u>: when we surrender into God's hands, willing to take the negative outcome if that is to come, God acts. Abraham was willing to sacrifice Isaac. God intervened. Sometimes the outcome is still negative, but in the dark trial, God will speak. His word will sustain us, bringing supernatural peace, and He blesses us (Job 42:10). Jesus requested that the cup of suffering be taken from Him, but then said, "Not My will, but Yours be done." He accepted the will of God and an angel from heaven came to strengthen Him (Luke 22:42, 43).

Intimacy in warfare

Our human tendency is to get the formula and then use it over and over again. But God is not a God of formulas. He is a God of unique strategies. Only once did He tell the children of Israel to walk around a city, blow trumpets, and shout.

David was very intimate with God, having a deep friendship with Him. He asked God for strategies for the wars he fought. In one chapter, two separate wars are written about. David asked God for instructions and He gave a different strategy for each. (2 Sam. 5).

David, the mighty warrior, would draw aside to encounter God in intimacy. This great man of war said, "One thing I desire and that I seek after, that I may dwell in the house of the Lord all the days of my life, to inquire in His temple and to gaze upon His beauty" (Ps. 27:4). He not only inquired to get direction for battles, but also just enjoyed God and His beauty. He said, "You prepare a table before me in the *presence* of my enemies" (Ps. 23). Even though he was fleeing from Saul for many years, he experienced deep encounters with God that were like feasts. He knew he could be weak and trust God when His enemies were too big for him. When things were too difficult for him he said, "Surely I have calmed and quieted my soul, like a weaned child with his mother; like a weaned child is my soul within me" (Ps. 131).

God wants us to do this too, knowing that it's not always warfare praying. We have times of "gazing upon His beauty" like David. We move in times of intimacy, intercession, intimacy, intercession, intimacy, intercession. It's in the place of intimacy God gives us strategy for our next assignment, to intercede and war. Then He brings us back to the place of rest and refreshing. Then we rise in intercession again. We partner with Him, not running off fighting the battle in our own understanding but being led by His Spirit. He is the Captain of the Hosts. God likes to keep us close to Him, clinging to him like a waistband clings to a man (Jer. 13:11). He wants us at His side, doing these things together.

I learned the hard way that we need to be wise in warfare

I made the mistake of beginning to war against the principality of abortion over Canada on my own after travailing for a long time about this atrocity. I had brought it to our leaders but they didn't seem to pick it up the way I was burdened by it. It wasn't that they were against it, but it was not laid on them like it was on me. In my deep grief, often weeping about it at home in my prayer times, I finally foolishly thought that if others are not joining in this, I will stand up to this principality myself. I could no longer bear the knowledge of babies being murdered in the womb, so I began to bind this principality. Terrible night visitations of darkness began to happen. I would wake up to a cold, evil presence in my room. Within seconds I was cold and began to shake uncontrollably. I was gripped with dread. It went on for a long season and I was getting drained of any joy in my life. The future looked dark and bleak. After three years or so of this terror, I knew I had to have a breakthrough from this, just to be able to raise my kids. I asked my husband to pray to break its power off me. I had thought it out—that my husband is my covering—so I have confidence that his prayer will be answered. I remember the two of us sitting up in bed. He placed his hand on my head and prayed a simple prayer of breakthrough and protection. From that day on, these dark visitations began to recede and eventually ended.

I have seen people who have claimed they have authority over the principality of a city, to call it down. One person went on a high place above our city to "cast down" the ruling principality. His life quickly spiraled downhill. Another person did the same. I warned both of them not to do it. They did not listen, but rather intimated that the rest of us were lacking faith in the authority of the believer. I tried to tell them that I have been there and done that. I know. But it was to no avail.

If we fight certain principalities (i.e. the ruler over a city or country) alone, we will come under severe attack. This level of battle should be done in corporate settings led by spiritual leaders. One should never enter battle lightly. Never underestimate the enemy. Cindy Jacobs, who is a prophet, teacher, author, and a leader of national and international prophetic prayer and spiritual warfare, says that you need to have a healthy respect of the enemy. She knows. She has walked it.

We have the power and authority to handle some enemy fronts alone (enemies that come against our family) but the bigger the principality and its stronghold, God calls for a corporate effort.

Five of you shall chase a hundred, and a hundred of you
shall put ten thousand to flight; your enemies shall fall by
the sword before you. Lev. 26:8 nkjv

A wise man scales the city of the mighty, and brings down
the stronghold in which they trust. Prov. 21:22 nasb

How God directed in a city level warfare strategy

Our prophetic intercessory group prayed weekly for many years for our city, for unity of the churches, for our pastors, and for revival.

God began to reveal a stronghold over our city and region through various dreams and visions. When I shared a dream God had given me, there was quite a stir as a number of prophetic intercessors had gotten the same message. Around that time, a visiting pastor asked us what we were hearing from the Lord, so we told him these dreams and words. A few days later he contacted me saying he had met with a group of intercessors in another community not far from our city, and one of the men had had a dream almost identical to mine. Confirmation.

We knew, that though God had revealed and confirmed a stronghold over our region, we were not to tackle it alone as intercessors. We sensed it was to be done in a corporate setting by a corporate leadership of apostles and prophets. We kept praying that God would set the stage for this. We thus prayed *about* this situation but *did not confront* the stronghold. We also did not go about trying to organize a corporate gathering, but rather prayed for God to do this. After praying into this for about a year, God divinely led during a conference. Two hours of worship warfare took place to specifically target this stronghold under the leadership of apostles and prophets.

Several years later, a visiting minister, who spoke at one of our ministerial retreats, said that our city has an unusual level of unity and a feeling of "safeness" on the ministerial level. It was not the norm in many cities. Something had come down through that time of corporate warfare.

We should not engage in every battle that comes our way

There is a story with a sad ending of a very godly king in 2 Chronicles 35:20-27. He entered a battle that God did not ask him to, and died as a result. We need to be careful we do not ride on past victories and assume God will do it again in a similar way. We always need to seek His face for instructions because they are different for each battle.

Chapter Forty-Nine

A Time to Say, Not Pray

Why was I shouting, "Here is your God", with excitement?

I was in my early twenties, a tired mom with several small children. One day I was reading Isaiah in the living room—it must have been nap time because I had a moment of quietness. As I read the verses, I suddenly came alive with a powerful stirring of the Holy Spirit, invigorated from tiredness to such an anointing that I got up and began shouting with exuberance. What had I read? What was I shouting?

> *Get yourself up on a high mountain, O Zion, bearer of*
> *good news, lift up your voice mightily, O Jerusalem, bearer*
> *of good news; lift it up, do not fear.*
> **Say to the cities of Judah, "Here is your God!"**
> *Behold the Lord will come with might, with His arm*
> *ruling for Him.*
> *Behold, His reward is with Him and His recompense*
> *before Him.*
> *Isaiah 40:9-10 nasb*

Though my mind did not comprehend why I was so alive, energized, and empowered that I was shouting this verse, my spirit knew beyond a shadow of a doubt that something significant was happening in the spirit realm. No one had taught me how to prophesy. The Holy Spirit just fell on me and I did what He was stirring me to do. It was years later that I read about these kinds of things in books, or learned by attending prophetic teaching conferences. Those were times of bringing understanding to my mind what the Spirit had already taught and led me to do.

The full extent of what this anointed shouting to the cities of Judah was not revealed until 25 years later.

In 2001, I was praying and preparing to go on the *Watchmen for the Nations Journey of Hope* to Israel—the journey of 550 Canadians asking Israel's forgiveness.

God directed me in a very profound way to be a part of this. As I was preparing, I received prophetic words from several intercessors. At one point I was discouraged as there were significant obstacles hindering me from going. I spent much time praying alone, but one time I felt to call a friend who lived in another city and who was not aware of my plans. She was soaking in her bathtub, but took the call and before I spoke many words, she had a "word" for me. She called her daughter to bring her Bible and then fluently and precisely read Isaiah 40, having no idea what that chapter meant to me! It was the *very chapter* containing the verses I had shouted 25 years earlier, and now I was going to actually be in Israel, the country these verses were literally for. I didn't say anything while she read, only listened intently, taking in every word. I felt God strongly confirming that I was definitely to be on this trip and the obstacles would be removed.

Later another friend contacted me and said she had received a word from Isaiah 62:10-11 for me. When she read it, speaking it prophetically, I was surprised and excited because it was a parallel passage to Isaiah 40:2-10.

> *Go through, go through the gates, clear the way for the people; build up, build up the highway, remove the stones, lift up a standard over the peoples.*
> *Behold, the Lord has proclaimed to the end of the earth,*
> **say to the daughter of Zion, "Lo, your salvation comes;**
> *behold His reward is with Him, and His recompense before Him.*
> *Isaiah 62:10-11 nasb*

Out of the mouths of two or three witnesses a matter is established. I had no idea where I would speak this in Israel, but I knew I carried a message for them in my spirit.

In Israel, we traveled as a large Canadian company of 550 people, to various sites to repent, pray, and decree, one being the Knesset. I wrote of this in another chapter, so I will fast forward to where the message God had given me was released—near the end of the journey when we headed to Bethlehem. We were going to the very fields and hills where the shepherds watched their sheep when the angels appeared to them announcing the birth of Jesus. The day before, it was announced that prophetic decrees would be released there. I got excited, as the word from Isaiah 40 was, "Say to the cities of *Judah*, Your God reigns". Since Bethlehem is a city of Judah, I knew this was the place I was to **"lift up my voice mightily"**, to **shout** it out.

However I struggled in my spirit on how to bring the word forward. There were so many prophetic intercessors in this group, I being one of many. But I also knew if God had gone to all that trouble to give me this word 25 years earlier, and confirm it in such profound ways, He would also make a way. Sure enough, the evening before we went to the Judean hillside, we were told to be prepared to decree if the Lord had given us a word. An open invitation.

The next day we had to pass through a security check at the West Bank border. We disembarked, left our buses on the Israeli side, and walked to the West Bank side to board other buses to ride to Bethlehem.

After we gathered in the fields, and after some speaking done by the leaders, we were invited to go forward to decree prophetically. I was standing at the back of the crowd and again felt discouragement about going forward (that battle we go through before delivering a prophetic word). I felt a gentle tap on my shoulder—it was one of the leaders. He prompted me to go forward. It was exactly what I needed.

A megaphone was thrust into my hands. I began to decree Isaiah 40:9-10, turning it into a prophetic declaration for the present time. David Demian, who was leading, told me to shout it out louder. So I **"lifted up my voice mightily"** and **shouted** what the Lord had given me 25 years earlier, saying to the cities Judah, "YOUR GOD REIGNS! YOUR SALVATION HAS COME!" and the rest of the verses. These very words I had shouted in my living room as a young woman, I now shouted on the actual hills of Judah to the cities these words had literally been written for. God's ways are beyond comprehension. What He begins, He completes, though His timetable is often different from ours.

Every word which God tells us to speak into the atmosphere is creating something, and will manifest in due season. We are created in the image of God. At creation, Jesus **spoke**, He declared **words**, which brought the worlds into existence saying, "Let there be…" He walked and talked intimately with His Father speaking out the dreams of His Father's heart. Because we are created in the image of God, we have this same mandate to speak and create, speaking out what He whispers to us.

What is whispered in your ear, proclaim from the roofs.
Matthew 10:27

Don't Pray About the Storm, Speak to It!

A freak snowstorm hit as I drove to my son's place 75 km away. He was alone and very sick in bed so I was going to cook for him. The snow came down heavily making it difficult to see, and the mix of ice and snow made the roads treacherous, so I crept along slowly. I stopped for groceries and seriously contemplated turning back. Getting back into the car, I was still unsure of what to do. As I was pulling out of the parking lot, I noticed a snow plow clearing the road and going in the direction I was to drive. I thought, *I will follow at a distance and see how the highway is. If it is bad, I will turn back, but if it seems better because of being plowed, I will continue.*

As I got onto the highway, I quickly assessed the situation as *not good*. The road was icy and treacherous even though the plow was removing the snow. But there was no place to turn. If I pulled to the side to do a U-turn, I would get stuck in the snow, so I had no option but to keep following the plow. Slowly, in heavily falling snow, we trudged along.

I was anxiously praying constantly, asking God to help me. Then this thought came to my mind that Jesus spoke to the storm, saying, "Peace, be still" and the weather obeyed Him. I remembered the prophet, Bob Jones, saying God is training His people to do the same (speak to the weather) more and more as we move into the end times. I have done this from time to time over the years, and remembered a specific instance. So I began to speak to the snowstorm, telling it to change into rain to wash the roads clear of snow and ice. I didn't shout, just thought out what to say, and then told it what to do. I kept driving and got safely to my son's place. Normally the trip takes less than an hour, but it took almost 2 hours.

As I cooked, I told my son about the weather conditions. He said I could stay overnight. I thought and prayed about it as I had a couple of important things happening the next day which I felt God wanted me to do. Finally, at 10:30 pm, when I was finished cooking and visiting, I told him I would go home. Secretly I wondered if I was out of my mind. I ventured out and found that all along the route it was RAINING! Even the very worst sections of highways and roads were washed clear of snow and ice.

The next day I attended two corporate prayer gatherings for a critical international situation that was affecting Israel. Thousands of groups of people all over the world were praying. I felt a strong anointing on our prayer gathering, *knowing* that God was shifting things in the nations. Within a few days, the results of these prayers were coming out in the news! God had moved according to how He had directed us to pray!

The enemy tried to prevent me from getting to my son's house and to these prayer gatherings, but God is greater than any enemy. And God doesn't always answer our prayers but rather tells us to do what Jesus' did: speak to the situation instead of praying about it.

Speaking Blessings on People, Cities, Nations

Aaron and his sons, who were priests, were instructed by God through Moses to *speak, not pray,* this following blessing on the sons of Israel:

> *"The Lord bless you and keep you;*
> *The Lord make His face shine on you and*
> *be gracious to you;*

The Lord lift up His countenance on you and
give you peace."
So they shall invoke My name on the sons of Israel, and I
then will bless them. Numbers 6:24-27 nasb

We who are born again, are called a royal priesthood (1 Peter 2:9), so as priests, we can invoke blessings on people, cities, and regions. My dad often does this over us, his children and their families. I feel the grace of blessing when he does and I am thankful for it. You may not have a dad who speaks over you, but God speaks blessings over you directly as He is your Heavenly Father. You, in turn, can speak blessings on others.

Some of this we do in our prayer times alone with God and other times in corporate settings. It is good to speak over the city or town we live in, over the nation we live in, over those in authority, and even over difficult people and "enemies". We are told to bless them.

My husband and I often speak blessings over the neighborhood, city and region we live in, praying shalom over it (shalom meaning peace, prosperity, well-being, stillness, and calm into chaos).

Seek the shalom of the city where I have caused you to be
carried away captive, and pray to the LORD for it; for in
the shalom of it shall you have shalom.
Jeremiah 29:7 hnv

Prayers of blessing over Poland under martial law

Poland was under martial law led by General Yaruzelski when my brother-in-law began making trips there to minister in 1981. At each church, being aware there were government observers attending the meetings, he would have everyone stand up, saying, "We Christians have authority to bless our governments. I am here to bless Poland and the government leaders. I want everyone to shout 5 times: God bless Yaruzelski!" A year later, by government invitation, my brother-in-law was asked to go to minister in the big city of Wroclaw because they had been following his ministry and saw the change in the lives of prostitutes and alcoholics.

They said Wroclaw needs this. God moved mightily in those meetings and thousands came to Christ. Also, Poland led the way to freedom for the East Bloc countries because of the power of the believers continually blessing the government.

Declaring blessings over an evil regime

Romania was under the grip of an evil regime for many years. My brother-in-law made trips into this communist country also, to encourage the believers. Not only are we commanded in scripture to pray for kings and those in authority (1 Tim. 4) but to also bless those who persecute us and not curse them (Rom. 12:14). He led them to bless the national leader, Nicolae Ceausescu, as well as the other communist leaders. They would open each service by shouting, "God bless Ceausescu!" They did this for several years. It was not easy for these believers to do because they had suffered greatly under his regime, but they obeyed God's word.

Ceausescu did not repent from his evil deeds, so the blessing came to the people. The communist government was overthrown (1989), he was executed, and they are now a democracy. I'm sure there are many others who earnestly prayed for many years, but we are aware of this group of Christians who did that which is totally contrary to human nature—to bless their oppressors—and God worked a mighty break-through. Praise the Lord!

Part Seven

Hearing God Speak

He awakens My ear to listen as a disciple.
Isaiah 50:4

Your ears will hear a word behind you,
"This is the way, walk in it."
Isaiah 30:21

I will keep watch to see what He will speak to me.
Habakkuk 2:1

My sheep hear My voice. John 10:27

In the latter days you (Israel) will return to
the Lord your God
And listen to His voice.
Deuteronomy 4:30

Chapter Fifty

How God Speaks

Prayer is a conversation, meaning there are *two* people talking. We often pray, pray, pray, telling God all the things on our heart and mind, but we forget to stop and listen to what He has to say.

A number of my grandkids have expressed frustration because they can't "hear" God's voice. How delighted God must be because it spells out that they *want* to hear His voice.

God doesn't always speak with words. He speaks in many different ways and as we grow in knowing Him over the years, we get more and more familiar with His voice and language.

"Look Up!" I heard on the phone

One day I was feeling rather discouraged—I just couldn't seem to pick myself up. It was one of those days where you have responsibilities and you keep trying to press through to get them done, but it feels like you are walking through sludge. The inner spark was missing.

The phone rang. I picked it up and heard my son, Steve's voice, saying, "We're outside, Ivan and I." Ivan was four years old at the time. I thought they must have parked outside, so I went out on the steps but saw no car in the driveway or at the curb. Puzzled, I said into the phone, "Where are you?"

"Look up," came Steve's reply.

I looked up and there, flying above our house, was Steve's plane!

My heaviness broke in an instant. I always love to hear from my kids and grandkids, for sure. But the double meaning rushed into my spirit. It was God's brilliant way of reminding me to "Look up!"

Isaiah 40 is a chapter reminding discouraged Israel, or discouraged us, to look up and remember who He is, and that as we wait on Him He will renew our strength and we will mount up with wings as eagles.

> **Look up at the sky!** *Who created all these*
> *heavenly lights?*
> *He is the one who leads out their ranks; He calls them*
> *all by name.*
> *Because of His absolute power and awesome strength,*
> *not one of them is missing.*
> *Do you not know? Have you not heard? The LORD is an*
> *eternal God, the creator of the whole earth. He does not get*
> *tired or weary; there is no limit to His wisdom. Do you*
> *not know? He gives strength to those who are tired; to the*
> *ones who lack power, He gives renewed energy.*
> *Even youths get tired and weary; even strong young men*
> *clumsily stumble.*
> *But those who wait for the LORD's help find renewed*
> *strength;* ***they rise up as if they had eagles' wings,***
> *they run without growing weary,*
> *they walk without getting tired.*
> *Isaiah 40:26-31 net*

The airplane itself was a picture message about mounting up with wings as eagles. God is clever in how He speaks to us!

A broken windshield wiper in a blinding downpour and heavy traffic

I heard the email ding. I opened it, and there was a verse. I immediately knew this was the word for us for that exact day.

The Lord will guard your going out and your coming in
from this time forth and forever. Psalm 121:8 nasb

Our moving truck and car were almost packed. Within a few hours we would be on the road heading to Vancouver Island, leaving Prince George which had been our home for 44 years.

I love it when God is alongside you whispering these perfect words to suit the situation. Little did I realize He had much more reason for giving them.

We had only travelled a little over an hour when both vehicles began to stall. First the moving truck. Tuomo was barely able to get it to the Canadian Tire parking lot in Quesnel where he could work on it. I parked nearby. It was an extremely hot August day and there was no shade. Because the heat was getting to me, I thought I better move the car into the shade of the truck, the only shade available. But the car would not start. After a few failed attempts, I got it started, but it didn't sound normal and it only inched forward slowly.

It was frustrating. Two vehicles down and we had barely started. However, because of the shade, I felt immediate relief. I thought I better do some praying for Tuomo while he worked on the truck in the blazing sun.

I pulled out my prayer journal and Bible. When I opened my Bible to Psalm 121 to write out verse 8, which the Lord had given me that morning, I laughed because the previous verses say:

The Lord is your keeper; **The Lord is your shade on your**
right hand. *The sun will not smite you by day, nor the*
moon by night. Psalm 121:5-6 nasb

The shade of the truck was on my **right hand side**. Then, I read my devotional book, and this was the verse.

Because He is at my **right hand** *I will not be shaken.*
Psalm 16:8 nasb

Tuomo, along with a mechanic, was able to get the truck fixed after a few hours of work, and my car broke out of its stalling as well.

For the rest of the trip, everything went well until just before the Port Mann Bridge going into Vancouver. We were maneuvering through heavy, three and four lane traffic at rush hour. To add to the stress, it began to rain —a downpour. I was leading but kept an eye on Tuomo through my rear view mirror. I noticed he was way behind and seemed to be going slower and slower with vehicles rushing past him on both sides at high speeds. In the rushing traffic, I managed to maneuver into the right lane and pull over just before the bridge to wait. He didn't come, so I phoned him. He said his windshield wiper had broken and he could not see. After half an hour or so we were back on the road as he had invented something to make the wiper work. It was the most stressful part of the move, driving in heavy traffic in that blinding downpour. But we arrived at our destination late that evening, safe and sound.

I realized why God had gone out of His way to be very specific in speaking to me: I was going to need the assurance that He would be guarding our coming and going, the sun was not going to smite us, He would keep us, and we would not be shaken.

Sudden change of direction from Heaven's headquarters

I thought I would be writing steadily for three days. But when I read the devotional that morning, it caught my attention. The article said God might have something new and different from regular routine, and to watch for it. It felt like a "word" from the Lord.

Sure enough, when I tried to get on my weekly prayer conference video call, the internet was down. I tried several times to no avail. There was something going on outside—a truck parked across the street and a work crew doing some electrical repairs, or something. I didn't know if that was the cause. Regardless, the internet was down.

The phone rang. It was Abe, our son-in-law. That was new. He doesn't usually call; it's Helena who calls. He is a truck driver working between Alberta and the Lower mainland of BC. However, this time, a very rare occasion, he was bringing a load to Vancouver Island. He wanted to see if family could come up island to meet him for breakfast the next morning at Tim Horton's in Parksville while his truck was being unloaded. He knew it was a long shot, as it was an hour plus drive for most of us, but he took the chance to call and see if it would work because he could not come down.

Amazingly, it worked for all three families at short notice. We had a wonderful time having breakfast together and walking along the ocean.

When God whistles, the troops gather! It was a plan put together by God. For me, instead of three straight days of writing, God had another plan and it was a blessing. God cares about family—it is high on his list of priorities because He created family.

Also, one of our sons was actually heading up towards Parksville for a day of work, so it wasn't even out of his way. When God's Spirit is behind things, He moves the troops quickly.

I will whistle for them to gather them together.
Zechariah 10:8 nasb

Cavorting elk calves and a remarkable jump in temperature

God often speaks to me through creation. Over the years I have learned to listen for His voice in this way.

It was before six the morning of May 24, 2017. I stepped out on our wooden patio to "feel" spring—to deeply breathe in the ardently-longed-for sensation of spring after prolonged months of unseasonably cool weather. *Finally* the weather prediction was showing a whopping 24 C for the day with full sunshine. It had hovered around 11 to 13 C far too long. Suddenly overnight, it jumped a whole 13 degrees to 24 C. I had checked the extended weather report, and, strangely, it was dropping back to 11 degrees the following day. 11 degrees one day, 24 degrees the next, and back to 11 degrees again. Strange!

Why was this one day standing out with such an exaggerated jump in temperature?

As I was enjoying the moment out on the patio, my reverie was broken by clatter and commotion to my left. There, to my surprise, I saw three yearling elk cavorting on the road. They ran recklessly and disappeared around the side of the house. Then as quickly as they disappeared, they raced back, turned 180 degrees and ran out of my vision again. They raced back again, this time with two more young elk in tow, making it five. This went on a few more times. At one turn, one of the elk lowered his head and shook it in sheer joy and abandonment. What a spectacular show—even these romping, frolicking yearling elk were rejoicing in this "for-real" spring day! Scattered in some of the neighbors' yards across the road were the more dignified mother elk, browsing and eating with their heads down, totally ignoring their boisterous youngsters' antics.

A sign and a wonder—creation was celebrating! But celebrating what? Something was up. My antennae was up, scanning.

Later that day I caught up on news. That very day President Donald Trump hosted the National Day of Prayer for USA in the Rose Garden of the Whitehouse. 150 faith leaders had been invited to this event where prayers were lifted up for the United States, and the government leaders were prayed for. After the prayer time, the President signed an executive order to protect and defend religious liberty and free speech, saying, "*We will not allow people of faith to be targeted, bullied or silenced again, and we will never stand for religious discrimination.*"[16] He went on to say that pastors were free to speak what was on their hearts, that no one should be censoring sermons or targeting pastors, and that freedom is not a gift from government but a gift from God. He included cathedrals, synagogues, and any other houses of worship in this executive order.

When I read this news and watched the video clips, I knew God was pleased. *This* was why creation was celebrating. There was cause to celebrate, on that glorious spring day, because the purposes of God were being revered, upheld, and advanced.

God is a rewarder. I believe there is blessing in store for President Trump for this act as this scripture says:

> *Preserve justice and do righteousness, for My salvation is about to come and My righteousness to be revealed. How blessed is the man who does this.*
> Isaiah 56:1-2 nasb

The celebrating elk calves were a prophetic picture of the ultimate breakthrough when Jesus returns to establish His earthly kingdom, bringing justice and removing all that hinders His love and purposes.

> *"For behold, the day is coming, burning like a furnace; and all the arrogant and every evildoer will be chaff; and the day that is coming will set them ablaze," says the Lord of hosts, "…but for you who fear my name, the sun of righteousness will rise with healing in its wings; and **you will go forth and skip about like calves from the stall.** You will tread down the wicked, for they will be ashes under the soles of your feet on the day which I am preparing." Malachi 4:1-3 nasb*

The extreme jump in temperature, and a beautiful sunny day after many cool, cloudy, rainy ones, was a picture of the day when the son of righteousness will rise with healing in its wings. And the romping elk showed how we will feel when Jesus finally returns to set things in order, making all the wrong things right. It *will be* a Great Day of Celebration!

Chapter Fifty-One

Cast Your Crowns at My Feet

"Cast your crowns at My feet. You can't move to the next level until you do."
The worship leader prophesied these words in the middle of worship. I was lying down on the floor at the 2003 Dominion Conference in Lethbridge, at the side of the semi-darkened auditorium. I began to weep and shake. Those words were for me, though he prophesied them to the crowd.

I had been serving as the prayer pastor of our church going on eight years. It had been fulfilling and satisfying. We had prayed through many things as a church, and God had moved in wonderful ways in the city and nation.

But I was exhausted. I was drained. The year and a half leading up to this time had been excruciatingly busy and intense, both in ministry and family responsibilities. In the middle of being a prayer pastor, I was still a wife, mother and grandmother. Each of our five children had major events in their lives during that season: a wedding, a return home from the mission field in Africa, two graduations, a move from USA to Canada, a grandchild born to make it four, and another on the way. As a parent, you carry your children in your heart and support them. On top of this, Tuomo's mother passed away at the age of 92. We bought an old house and renovated it (with help from family and church family). Also I was officially ordained into the ministry in April of 2002. I counted 13 major life events.

Also that year our ministerial hosted a city-level thrust for Cross-Canada Alpha, an inter-denominational event. I was on the conference committee to train altar ministry people to pray for the baptism of the Holy Spirit.

And, now, here I was on the floor in Lethbridge at the Dominion Conference, hearing this prophetic word that pierced my soul.

Tuomo and I had come to see our daughter graduate from the Miracle Channel Master's Commission program, as well as to participate in the conference itself. I did not expect a prophetic word that would shake me this much. I sensed a change was coming. Transition was in the air. What was God saying?

I'd had great joy in serving in our church as a prayer pastor, but was God saying something new was on the horizon?

When you come, you will stay at my house!

Six weeks earlier I had attended a Regional conference for our church denomination, and several of the messages had been about sabbaticals. I felt God speaking to me. During that time I was billeted at my relative's place, sleeping in their basement family room. They told me I would have to share the space for one night because a woman friend of theirs was coming into town for an appointment. I was amazed when they told me who it was. I knew her. I had met her the year before in Calgary when I attended a prayer conference that paralleled the G-8 Summit in Kananaskis, where world leaders met. Five hundred or so intercessors worshiped and prayed doing spiritual warfare for God's agenda to unfold for the nations.

When I met her there in Calgary, I found out that her family was moving to the International House of Prayer in Kansas City to be on staff. I was excited to meet someone who actually knew about IHOPKC because not too many did. I told her I was also planning to go there for training to establish a house of prayer, one day in the future. She pointed at me, saying, "When you come, you will stay at our house!"

Now, a year later, here she was. Her bed was on the other side of the big room. We talked and talked in the dark. I told her I had been crying out to God, "When are you going to open the door for me to go to IHOPKC?" I jumped up and turned on the lights. Finding my journal, I read my prayers to her, prayers I'd just recently written about wanting to go there. She again pointed at me, saying, "You are going to stay at our house!" Her purpose for being in Vancouver that day was to get her family's visas arranged at the consulate for their move to the USA.

On a side note, if you have heard negative things about Mike Bickle and IHOPKC, please read what I wrote in the extra writings under the title *The Mystery of God's Grace,* after the Epilogue at the end of this book.

It was time!

Because sabbaticals were spoken about in several sessions at the regional conference, and because of this encounter with Cheryl, I knew God was speaking loud and clear. It was time! After returning home, I made an appointment with my senior pastor to talk about this. I asked him if he and the board would release me to go to IHOPKC for 3 ½ months the following year for training to establish a house of prayer. I felt I needed to get away to a place like this to be recharged, a place to be by myself, and at the same time to receive training.

Three years earlier in the fall of 2000, I'd had the privilege of travelling to Kansas City with an intercessor friend to attend a Harp and Bowl Conference hosted by IHOPKC. I had read Mike Bickle's book, *Growing in the Prophetic* and felt a strong draw to go there. It was a downpour time of refreshing and confirmation of things God had been talking to me about for a long time. They had just opened up the house of prayer the year before (1999) and at the conference they spoke about a 3-month training program which was to begin soon for people who were called to start houses of prayer. When I heard this I knew *I was to go.*

Eight years earlier the vision had been written on my heart

Backing up to 1996 when my pastor asked if I would consider taking on the prayer director role at the church, he asked me to write a proposal of what my job description would entail. I prayed about it and began by writing that God had spoken to me the words, *My house shall be called a house of prayer for all nations.* He had spoken those words a year before during a three-week fast our church was doing. One day during the fast, my son was playing his guitar and singing in our living room, totally lost in God. I joined him. Suddenly those words were emblazoned upon my heart. I knew that I knew I was called to be a part of a house of prayer one day. I had no grid for it at the time, no idea what it would look like because there were very few houses of prayer in the world back then, and google hadn't started. Neither did I know how all this would unfold, but those words were burning in my heart. I wrote in the proposal that I felt I would somehow be involved in a house of prayer in the future, but I did not have any other details from the Lord except that. Then I wrote out the rest of the vision of prayer the Lord had given me for our church.

When I met with my pastor, he said he could see a house of prayer established at our church. I was open to that if it was the Lord's will. I knew God would light the path a step at a time.

Now the time for birthing was at hand

That is how I had come to this point, lying on the floor at Dominion Conference in Lethbridge, Alberta and hearing those words: *"Cast your crowns at My feet…you can't move to the next level until you do!"*

What are you saying, Lord?

The following week I was back at my home church. One of the pastors preached on Sunday and used an illustration almost identical to the prophetic word I had heard the week before. He told a story about a little girl who had a plastic necklace she had bought with her saved nickels and dimes. She wore it all the time, everywhere, even to bed. Night after night her father would tuck her in and pray with her, and then ask for her plastic necklace. She'd cover it with her hands and say, "No, it's my necklace!" He continued to do this every evening. One night she said, "Here, you can have my necklace. Why do you want it?" Her father took it and walked out of the room. A few minutes later he returned holding a black velvet box, which he gave to her. She opened it and was amazed to find a pearl necklace.

It was the same message! God was asking me to give up something to give me something in return. When it was altar ministry time, I went forward. I told the pastor what God had spoken to me the week before and now it was repeated, and saying I didn't know what He was asking me to give to Him. He said, "Don't worry. God will tell you what it is, like the father in the story specifically asked for the plastic necklace." Wise words.

That summer, the following scripture was highlighted to me twice. Once a friend called, saying this word was for me. A few days later, one of our associate pastors preached, using this same scripture as his text:

> *"Do not call to mind the former things, or ponder things of*
> *the past. Behold, I will do something new."*
> Isaiah 43:18, 19 nasb

Some weeks later the board and our pastor released me to go to IHOPKC.

I was very excited. That fall I did all the necessary reams of paperwork, and soon I received word I had been accepted.

Our pastor often spoke to those in leadership that we should have someone shadowing us who can rise up to do the ministry we carry if we are no longer there to do it. I knew exactly who I to ask—she was the one who had been powerfully touched by God at the Fan the Flame meetings. I had previously asked her, a few years earlier, if she would want to walk alongside me to be equipped for leading the prayer ministry. She had declined because she worked full time. However this particular year her job position was eliminated and she was given a severance package. She was ready. Thank you, Lord, for providing! Everything was lining up.

The gauntlet

The course at IHOPKC was to begin in early February. I made a stop in Denver, Colorado to visit my youngest daughter who was interning at the Hyatt Regency Hotel in hospitality administration. From there I took an overnight bus to Kansas City. The bus, which was packed full, was the worst bus ride I have experienced. There was a presence of dark evil, fueled by demons, but God also showed up. He has promised that when darkness covers the earth, His glory is revealed.

Three young men who sat at the very back, constantly harassed the passengers, openly and loudly ridiculing, degrading and calling people down, making fun of their appearance and other things. Another young man who sat across the aisle, started up a conversation with a university student who was reading a Bible. He calmly, and with seeming scriptural knowledge, proceeded to discredit the scriptures. He directed her to specific passages to show her how "cruel" God was. I prayed silently for wisdom to know what to say, but I didn't get clarity on how to step into the conversation and the girl did not seem disturbed. After the young man stopped talking, I asked this young student about her Bible reading and if she was a Christian. She said no, she wasn't. She was reading it as a part of her university course, studying the Bible for its literary content. I prayed for a spirit of revelation to rest on her as she read. I didn't feel the need to talk further as there was no contest with the Holy Spirit resting on her while she read God's word.

However, I struck up a conversation with the young woman beside me on the other side. Before long, in the middle of all this warfare, she gave her heart to Jesus! God prepared a table for us in the *presence* of our enemies.

Also, a woman further ahead on the bus talked boldly, and with wisdom, about the Lord to a young person across the aisle from her. She was quite loud so others around her heard the gospel, too. It was such a mixture of darkness and light on that bus, reminding me of Isaiah 60:1-2: "Arise shine, for your light has come, and the glory of the Lord has risen upon you...darkness will cover the earth, and deep darkness the peoples; but the Lord will rise upon you, and His glory will appear upon you."

Because the Lord had taught me about birth pains—about the depth of suffering equaling the height of glory—I had a sense that something very good was coming since the dark world was manifesting. These 12 plus hours on the bus were truly a gauntlet.

I loved being at the International House of Prayer

Indeed, my sense was right. My time at IHOPKC was a highlight in my life and still is. I am at a loss to express how impactful and meaningful it was, except that it was an open heaven time.

The Global Prayer Room, which seats around 700, is in a large room, part of a renovated retail plaza which they had purchased. Some of the other "shops" were converted into offices and seminar rooms, and a delightful coffee shop called Higher Grounds. There is also a nature park area with several lakes, called Shiloh, where one can walk or sit to pray. I walked there often—that was where I had the encounter with the "gazelle".

The prayer room is open 24/7 with 2 hour "Worship and the Word" and "Intercession" sets, back to back. The WWW sets are meditational, with quieter music, and the worship team sings through a scripture passage. The presence of the Lord is tangible. It is hard to leave at the end of a set.

Each intercession set has a main focus: some for revival, others for breakthrough in high schools, for Israel, human trafficking, the ministry at IHOPKC, nations, etc. During the prayers, the worship team continues to play and sing phrases echoing words the person at the microphone has prayed. I am using present tense because the prayer room is continuing on—it has not stopped.

I loved the prayer room! I had no problem spending hours there. I was prepared to pray for each of our kids, my husband, our church, our pastors, the Prince George city pastors and churches, for Canada, Israel and the nations. I loved that I was able to spend many hours doing that with no commitments to organize or administrate anything.

The Psalm 27 calling confirmed

The classes started. Again, I was awed because the main theme taught was the message of Psalm 27, and especially verse 4. I had memorized that very psalm twenty years earlier after my intercessory group prayed for me on the day I could not lead but only weep. When the youth pastor's wife read the psalm, I had clung to every word because it was a life line from God. Now here it was again—the main theme! It was a profound confirmation that God had sent me there and was building on what He had spoken years earlier. I felt at *home* knowing I was in the center of God's will. I had no idea, 20 years earlier, that there was more to why He had me memorize it.

> *One thing I have asked from the Lord, that I shall seek:*
> *that I may dwell*
> *in the house of the Lord all the days of my life, to behold*
> *the beauty of the Lord and to meditate in His temple.*
> *Psalm 27:4 nasb*

The message of that chapter is an end time message. It is about the place of hiddenness from hostile hordes and evil armies when they come against us. This hidden place, this secret place of His tabernacle, where we gaze upon His beauty, is the place of intimacy with God, of hearing His voice directing our lives through whatever we may face.

Verse 13 says, *"I would have despaired if I had not believed I would see the goodness of the Lord in the land of the living."* That had been my desperate prayer when I was in the season of overwhelming warfare 20 years earlier. I was indeed seeing the goodness of the Lord unfolding.

During one of the prophetic ministry times, it was prophesied over me that I had the "One Thing Psalm 27:4 calling". God kept repeating this, confirming what He had spoken many years earlier.

I was afraid of the end times

The two main tracks taught there were: Intimacy with Jesus, and end times. And the main and plain meat of the word of God was taught, as well. I liked intimacy with Jesus. When I had been at IHOPKC in 2000, I had purchased the *Song of Solomon* teaching series and brought it to our church, where it was taught as a course and many people took it. It was life-giving to me. It released me more in my walk of faith knowing how much I am loved by Jesus and the Father.

However, I was very afraid of the end times and didn't particularly enjoy reading about it in the Bible. Matthew 24, Mark 13, Luke 21, 1st and 2nd Thessalonians, Daniel and the Book of Revelation scared me. All those passages about the antichrist and the plagues! I braced myself to go through this gauntlet of end time courses.

I began to understand it was mostly about His wedding day

As the weeks and months progressed, my dread of end time teaching began to shift into anticipation for more. I had never heard it taught from the angle presented there, that the end times were actually about a bridegroom God in heaven who was longing for His bride—about Him coming for her. Together they would rule in the 1000 year reign. It was about the gladness of His heart for His wedding day, a day He has been looking forward to for a long time (Ps. 45). I saw how the scriptures were about a wedding. The Bible begins with a wedding in the garden, and ends with a wedding, the Marriage Supper of the Lamb. The church is called His bride. I knew about these scriptures before, but never understood the emotion of God's heart behind it all.

I later wrote a book about this titled, *A True Tale of a Returning King*.

What crown are You asking me to cast at your feet, Lord?

As I settled into many hours a day in the Prayer Room, I asked God, *"What "crown" are You asking me to cast at Your feet?"* It was my number one prayer. The worship team sang in the background while I journaled. My ears perked up when I heard them sing, *"Let go of the past and reach out to the new!"*

One day after my normal 25 minute walk to IHOPKC, I settled in to wait on God. *The presence of the Lord is in the house!* I could feel it. The worship team began singing, *"Cast your crowns at His feet."* I wept. Here it was again.

This continued to be repeated many times as well as Isaiah 42:9, *"Behold, the former things have come to pass, now I declare new things…to you."*

One Saturday evening, Mike preached about end times, saying God was calling forerunner messengers who would speak boldly what God says in His word about the end times. To prepare the bride. Many churches avoid speaking about these passages in the Bible, but God wants the whole Bible to be preached. He went on to say, most would not speak at a microphone on a platform, but rather in conversations, one on one, or through short email messages (and now it would be other forms of social media as well) that may unexpectedly go far and wide. At the end he opened up for altar ministry for those who felt God calling them to this. I went forward along with others as it was something God had been calling me to for several decades. With the worship team playing and singing in the background, Mike began to prophesy over the group, saying: "*It is time to* **let the past go**, *the yesterday, because* **I have brought you to a new beginning.**"

The next day, when talking with Tuomo over the phone, *I finally got it!* I was to give up being the prayer pastor at my church to establish a house of prayer in Prince George, separate from our local church because it was a city vision. Tuomo affirmed it, having planned to call me to say exactly that.

It was to be a separate ministry. *Cast your crowns at my feet. That's what God was asking me to give back to him: being on staff at my church.* What I'd heard at Dominion Conference the year before, now made perfect sense.

A baby was born!

I wrote this story to share how God speaks to us in hints, clues, and riddles at times, keeping us running up the mountain after Him. He unfolds His heart plans to us a step at a time, as we stay close to Him. He wants relationship, intimacy. He wants us close, and as we stay close, He speaks.

Chapter Fifty-Two

Miracles Unfolded as We Stepped Out in Faith

Before the 3½ months of training and being sequestered in a time of prayer were over, I received many other confirmations. I knew there would be a battle involved to establish this house of prayer because the enemy hated this "baby" that was born. I was greatly strengthened by all the ministry and preaching that still took place after this clarity came. I highlighted words and sentences in my journal from both preaching and prophetic words, to remind myself in the days to come, not to doubt in the dark what God had spoken in the light.

We are to be obedient to the heavenly vision. These words were written in my journal, and on my heart. I was willing, though I sensed a storm brewing.

Tuomo received strong confirmation about this also, and was fully supportive. He made a trip to Kansas to attend the Marketplace Conference that spring. The teaching and prophetic ministry were overwhelming. God encountered him with such force, it launched him into intercession in a whole new way. When he traveled home, he continued in that presence of God for many days. God sealed this transition to both of us. It was another sign to me, watching what God was doing in Tuomo.

Stepping down from staff

When I returned home, we submitted what God had been speaking to us to our leaders and I transitioned to a very part time role at our church, to spend more time praying for God's leading. At the end of summer it was mutually decided that September 30th was to be my final day on staff. That month I mentored the person God had raised up to lead the prayer ministry.

On September 30, we received a call that Tuomo's dad, who was 95, passed away. It was a sad but sweet time knowing that, though he was not with us anymore, he was in heaven with Jesus. It was a further sign to me: the end of one era and the beginning of another.

Miracles of provision

Our pastor advised us not to officially begin the house of prayer for a year. That was exactly what I wanted and intended to do.

Because I had no resources, I looked forward to diving into a season of prayer. I was no longer asking God *what* He was calling me to, but rather I was praying for a building, for the people God wanted to send to be a part of this ministry, and for finances. I had no money, no people, no building, but I knew that God had called me so I knew He would provide.

All these things began to come in miraculous ways. I prayed at home for several months. One day Tuomo called from his office and said the owner of the building where his office was, had generously offered the upstairs rooms to be used by Prince George House of Prayer (PGHOP), free of charge, if these rooms were suitable for us. They were very suitable and we gratefully received this gift. I began to pray there on site for the next 9 months, mostly alone, praying for everything to come together before we would open officially.

There was great warfare during those months of preparation, but God's glory was also revealed in the midst of the trials. I was on the ministerial executive, and this team of pastors rose as one man to support the establishing and opening of PGHOP. One church, The Well, graciously invited us to use their charitable status until we became a registered charity ourselves. A board formed consisting of people from various congregations.

The finance angel

September 1, 2005 was a significant day. I spent that whole day at PGHOP in prayer alone. We had not opened yet. I was playing a Jason Upton worship CD and God's presence increased in the room with each passing hour. The presence of an angel was in the room. In the spirit I could sense this angel and it was not a "normal" looking angel in white garments, the way we usually visualize them, rather it had armor on part of its body, the scales being like coins, like money. I knew it was a "finance angel". At one point I paced back and forth across the room as the worship played. I had a set of keys in my hand which I was subconsciously jiggling as I paced, worshiped, and prayed. All of a sudden I realized Jason was singing about *the key* of David, which is intimacy. Intimacy with the Lord is the *key* that locks and unlocks things because it is about hearing God's voice in each situation, hearing and obeying what He says to do. I sensed God's presence had come that day to unlock our finances. The finance angel was present.

Sure enough, from that day on, our finances took a steady upward turn—not only our personal finances, but finances flowed into PGHOP. God gave regular givers as well as some giving big lump sums. We were able to purchase sound equipment and a computer. My son, who was a recording engineer, gave advice and time to purchase and professionally install them. One couple provided financing for 8 people to travel to the Onething conference held in Kansas City, an annual event attended by 20,000+ people. This offer was for youth leaders of churches in Prince George. Several of the youth leaders who went, began to attend PGHOP and grow in their prayer lives. One of them now leads the ministry.

What God calls us to do, He provides for!

Web streaming the Prayer Room from IHOPKC

IHOPKC went global in 2005, beginning to web stream their Prayer Room 24/7. We were blessed because we could now stream to PGHOP, playing the worship sets in the background while people spent time in prayer. It was a wonderful resource since we did not have multiple worship teams like they did.

Even though they also streamed Sunday morning services, PGHOP was not open on Sundays. We encouraged everyone to be a faithful part of their church family. PGHOP was not replacing church.

Chapter Fifty-Three

Opening Prince George House of Prayer

On October 2, 2005 Prince George House of Prayer opened officially. One man blew a ram's horn to announce the Feast of Trumpets and the opening of PGHOP. I was awed that God had arranged our opening to fall on *that day* without me planning it, another sign. Prince George ministerial was represented and they prayed a blessing over us.

We began our weekly prayer schedule and hosted many web-streamed conferences from IHOPKC. I sent out a monthly newsletter to announce weekly, monthly, and conference events.

Finances flowed as we blessed Israel

One of the annual conferences we streamed was the Israel Mandate conference. I was thankful to be able to share God's heart for Israel this way. He is not finished with Israel.

> *I am exceedingly jealous for Zion, yes, with great wrath I am jealous for her.... I will return to Zion and dwell in the midst of Jerusalem. Zech. 8:2, 3 nasb*

> *When you (Israel) are in distress and all these things have come upon you, in the latter days you will return to the Lord your God and listen to His voice. For the Lord your God is a compassionate God; He will not fail you*

nor destroy you nor forget the covenant with your fathers
which He swore to them.
Deut. 4:30-31

If this is what God thinks about Israel and Jerusalem, I want to be aligned with Him by having the same heart towards them.

Tuomo had the largest sales he'd ever had in his business during the first two Israel Mandate conferences. We were astounded at the blessing that flowed as we made God's heart for Israel known. God promises that if we bless Israel, we will be blessed.

I will bless those who bless you. Genesis 12:3 nasb

Pray for the peace of Jerusalem. May they prosper
who love You.
Psalm 122:6 nasb

We streamed many other conferences and summits from IHOPKC: Marketplace, Prophetic, Passion for Jesus, Children's Equipping, and the annual Onething Conference at the end of each December. The worship, teaching and ministry times were greatly enriching.

The Move of God's Spirit

In 2009, a move of the Spirit broke out at IHOPKC while four of us from Prince George were there for a few weeks. One evening, two days before we flew home, I was turning off lights in our rental suite. My eyes fell on the microwave clock. It said 11:11. I thought, *that is interesting because today is November 11, so it is 11:11 pm on the 11th day of the 11th month (11:11 pm, 11/11).* It was a sign. My spirit was stirred. Next day we heard about a breakout of the Holy Spirit at the IHOP University—teachers and students had continued meeting for hours and moved the meeting to the church auditorium. So *that's* what I'd felt the evening before! We made sure we got in on it because we were flying out the next day. The auditorium was filled with people getting powerfully touched by the Holy Spirit. Many were lined up to give testimonies of what God had done—repentance, healings and breakthroughs of many kinds. These meetings continued nightly for many weeks. Flying home, we streamed them at PGHOP. Many people came to soak in this outpouring and receive powerful touches from the God. One man gave his life to Jesus.

Prayer and teaching at PGHOP

On a weekly basis we were open 9 am–1pm for people to wait on God, praying on their own while quiet worship played in the background. In the evenings we had different focuses each night, led by various leaders—men's prayer, Canada and the nations, our city, and for youth. Wednesdays we streamed from Dominion Gateway church in Lethbridge, Alberta as they had a weekly worship and prayer night focusing on revival for Canada. Thursday was a teaching night. Courses offered were: Song of Solomon, Book of Revelation, and many others. Once a month we had prayer for Israel and the Middle East. People attended from many churches, some once a week, some several days a week, others once a month, choosing the meeting that drew them the most.

Overall, we prayed incessantly for our ministerial, the churches of our city, for the pastors, for revival, and for unity because the commanded blessing comes when brethren dwell together in unity (Ps. 133). Our ministerial had two prayer retreats a year which PGHOP covered with prayer.

Global Day of Prayer six years in a row

From 2005 to 2010, our ministerial and PGHOP joined with the Global Day of Prayer worldwide. We hosted a citywide corporate worship and prayer event for Pentecost Sunday each year at the CN Center and Civic Center, larger venues to accommodate the numbers of people. Leading up to those times, PGHOP organized 10 days of fasting and prayer, which many churches participated in. These gatherings were very impactful in building unity and adding to the golden bowls of prayer for global revival.

A helicopter repentance and reconciliation assignment

Back in the year 1745, a horrific massacre happened in a place named Chenlac, some 60 km west of Prince George. The Chilcotin and Carrier tribes had been at war. The Chilcotins, from William's Lake area, traveled north up the Fraser and Nechako Rivers and massacred a Carrier village where only women and children were present because the men were fishing. The children were cut open and hung on poles like salmon, a gruesome massacre. The men returned home from fishing to find this horrific devastation of their families. These grieving and angry men waited several years without retaliation to lull the Chilcotins to thinking none would take place. Then, suddenly they attacked, coming upon them unawares. Thus, another slaughter took place.

Two First Nations ladies, a mother and daughter, came to ask if PGHOP would join for a repentance and reconciliation event regarding this horrific massacre and to host the meetings at our facility. They had invited a guest minister and team to officiate this reconciliation. After praying, it seemed the Lord's direction was clear that we were to participate.

We had some meetings at PGHOP and the main event on site in Chenlac, at the confluence of the Stuart and Nechako Rivers. The only way to reach this location was by helicopter (otherwise, a long and difficult hike). Seventeen of us were flown to the site in small groups.

When our little group was descending, I saw periwinkle blue flowers covering the whole area of the now non-existent village. It was hushed, beautiful, and ethereal, with a sense of angelic presence. God's glory was there, waiting for this moment. Weeping travail hit me when I thought of those children who had been massacred in this location. I ducked under the whirling blades and ran for the river bank where I fell on my face and wept uncontrollably for a long time. It was a deep agonizing of the spirit, groans too deep for words.

A representative for each tribe had been invited and these two repented to each other identificationally, asking forgiveness for these atrocities and releasing forgiveness so the land could be cleansed and healed. The words of a Christmas carol rose up in my spirit. It was full summer, July 7, 2007 (7/7/7), and a Christmas carol was ringing inside me?!

> *Joy to the world! The Lord has come…*
> *No more let sins and sorrows grow*
> *Nor thorns infest the ground*
> *He comes to make His blessings flow*
> *Far as the curse is found*
> *Far as the curse is found*
> *Far as, far as the curse is found*
> *~ Kevin Kern*

We sang this song, the words decreeing what had happened through this repentance and reconciliation. Where there had been a curse, God was now releasing a blessing between these tribes and upon the land.

A group of intercessors had remained at PGHOP to pray during this whole time. When we told them about the Christmas carol, they told us *they had sung the same carol at PGHOP!* Wow! It was a beautiful confirmation that heaven was mightily working behind the scenes and had accepted our offering of repentance and reconciliation.

Young intercessors rising

In Chapter 39, I wrote about the prodigal who became an intercessor, and served for 13 years as an intercessory missionary at IHOPKC.

He has also served on the PGHOP board for many years, and was our guest speaker for one of our conferences. It has been a great blessing to have a younger person who understands, values, and supports intercessory prayer.

We hosted three local conferences with guest speakers to further equip people in prayer and intimacy with God. For two of the conferences, guest speakers were young adults who shared from lives of walking in a place of faithful intercessory prayer, worship, and the word. We included 8 hours of worship and intercession during one of the events, with worship teams from a number of churches participating, one after the other.

A children's track also took place simultaneously. During one afternoon, we had prophetic teams ready to minister. God touched many lives in a significant way.

Chapter Fifty-Four

Keys to Eight Churches and Houses of Prayer Since I was a Girl

As I look back and reflect on how God called and led me, I realize that right from the early age of 11, I was given keys to "houses of prayer" all through my life.

As an eleven year old girl, I walked a mile to our little Finnish Free Church on John Street in Port Arthur, Ontario, to practice piano, summer, winter, fall and spring. I had a key because no one was there to let me in. It was in that sanctuary, being alone, where I felt the call to kneel and pray. As I look back, it was also there that the two themes of Psalm 27 (end times and His call to intimacy) began to unfold, though I didn't realize it at the time.

The explosion!

Late one winter afternoon, while I was practicing piano, a huge explosion rocked the church! I bolted up with shaking legs and saw the windows on one side of the church lit up like daylight. Something was very wrong because it was dark outside, darkness falling early in the winter, and now the windows were ablaze with light. With heart pounding I thought, *is it the end of the world! Is this the rapture?* Shaking, I ran to one of the tall, lancet windows. Something big had happened at the end of the street. A blazing inferno, so big I had never seen one like it, lit up the neighborhood. I quickly threw on my coat, hat and mitts, ran outside and locked the door. People were gathering, looking up the street. I asked someone what had happened. They said a house exploded. It turned out an excavator accidentally broke a gas line. I later read in the paper that at least one person had died.

Adrenaline had kicked in and my heart pounded because I thought the rapture was happening. God has kept the end times a theme in my life right from childhood.

The call to meet Jesus in the Garden of Prayer

As I wrote earlier, one of the songs I loved was *I Come to the Garden Alone.* I practiced hard to learn to play it because it was so beautiful and spoke deeply to my heart. This again, I realized later, has been an embedded theme in my walk of prayer all through my life: intimacy with Jesus. Already back then, in that little, old-fashioned church with lancet windows, He was calling me to come to the garden of prayer, to meet Him alone on a regular basis. I began kneeling and praying for 15 minutes after practicing—for a week or two.

Keys to other Houses of the Lord

Later, when I was a young adult already married and attending the Full Gospel Tabernacle on Ospika Boulevard in Prince George, I was given a key for that same purpose. I practiced the piano because I occasionally played during services. At that time I had already begun my life of prayer, so after practice, I would pray, walking up and down the aisle and literally crying out *loudly* to God for a great move of His Spirit in our church.

Years later I became the prayer pastor of Gateway Christian Ministries (same church but with a new name and a new location) and held keys to both the church and the chapel. The first prayer room was in our chapel building, a block away. I was often completely alone in the mornings after the early morning prayer teams left. I would put on worship music and pray in the large prayer room as well as in the adjoining chapel, walking back and forth, calling on God for His glory to break through in our city, churches, Canada, Israel, and the nations.

Nine years later we started a house of prayer in Prince George (PGHOP) in an office building on Pacific Street, to which I had a key. After five years, we moved PGHOP to the All Nations Church. They had invited us to rent their facility, so I had a key to their church building. A few years later, they moved to a larger building complex and PGHOP moved with them, and a new set of keys was given to me.

Later I was part of the prayer ministry at Timbers Church in Prince George and was given a key.

When we moved to Vancouver Island in 2016, I had a key to Lake Cowichan Christian Fellowship where I led prayer ministry.

It was years later that I realized God had given me keys to the Houses of God all through my life. I have…

…loved the habitation of Your house, the place where
Your glory dwells.
Psalm 26:8 esv

The lingering presence of God in places of prayer and worship

In each of these places I especially loved being alone, walking through the church, feeling God's presence and praying. I know it is said you can meet God anywhere because His presence is everywhere. It is true. But I especially sense His presence in buildings where God has been worshipped and where there has been prayer for many years. I also felt this grace to pray easily in my son's office in his home. It is his place of worship and prayer. Is there scripture to back this up? I think of Elisha who died of a sickness and was buried. Later when two men were carrying the body of another dead man to bury him in the same graveyard, they saw a marauding band of Moabites approaching. They quickly threw the body into Elisha's grave and fled. As soon as the body touched Elisha's bones, it came to life! (2 Kings 13:20-21). Why? Because Elisha's body had the residual power of God in it even in death, having walked with God all his life. There is a lingering, residual presence in buildings where prayer, worship and proclamation of God's word have taken place.

Chapter Fifty-Five

The Shrinking Before the Explosion

During the difficult years it was impossible for me to imagine that I would become a pastor and travel and minister globally. There are many who have done much more than this, ministering to thousands and millions in many countries of the world. I am thankful for them and their obedience to the call of God on their lives, and have prayed for many of them. Mine is on a much smaller scale. However, God asked me to write this book, so I am obeying. Perhaps it will be an encouragement to you—you, who have been going through dark times, wondering if it will end, but sensing hints of something more God has for you down the road. You, who have felt like Joseph in the dungeon.

I read a book once called *Reaching Critical Mass* by Mario Murillo, where he writes that before an atomic explosion there is the opposite that takes place: a huge reduction, a shrinking of the atom. He goes on to say that God works this way, the opposite taking place before a spiritual explosion.

I think of the 120 that waited in the Upper Room. Where were the thousands that had followed Jesus? God pared them down to 120. The Holy Spirit fell on these few with such "explosive" power that the gospel was launched to the nations. Two thousand years later the gospel has gone almost to the ends of the earth, and the Bible is the best seller in the world. Similarly, Gideon, when faced with 135,000 enemy soldiers, went through this. He had an army of 32,000 but God pared it down to 300. This small army, under God's direction, routed the enemy.

If you have been going through excruciating circumstances for a long time, and there seems to be no give, you are a candidate for critical mass. Or if your congregation seems to be shrinking even though you have faithfully prayed and shepherded the flock under His leading, and have believed and prayed for revival along with your people, you are a candidate for critical mass. If you keep waiting on the Lord in your darkness, believing in His goodness, worshiping Him, praying faithfully, serving Him by serving the body of Christ, obeying His voice and His commandments, then God is about to do something very surprising. Wait and see!

> *For You have tried us, O God; You have refined us as silver is refined. You have brought us into the net; You laid an oppressive burden upon our loins. You made men ride over our heads; we went through fire and through water;*
> ***yet You brought us out into a place of abundance***.
> *Psalm 66:10-12 nasb*

And some may have the higher privilege of not seeing the fruit of their faithful prayers and labors take place in their lifetime, "men of whom the world is not worthy", as Hebrews 11 says. Their prayers, faith and labor are not in vain. The next generation may be the beneficiary.

> *"Blessed are the dead who die in the Lord from now on."*
> *"Yes," says the Spirit, "that they may rest from their labors, and their works follow them."*
> *Revelation 14:13 nkjv*

Epilogue

When I received my call to prayer as an 8 year old child, lounging on the floor and coloring in a shared coloring book with my sister, I had no idea what would unfold in my life. I didn't even understand the strange thing that happened to me, nor the song I heard.

God is like that!

He gives snippets of the puzzle in hints, riddles, and little flashes of revelation that make you wonder. They are profound enough that you don't forget. But often puzzling.

Over the course of life, He drops another clue, and another, and another. If you follow the thread, doing your part of pursuing Him and seeking Him with all your heart, you will find Him.

Later it becomes clear what it was He was telling you all along.

He is so brilliant that He can entrust a child with a hint. He knows it is a seed buried in the heart of that child, a seed which may be dormant for a season, but which in due time will break forth to the surface, growing up into fullness to blossom and bear fruit.

God does His part. We do ours.

He leads the Treasure Hunt as the Good Shepherd, giving us hints and clues. Our task is to seek Him diligently for increased revelation. The more we seek Him, the more He reveals, and the more the mystery unfolds.

It is the glory of God to conceal a matter,
But the glory of kings is to search out a matter.
Proverbs 25:2 nasb

He is a rewarder of them that diligently seek Him.
Hebrews 11:6 kjv

But above all else, in this journey we get to *KNOW HIM!*

*This is eternal life, that they may **know You**, the*
only true God,
and Jesus Christ whom You have sent.
John 17:3 nasb

Who is this coming up from the wilderness leaning on
her Beloved?
Song of Songs 8:5 nasb

The Mystery of God's Grace

God chooses imperfect people to carry out His purposes on earth. I wrote earlier in the book, that by reading the Bible, I saw that all the Bible heros, except Jesus, were flawed people. They had done things that were sinful, very wrong, like murder and adultery (David), marrying pagan women and idolatry (Solomon), running from God's call (Jonah), getting drunk (Noah), denying Jesus (Peter), lying and working out their own plan for birthing God's promised descendant (Abraham and Sarah), murder and disobeying God's instructions (Moses).

Yet God chose them and used them to advance His kingdom purposes significantly. He did not disqualify them. In fact, we read Psalms in spite of David's great sin. We read Song of Solomon, Proverbs and Ecclesiastes, all penned by Solomon in spite of his failures. We consider Abraham a father of faith, and Moses a great leader. Jonah did his assignment, though grudgingly, and his story is recorded, a story that children especially love.

I pondered God's assessment of David and Abraham in the Old and New Testaments. He called David a man after His own heart (1 Sam. 13:14) and having done the all the will of God in his generation (Acts 13:22, 36). He called Abraham His friend, and said his faith did not waver (Rom. 4:20-22, James 2:21-23). How could He say these things about these men? How could He list all the "heros" of faith in Hebrews 11 as such, not mentioning any of their failures, but calling them people of faith?

It is because God sees the heart of man. He sees the deep desire to love and honor God, and to do His will. He loves the heart that clings to Him and keeps an ongoing dialogue with Him, that considers Him. These ones had moments of failure, very serious failure, but their overarching desire was to please and serve God. He saw their hearts of trust, faith, love and loyalty to Him. When they sinned, they repented, agreeing with God about their sin. God is fully aware of our human frailty and imperfection.

My heart is relieved reading the stories of these people. If they did that and were still considered people of faith, then I fit in! Who of us hasn't sinned in some way?

I write this because there has been a controversy about Mike Bickle due to his serious moral failure. Voices have been raised vehemently against him and the ministry of IHOPKC that it should be completely shut down. Some wanting his years of teaching to be dismissed.

Why would we do that when as Christians, we, along with millions, read Psalms, Proverbs, Song of Solomon and Ecclesiastes and are strengthened and encouraged, and built up in our faith though them, even though the writers had big, disgraceful failures in their lives?

The grace of God is such, that God uses us in spite of our failure and weakness. His anointing and calling are without repentance if we have a heart of repentance and a heart after God.

In spite of these failures on Mike's part, God used him to establish, launch, and grow a powerful prayer ministry that went global with houses of prayer established all over the world. He didn't strive for this, for a global prayer ministry. He repented of his failures and spent hours seeking the Lord, obeying His directions. He didn't travel much, but rather spent time praying. As a result of these prayers and the prayers of the growing company of singers and intercessors, people started flocking to Kansas City to seek the Lord in the Global Prayer Room. People came from all over the world to learn to establish houses of prayer, even from Russia, China, and Korea. Many have been strengthened in their faith through his gift of teaching. He has equipped the body of Christ to be prepared for the end times, to have revelation of eternal rewards, to challenge us to live with eternity in our hearts, to have a revelation of God's heart for Israel, to know His affection and Bridegroom love for us.

How could a prayer movement like this have been birthed and gone global if God was not in it? Man could not have done it. It was God's doing and He moved on a flawed man who said "Yes" to God.

I acknowledge the bad that has been done, but I recognize and appreciate the good. God has moved mightily in this prayer ministry that has impacted the global body of Christ and the nations from behind the scenes. Many have found their callings by attending the training that has taken place there.

Instead of tearing apart, God wants us to have the spirit of Christ which is gentle and redemptive:

> *For man's anger does not bring about the*
> *righteousness of God.*
> *James 1:20 nasb*

> *Brothers and sisters, even if a person is caught in any*
> *wrongdoing, you who are spiritual are to restore such*
> *a person in a spirit of gentleness; each one looking to*
> *yourself, so that you are not tempted as well.*
> *Galatians 6:1 nasb*

May God's healing grace abound to restore all who have been wronged, and to all who have done wrong. May He redeem, heal, restore and bring new life, bring beauty from ashes. With God all things are possible.

About the Author

Marja Kostamo is a Canadian who was born in Finland and lived in Australia during her childhood. She is married to Tuomo and they have 5 children, 19 grandchildren, and three great grandchildren. She is an ordained minister, her main area of ministry being prayer – leading, encouraging, and teaching about the adventure and power of biblical prayer, which is the pathway to growing in the true knowledge of Jesus, our returning Bridegroom, King and Judge of the earth.

Books by Marja Kostamo

Power Perfected in Weakness – *Marja Kostamo*

Everything Jesus did was to be an example for us to follow. He who was the very Son of God, prayed. He spent much time alone with God in prayer—in enjoyable relationship, and to know what His Father wanted Him to do. To be fulfilled Christians, prayer is the main thing. It is, simply put, talking with our Bridegroom, Jesus (how hard is that?) He longs for our conversation with Him—He desires us, our closeness. Our lives begin to unfold with purpose, adventure, and destiny once we enter into this ongoing conversation.

To bring forth life, we must pass through the valley of death. This is what happens when giving birth to a child. This principle operates in every sphere of life—there is a birthing process that brings us to the brink of death first. If we do not go there, we remain unfruitful. Jesus said we are to take up our cross, deny ourselves, and follow Him. Otherwise we are not worthy of Him (Matthew 10:24-39). "If anyone wishes to come after Me, let him deny himself, and take up his cross and follow Me. For whoever wishes to save his life shall lose it; but whoever loses his life for My sake and the gospel's sake, shall save it." (Mark 8:34-35).

A True Tale of a Returning King – *Marja Kostamo*

There are many tales, written and in movie form, about a returning king who comes to rescue a princess who is imprisoned, threatened, or somehow oppressed by a villain. The king takes his rightful throne in the kingdom the villain has usurped. These are mere shadows of the amazing

True Tale of a Returning King. This is God's Story. He has a magnificent plan behind all the increasing shakings and conflict in the world around us. He is about to break into this earthly realm very soon to marry His Bride and to rule the nations justly from His throne in Jerusalem, Israel. He is the beautiful King of Israel and King of all the nations of the earth. He will reign with a Bride at His side preparing the earth for the return of His Father.

The Story of Helmi – *Marja Kostamo (my mom's story)*

When Helmi was a little girl, bombs fell and shook her house. At 4 years of age, she lost the loving affection of her mother. However, the winter winds of adversity could not crush her zest for life and learning. In this book she tells the story of how God's presence, love, and care guided her to a future and a destiny which unfurled in an amazing way. It ultimately lead her to travel around the world and live in three continents in answer to God's call on her life.

The Story of Usko – *Marja Kostamo (my dad's story)*

How did this Finnish farm boy, who left school in seventh grade, end up traveling completely around the world and live in three continents?

Read how a surprising prophetic word became a reality…

The Lord says, "I will send you across great waters. Your work is not ending here, but will continue."

I pondered these words – what do they mean? As the years unfurled, I found they weren't just symbolic, poetic words. They meant exactly what they said – we traveled the North Sea, the Atlantic Ocean, the Mediterranean Sea, the Red Sea, the Arabian Sea, the Indian Ocean, and the Pacific Ocean – all these great waters and ministered in both Australia and Canada, as well as originally ministering in Finland.

Books by Savannah Wiebe
(my granddaughter)
edited by Marja Kostamo

My Horse One Summer

Savannah Wiebe
Illustrated by Heidi Wiebe

This book is for all people who love horses, from beginner riders to experienced riders—and even for those who don't ride at all. I hope you have a great time reading about a girl and her love for a horse. Enjoy!

Mandy's Summer

Savannah Wiebe
Illustrated by Marja Kostamo

I am going to have the longest week of my life this summer! Violet, my annoying cousin is coming. She always complains if her nails are chipped or her hair is out of place. And we DON'T get along at all. We have been archenemies since we were born. What do I do? Do I just let Violet walk all over me, or…should I be her friend?

Mandy's Dilemma

Savannah Wiebe

This summer was going to be exciting! Violet was coming over and we were going to have great times with my horse Gracey and each other.

But I guess I didn't see the knock-out punch coming...

When Violet got really sick, it changed the rest of our lives—forever. As I watched Violet fall into bitterness and despair, I began to question everything I believed in. It was going to be a time of testing, perseverance... and holding onto the only stable thing in my life... God.

Endnotes

1   E. M. Bounds, "Purpose in Prayer", (Fleming H. Revell Company), p. 48.

2   MacMillan, John Mark, lyrics to song "How He Loves", 2005, from album *The Song Inside the Sounds of Breaking Down*, www.azlyrics.com

3   MacMillan, "How He Loves"

4   Dick Eastman, "Change the World School of Prayer", (Change the World Ministries, 1983), p. C-86.

5   Paul Billheimer, "The Mystery of God's Providence", (Tyndale House Publishers, 1983), pp. 63 and 64

6   MacMillan, "How He Loves"

7   Miles, "In The Garden, 1912

8   Paul Billheimer, "The Mystery of God's Providence", (Tyndale House Publishers, 1983), p. 16

9   Ulla Riutta, "Katso Mika Aamu", (Kustannuskeskus Paiva Oy, 1985) pp. 154-155

10   Paul Billheimer, "The Mystery of God's Providence", (Tyndale House Publishers, 1983), p. 69

11   Paul Billheimer, "The Mystery of God's Providence", (Tyndale House Publishers, 1983), p. 78

12   Dick Eastman, "Change the World School of Prayer", (Change the World Ministries, 1983), p. E-160

13   Wikipedia, "2023 Asbury Revival", retrieved from https://en.wikipedia.org/wiki/2023_asbury_ revival

14   Antero Laukkanen, "Kansanedustajan Salainen Elama", (Paiva Oy, 2023), p. 108

15   Antero Laukkanen, "Kansanedustajan Salainen Elama", (Paiva Oy, 2023). p. 109

16   Fox news, Trump marks National Day of Prayer, signs executive order on religious freedom | Fox News, May 24, 2017 http://www.foxnew.com/politics/trump-marks-national-day-of-prayer-signs-executive-order-on-religious-freedom

www.ingramcontent.com/pod-product-compliance
Lightning Source LLC
Jackson TN
JSHW021916120425
82425JS00001B/1